Thanks for the Mammaries

Sarah Darmody is the author of the prize-winning novel *Ticket To Ride: Lost and Found in America* (2005). After working as a journalist and film critic, she wrote a book about the Australian film industry called *Film: It's a Contact Sport* (2002), and later contributed to the short story collection *Take Me With You* (2005). Sarah is an ambassador for the National Breast Cancer Foundation, and underwent a prophylactic double mastectomy at the age of twenty-nine.

ABOUT THE NATIONAL BREAST CANCER FOUNDATION

The National Breast Cancer Foundation (NBCF) is the leading community-funded national organisation in Australia raising money for research into the prevention, detection and treatment of breast cancer.

Since the NBCF was established in 1994, over $48 million has been awarded to Australian-based researchers across every state and territory to improve the health and wellbeing of those affected by breast cancer.

Research programs funded by the NBCF cover every aspect of breast cancer, from increasing understanding of genetics to improving ways to support women and their families.

Underpinning the NBCF's approach is the National Action Plan for Breast Cancer Research and Funding, a blueprint for accelerating our knowledge and understanding of breast cancer. The National Action Plan centres on funding collaborations with other like-minded organisations including the state based Cancer Councils and Cancer Australia. This ensures a long-term, cost-effective and coordinated approach to research, while providing an opportunity to accurately monitor and report outcomes to supporters.

The NBCF does not receive any government funding, and therefore relies on corporate and community support to continue its work.

Key fundraising initiatives of the NBCF are October's Pink Ribbon campaigns, including Pink Ribbon Breakfasts, Pink Ribbon Day, Pink Magazine, Global Illumination and Pink Ribbon Licensed Product. In addition, the NBCF works with a range of corporate partners on cause-related campaigns.

The NBCF also works with third parties on major fundraising events, such as the Mothers Day Classic, a national walk or run for breast cancer held annually, and reaches the youth market through the Fashion Targets Breast Cancer campaign.

NATIONAL
BREAST CANCER FOUNDATION
FUNDING RESEARCH FOR PREVENTION AND CURE
FUNDRAISING SUPPORTER

Thanks for the Mammaries

Edited by Sarah Darmody

PENGUIN BOOKS

PENGUIN BOOKS

Published by the Penguin Group
Penguin Group (Australia)
250 Camberwell Road, Camberwell, Victoria 3124, Australia
(a division of Pearson Australia Group Pty Ltd)
Penguin Group (USA) Inc.
375 Hudson Street, New York, New York 10014, USA
Penguin Group (Canada)
90 Eglinton Avenue East, Suite 700, Toronto, Canada ON M4P 2Y3
(a division of Pearson Penguin Canada Inc.)
Penguin Books Ltd
80 Strand, London WC2R 0RL, England
Penguin Ireland
25 St Stephen's Green, Dublin 2, Ireland
(a division of Penguin Books Ltd)
Penguin Books India Pvt Ltd
11 Community Centre, Panchsheel Park, New Delhi – 110 017, India
Penguin Group (NZ)
67 Apollo Drive, Rosedale, North Shore 0632, New Zealand
(a division of Pearson New Zealand Ltd)
Penguin Books (South Africa) (Pty) Ltd
24 Sturdee Avenue, Rosebank, Johannesburg 2196, South Africa

Penguin Books Ltd, Registered Offices: 80 Strand, London WC2R 0RL, England

First published by Penguin Group (Australia), 2009

1 3 5 7 9 10 8 6 4 2

Cover design by Kirby Stalgis © Penguin Group (Australia)
Text design by Cathy Larsen © Penguin Group (Australia)
Typeset in 11/16 Janson Text by Post Pre-press Group, Brisbane, Queensland
Printed and bound in Australia by McPherson's Printing Group, Maryborough, Victoria

National Library of Australia
Cataloguing-in-Publication data:

Thanks for the mammaries/editor, Sarah Darmody.
9780143009078 (pbk.)
Darmody, Sarah Jane.

820.8

CONTENTS

INTRODUCTION

Do you ever get ribbon fatigue? Go on, you know what I mean. Or feel that breast cancer is one of those overly fashionable afflictions that must be close to cured by now because every product imaginable has already turned pink? I felt that way. Pink ribbons. Sigh. They put a hole in my favourite vintage T-shirt, or got lost in my handbag and spiked me like a horse injection when I scrambled for my mobile. They weren't doing anything except helping my conscience for a minute anyway, right? Right. But then it turned out it was just as well I'd bought some. They saved my life.

My Aunt Danni found a lump in her breast on her fortieth birthday. I'm glad she went ahead with her party that night, because for the next four years she had an ugly fight for her life. The day before she died, a medical team carrying out tests finally reached my family tree. It was a groundbreaking research group, funded entirely by public donations. Danni was able to give permission to be tested as part of a study into the BRCA mutation, which predisposes women to breast and ovarian cancer. On my twenty-eighth birthday, I was diagnosed with that same gene, and along with it, the extreme propensity to develop breast and ovarian cancer. At twenty-nine, I had my healthy breasts removed. If it weren't for all those tiny pink ribbons, last-minute coin donations, small bequests instead of funeral flowers, fun runs and pink socks, I would be walking around today with two ticking time bombs inside me. Radical surgery (my unsuspecting ovaries have to go next) might not seem like a gift, but I doubt I will ever be able to properly express my gratitude for the research that made it possible.

Unfortunately, I can't help thinking how many more handfuls of coins it would have taken for the study to have picked up Danni's genetic risk earlier, so she might have lived to see her daughter Sally go to 'big school'. Thousands of women in Australia have these life-threatening genes and at present will never get the chance to find out. One of my doctors likened the effort of locating these genes to 'finding a specific word, in a matching sentence, in a single book, in a massive library'. It takes time, and time costs money. Some small change, maybe a ribbon, means an army of doctors and scientists all over the world will continue to search for tiny clues every day. They need our money. They need our help. At the risk of sounding like a chain letter, *this really works*. The difference between Danni's death and my preventative surgery was just a few short years of research.

The news is good. International funding bodies support trials and studies that are bringing us closer to answers all the time. But they need to work faster. If we could stand over them in their white coats and shout, 'Go! Please! Massage? Here, more coffee . . . c'mon, COME ON!', then we would, but most of them already act out of a sense of deep, personal urgency. The next best thing we can do is gather the funds for more tests, more scientists, and more time spent in the lab. Those pink ribbons are not a metaphor – they're an actual equation. The more money we can raise, the more mums, best friends, daughters, wives, workmates and girlfriends we can keep in our lives for longer. It really is that simple. As soon as these funding groups reach a financial target, they pick up the phone, or hit send on an email, and kick off another round of life-saving studies. Until that time, they wait, doodling on graph-paper, and hope people will still keep giving.

This isn't supposed to be a book about breast cancer, though. Oh no! It's a book of wonderful stories to reward you for making a difference, and to help you celebrate the boobs in your own life – the boobs that once nourished you, the boobs you have now, the boobs you wish you had, or the lovely set you lie next to at night. These are stories donated from the hearts of some of our best-loved and internationally recognised female authors. They are cheeky, silly, sexy, funny, poignant, sad, simple and complicated – which probably covers how most women feel about their breasts over the course of an average day.

So thanks for buying this. If you haven't, what are you waiting for? And if you've bought an extra one as a gift for someone you love, a big thanks on behalf of Danni too. She really loved to read.

Sarah Darmody
Melbourne, 2009

Bra Sizes They Need to Make

CATHY WILCOX

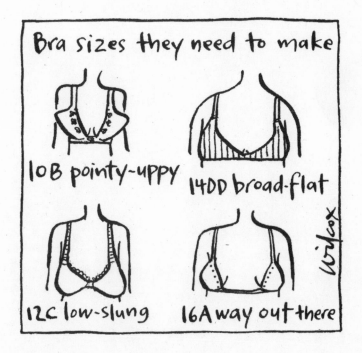

Bra sizes they need to make

10B pointy-uppy

14DD broad-flat

12C low-slung

16A way out there

Wilcox

Storm in a G-cup

MAGGIE ALDERSON

Caroline took a deep breath, pulling herself up from the base of her spine as instructed by her yoga teacher – pelvis tucked under, shoulders back, breathe out, aaaaahhhh – and walked into the lingerie department.

Trying not to look left or right, where she knew gorgeous wisps of lace and silk lurked, she made straight for the counter where a sensible-looking woman with nimble fingers was sorting through a pile of café au lait chiffon balcony bras.

'Can I help you?' asked the woman brightly.

I don't think so, thought Caroline, but we'll give it another go.

'I'd like a fitting, please,' she said.

The assistant smiled warmly and gestured towards the row of cubicles on the opposite wall. Caroline walked towards them, her stomach sinking with every step, her eyes glancing disobediently at the racks of shocking pink silk-mesh half-cup bras and mere scraps of matching knickers.

The assistant, who according to the badge on her black blouse was called Maureen, opened the door to one of the middle cubicles and ushered Caroline inside.

'I'll just leave you to get undressed,' she said, 'while I go and get the tape measure.'

Caroline took off her jacket, her rows of long beads, her V-neck T-shirt and her dirty grey bra, which had once been white. She hung them all on the hook, hiding the shameful bra beneath the other clothes. Then she turned and looked at herself in the mirror. Tears pricked the backs of her eyes. She grabbed the satin robe hanging on another hook and tied it tightly around her waist, folding her arms over the top.

Terrie walked determinedly out of the lift and turned right towards the lingerie department. For a few steps she maintained her resolve, but as the racks of lacy confections became clearer to her short-sighted eyes, she let out a quiet groan.

'Bliggery fumps,' she muttered under her breath, hoping her kindergarten swearwords would make her feel braver.

Against her better instincts, Terrie stopped at a display rail of chocolate-brown satin scanties, set off with pale-pink ribbon trim. She reached out and fingered the cups of a balcony bra, stroking the ribbon threaded round the edges. Remembering her mission, she made herself pull away and keep walking.

There didn't seem to be any assistants around, so she went over to the cash desk to wait. Someone was crouched down behind it, scrabbling around in a low drawer.

'Now, where on earth . . .' the crouching figure muttered.

Terrie cleared her throat and a woman's head shot up to look at her.

'Oh, I'm so sorry,' she said, standing up and smiling at Terrie. 'I didn't know you were waiting. I was just looking for the tape measure. It's gone walkies, as usual.'

Terrie smiled back at her. She looked like a nice lady. 'Maureen', it said on her badge.

'Well, I hope you find it, Maureen,' said Terrie brightly. More brightly than she felt. 'Because I was hoping to have a fitting myself.'

'Won't be long,' said Maureen, smiling back and bobbing down again. She tipped the contents of the drawer onto the floor.

'Aha!' she said after a moment. 'Here it is.' She stood up, holding the tape between her thumb and finger, and

Terrie saw it was one of those pull-out ones, with an ornate brass case. It looked very old.

'Let's get you over to the change rooms,' said Maureen, throwing the tape measure playfully in the air and catching it neatly in her hand.

She led the way, weaving through the display stands to the row of cubicles. Following behind, Terrie let one hand run along the rows of bras dangling from their hangers, feeling the textures of the different laces, satins, chiffons and silks.

'Now,' said Maureen when they got to the cubicles. 'I've got a lady to look after in number three, so I'll just pop you in number four and by the time you're undressed, I'll be back to see you. Okay?'

Terrie nodded. There was something so kind and nice about Maureen. She reminded her of the kindy teacher who'd taught her to say 'bliggery fumps' rather than the more graphic phrase three-year-old Terrie had come out with one morning after dropping her peeled apple in the sandpit.

Right, Terrie told herself. Get undressed, that's what I've got to do.

She took off her jacket, her strings of beads, her V-neck T-shirt, and her dreadful old grey bra, hanging it underneath all the other clothes so Maureen wouldn't see it. Then she turned and looked at herself in the mirror. Tears pricked the backs of her eyes. She grabbed the satin robe hanging on another hook and tied it tightly around her waist, folding her arms over the top.

Caroline heard a knock on the cubicle door.

'Come in,' she said, and Maureen's smiling face appeared.

'Right,' said Maureen. Undoing the belt of the robe with one hand, she deftly threaded a tape measure around Caroline's rib cage while still managing to keep the robe covering her up. 'Can you just hold your arms out a little? Hope it's not too cold . . . there we are.'

Whipping out the tape measure, Maureen looked at it quickly, then wound it round Caroline's body again, still underneath the robe but this time gently resting at nipple level.

'Okay,' she said, whisking the tape out again and looking at it. 'I think I know what size you need. Just tell me what you're looking for – something special for the evening? Or daywear?'

'Just something that makes me look normal,' said Caroline, looking at Maureen in the mirror.

'Won't be long,' said Maureen, and she was gone.

'Come in,' said Terrie, when she heard a gentle tap on the door.

'Okay,' said Maureen. 'Sorry to keep you waiting, now let's see . . .'

In one move she seemed to untie the belt of the robe and wrap the tape measure around Terrie's ribs.

'Shouldn't be too cold,' said Maureen. 'I warmed it up on the other lady.'

She pulled the tape out, glanced at it and round it went again, this time on a level with Terrie's nipples. Then it was gone again.

'Lovely,' said Maureen. 'I think I know what would suit you. Just tell me what you have in mind. Is it for a special occasion? Or just for everyday?'

'Just something that makes me look normal,' said Terrie, her eyes meeting Maureen's in the mirror.

'Won't be long,' said Maureen, and she was gone.

Caroline combed her hair and re-did her lippie to pass the time. She was just about to get her newspaper out of her bag when there was another tap on the door.

'Sorry about the wait,' said Maureen. 'It's just that I'm trying to do you and the lady next door at the same time, so I had quite a bit to find. Now, I think you'll like some of these.'

She reached up and put several hangers onto the peg where the robe had been.

'You try them on, and I'll come back in a jiffy and see

how you're going, okay?'

Maureen disappeared just as Caroline's eyes took in what was on the hangers. It was like looking at a plate of the most frivolous cupcakes. There was sugar-pink silk, pale-blue pleated satin, and one of the café au lait chiffon ones Maureen had been sorting out earlier.

She frowned at them. Maureen had seemed to know what she was doing, but had brought Caroline these tiny little wisps of fabric. It didn't make any sense.

While her conscious brain was still trying to figure it out, her hands reached up to touch the bras. She slid the sugar-pink one off the hanger, just to look at it more closely.

She sighed. It was so pretty, just the kind of bra she had always dreamed of wearing, but it couldn't possibly fit her. It didn't even have underwires.

Oh, what the hell, thought Caroline. She's clearly lost the plot and given me the bras meant for the girl in the next cubicle, who's clearly some kind of slender supermodel. I might as well try them on just for fun. Just to see what it feels like to have such delicious things against your skin.

Without looking in the mirror – something Caroline did as seldom as possible when she was naked – she put the straps over her arms, pulled the bra roughly into place and reached behind her to do up the clasps, just as she had been taught when she'd gone for her first bra fitting, aged fourteen.

At least it does up, she thought. That's something.

Leaning forward, she went to stuff her breasts in as she always did. But for once they seemed to go in quite easily.

This bra must be bigger than I thought, Caroline told herself. Then she looked in the mirror.

The bra was exactly the slip of silk she had thought it was. But the amazing thing was that her breasts fitted perfectly into it. She stood and gazed at the mirror, speechless with amazement. There was no flesh spilling over the top of the bra, or splurging out under her arms. Just two small mounds of flesh, each mound neatly covered by a triangle of light fabric. The bumps of her nipples poked against the silk.

Caroline stared a bit longer and then, in a rush, took the bra off and looked at her breasts, feeling almost faint with surprise. She turned sideways, and instead of following afterwards on a swinging trajectory of their own, her breasts moved with her. Tentatively she reached up and touched one. It was just a small roundel of flesh that hardly moved. More of a swelling than the great appendage she was used to.

Terrified they might change back at any moment, Caroline frantically tried on the other tiny bras and they all fitted just as perfectly. Then she grabbed her T-shirt and put that on without any of the bras. It looked fine. She jumped up and down on the spot and her breasts stayed where they were.

It was only then that she thought to look at the size on the bras Maureen had brought her. There it was in clear black on the white labels: 32A.

Too happy to question what was happening, Caroline put the pink bra back on again – snapping off the price tag first – and got dressed again. The last thing left on the hook was her dreadful old grey 34G bra. She pulled it off and threw it in the bin in the corner of the cubicle.

Then she scooped up all the other bras and went out to find Maureen.

'Sorry to keep you waiting, dear,' said Maureen, this time not bothering to knock. She looked a bit pink. 'I'm here on my own and I have two of you to look after.'

She reached over Terrie, who was sitting on the floor in a near-foetal position, and hung several hangers on the spare hook.

'Now try these, and I'll pop back in a minute to see if we need to make any adjustments. Okay?'

Terrie nodded dumbly, resisting a very strong compulsion to suck her thumb. For a moment she just sat there. Then she forced herself to look up at what Maureen had brought in. Blinking, she put her head on one side, tried to re-focus and then stood up clumsily, like a baby giraffe.

The bra on top was the chocolate-brown satin balcony with the pink ribbon detail.

Great, thought Terrie. She's got my bras mixed up with whoever's in the next cubicle – clearly some kind of glamour model judging by the cups on these babies. You could rear an orphaned roo in one of them.

Groaning again and pretending to bash her head against the wall in frustration, she looked sideways at the bras. They were gorgeous. As well as the chocolate-brown satin, there was a heavenly thing in black lace and another in shocking pink. She looked at the size on the label of the brown one and snorted in disbelief: 34G.

Yeah, right, thought Terrie. Maybe if she gave me a pair of football socks to stuff them with. Great.

Terrie wondered whether she should just abandon the whole idea and leave. Then her hand reached out to stroke the pink ribbon on the bra. It was so gorgeous. Just the kind of thing she had always dreamed of wearing.

I'll try them on for a laugh, she thought.

Shrugging off the robe, Terrie reached for the dark-brown bra and put it round her waist, fastening the clasps in front before turning it round and wiggling into it, pulling the straps up over her arms.

She knew it wasn't the way you were supposed to put on a bra, but she'd always found that instruction to 'let your breasts fall into the cups' very insulting. What was supposed to fall exactly? And where?

She looked down to laugh at herself and stepped back in shock at what she saw, bashing into the cubicle door. Where she'd been expecting to find underwires supporting two empty bra cups, she found two round brown mounds and a deep line of cleavage. Soft flesh spilled ever so slightly over the edge of the cups, just where the pink ribbon was threaded through.

'Bliggery fucking fumps!' she said quite loudly.

Terrie stared at herself in the mirror. Reaching up, she ran her hands over the satin-soft skin of her breasts. She took the bra off and held one in each hand. They had weight, they moved independently. She bent forward and they swung away from her. She jumped and they jiggled.

Jiggle, thought Terrie. I've got jiggle!

She put the bra back on and put her T-shirt on over the top. As she turned sideways, her breasts stood out clearly from her body. Very clearly. Nobody could miss them. They'll probably cast their own shadow, she thought, grinning. They might need their own postcodes.

Too happy to question what was happening, Terrie reached under her T-shirt, snapped the price tag from the bra and got dressed again. The last thing left on the hook was her sad old grey 32A bra. She picked it up and threw it in the bin in the corner of the cubicle.

Scooping up all the other bras, she went out to find Maureen.

The heat of the afternoon hit Caroline in the face as she left the store. She looked reflexively around her for a taxi and as she raised her hand to hail one she realised it felt different. There was nothing getting in the way of her arm as she lifted it.

Beaming from ear to ear, she dropped her arm, took off her jacket, then stepped out to walk home, swinging her arms and holding her head up high. When she reached the park she broke into a jog, revelling in the freedom of it.

Turning right towards the station, Terrie was so preoccupied with looking down at the splendid swellings under her white T-shirt that she walked right into a young man in a suit – and then seemed to bounce right off him again.

'Sorry, mate,' she said, glancing up at him as she picked up the carrier bag of bras she'd dropped in the impact.

'That's alright,' said the man, his eyes dancing with mischief and staring fairly blatantly at her chest. 'I enjoyed it. Wanna do it again?'

Terrie felt herself blush and hurried off.

Caroline wondered what Bill would say when he saw her. He wasn't 'a dedicated tit man', as he'd told her when they met, but he had always seemed to like her breasts. Especially in bed.

She wore a fairly loose silk shirt, so it wouldn't be too obvious at first, and right through dinner he didn't seem to notice anything was different. Typical, thought Caroline, remembering all the times he hadn't noticed when she'd had her hair cut.

But he was going to find out soon, she thought after the meal, as they snuggled against each other on the sofa, watching a film. Bill was clearly getting frisky. He nuzzled her ear, and his hands began to creep up inside her shirt.

Caroline froze as they reached her breasts – or the area where her breasts used to be – expecting him to shriek with amazement at any moment. But he didn't. Instead he rolled her nipples firmly between his fingers.

'Let's have an early night, shall we?' he said.

Terrie wondered whether to hit Michael right up front with the full package, or let him find out later as a nice surprise. But when she got dressed ready to go and meet him, she realised she didn't have much choice. Everything she put on, from her most demure little black dress to a baggy band tour T-shirt, now shouted out: 'Look at my boobs, everybody!'

Oh well, thought Terrie, I've always wanted them, so

I might as well show them off. She put on the shocking-pink bra and then buttoned a tight short-sleeved shirt over the top – well, she buttoned it as much as she could. The edges of the bra and the round humps of her cleavage were on full display.

Walking into the restaurant, Terrie felt a bit self-conscious. The maître d' seemed to be talking to her cleavage rather than her face. As he led her through the crowded room, ranks of male eyes rested on the area south of her neck and north of her waist. And quite a few female ones did too, but they didn't look so friendly.

The only person who didn't seem to be staring at her tits was Michael, who was more concerned with telling her about his tough day at work.

Oh well, thought Terrie, he's got a treat in store.

While Bill turned off the TV, Caroline raced up to the bedroom and put on the black silk slip she always wore when love action was on the cards. It was wonderfully slippery against her skin. Bill loved to stroke her curves through it, before gently peeling it away to find what lay within.

But as he came up the stairs, she caught sight of herself in the mirror. The slip hung on her like a baggy sack. Horrified, she took it off, jumped into bed and pulled the covers up to her neck.

Dinner and a few glasses of wine had relaxed Michael enough to forget work and put him back into his usual amorous Friday-night state of mind.

He had Terrie half-undressed on the stairs up to her front door and by the time they were in the kitchen they were both naked. Michael pressed her against the bench top and did what he liked to do. Terrie normally liked to do it too, but found she was having a few problems this time.

'Michael,' she gasped, finding it hard to catch her breath as her breasts were pressed painfully back into her chest by the granite worktop. 'This is really uncomfortable . . .'

She pulled back so that just her arms rested on the benchtop and her breasts slapped against the kitchen unit in rhythm with Michael's hips.

'Mike,' she said, pulling away from him. 'Can we just go to bed?'

By the time she joined him there, he was already asleep.

The next day Caroline hit Oxford Street early. She and Bill had a big party to go to that night. It was a swishy black-tie charity fundraiser at Bennelong, and she wanted to look amazing. Her hair and nails were booked for two p.m., so she had the whole morning to find the perfect dress.

Something backless, she thought, pushing open the door of her favourite boutique. Halter-neck. Plunge front. Sideless. I can wear anything now without being restricted by bra straps and bulges.

She tried on loads of dresses for the hell of it and then found the one: full-length chocolate-brown jersey, with a halter-neck and a plunge back. Looking over her shoulder at the reflection of her bare back in the mirror, Caroline revelled in the wonderfully free and easy feeling of being braless.

Still hardly able to believe it, she cut a few dance moves to see how great she was going to look at the party. While nothing jiggled, she was horrified when she realised the dress had slid across her body, leaving one nipple completely exposed.

The sales girl told her about some special tape that would stop the fabric moving independently from her body, so she bought the dress and then dashed to Bondi Junction to get some before her hair appointment.

Terrie left the house early on Saturday morning to meet her personal trainer in the park. She liked to jog there first so she was warmed up and ready for the workout, but before she reached the end of her street she realised something was very wrong.

Not only were her breasts feeling as though they were

being repeatedly punched, but two teenage boys standing at a bus stop were nudging each other and pointing at her, red in the face from barely suppressed hysteria.

She jogged a few more steps, looking down to see what was amusing them so much. Her breasts were bouncing about under the T-shirt like two puppies fighting in a sack.

'Hey, lady,' called out one of the boys as she ran past them. 'Want some help with those? I could hold them for you if you like . . .'

Terrie sprinted back to her flat with her arms crossed and tried on all the bras she had bought the day before. None of them stopped the deadly jiggle. She rang her trainer to cancel her session – that was sixty dollars up the spout – and headed off to the nearest sports shop to buy a jogging bra.

Caroline was thrilled with her hair. She'd had it put up in a loose style, all the better to show off her bare back. Her finger- and toenails were painted a burgundy as dark as the brown of her dress.

With a long gold pendant that hung down nearly to her navel, some high strappy gold sandals and a dark-brown and gold lizard-skin clutch bag, she knew she looked seriously chic and wondered, as she got into the taxi with Bill, why she didn't feel more excited about it.

Even after a few glasses of champagne, her mood didn't lift. The metal chair was painfully cold against her bare back and when it was time to dance after dinner, she just couldn't get into the groove.

One side of the tape had come adrift and she just couldn't get it to stick back onto her skin. She had to dance with one hand on her waist to keep the dress from sliding open.

As Bill held her in a clinch on the dance floor, she sneaked a look at his watch and hoped they could soon go home.

Terrie couldn't believe she was already back trying on bras. She wished she had someone as nice as Maureen to help her, but the young woman in this shop was clearly far more interested in serving the hunky footballer who was trying on running shoes than looking after Terrie.

'This is the biggest one we've got,' she said, thrusting what appeared to be a large black tarpaulin at Terrie.

It took her a few goes to work out which way up it went, then she finally got her arms through it and tried to pull the front together. It had a zip and looked like some kind of gothic surgical appliance.

After a Herculean effort she got it done up. Looking in the mirror, she wasn't sure whether to laugh or cry.

Her splendid new breasts had been flattened like road kill. She jogged on the spot. They didn't jiggle, that was for sure, but she couldn't breathe either.

On Monday morning Caroline arrived at the lingerie counter two minutes after Terrie. Maureen wasn't there. In her place was a young woman with short black hair.

'Can I help you?' she asked, looking at them both.

'Is Maureen here?' said Terrie.

Caroline's head snapped sideways to look at her. 'I've come to see Maureen too,' she said, surprised.

They both looked back at the dark-haired sales girl.

'Maureen?' she said, looking puzzled.

'Yeah,' said Terrie. 'She was here on Friday. She measured me and I want her to do it again, because I'm not sure these are the right size.'

She put a bag containing all the bras she hadn't worn yet on the counter.

'Same,' said Caroline, putting her shopping bag on the counter next to Terrie's. 'I wanted her to measure me again too.'

'Are you sure it was Maureen you saw?' said the young woman.

Caroline and Terrie looked at each other.

'Yes,' they said together.

'She was an older lady,' said Caroline.

'Really lovely and helpful,' said Terrie. Caroline nodded in agreement.

'No one called Maureen works here that I know of,' said the assistant, who according to her name badge was called Petra. 'But I can measure you if you like.'

'Okay,' said Caroline, trying to hide her disappointment.

Terrie shrugged and nodded. 'That's weird. There definitely was a Maureen here on Friday . . .'

'Well, come over to the cubicles and I'll see what we can do,' said Petra, and they followed her through the racks and rails of flimsy underwear.

Petra opened the door of a cubicle and turned to look at them.

'Okay,' she said to Caroline. 'Would you like to go in here?'

Caroline and Terrie looked at each other. Terrie raised an eyebrow. 'Your call,' she said. 'I was in the one next door on Friday.'

Their eyes met and then simultaneously slid down to study each other's chests. When they looked up again they were both smiling.

Caroline pointed at herself and then at the cubicle Terrie had been in before. Terrie gave her the thumbs up.

Caroline looked down at the tape measure as Petra slid it round her nipples. It was bright red plastic and clearly brand-new.

'Okay,' said Petra, as she whipped the tape away. 'That's you. I think you'll be fine in a 34G. Do you want something special for evenings, or just everyday wear?'

'Bring it all on,' said Caroline grinning.

Waiting for the lift fifteen minutes later, Caroline felt a hand on her shoulder. She turned round to see Terrie smiling at her, a large carrier bag in her other hand.

Caroline held up her own bag.

'34G?' said Terrie.

Caroline nodded enthusiastically.

'32A?' she said, pointing at Terrie's bag.

'Oh yes,' said Terrie. 'Yes, yes, yes.'

KAZ COOKE

Ah, bosoms. On the one hand there are the people who go 'Phwoaaarrr', and on the other people who worship them as sacred life-giving vessels of compulsorily acquired nourishment. Blimey. Get a grip. They're just bosoms.

~~~

Pregnancy diary, week 17
My bosoms are getting bigger, and none of my bras are comfy, even the bigger ones I bought. My bosoms used to stick out straight from my body, practically in opposite directions from each other. They were known as East and West. Now they're kind of bigger and lower slung, meaning there's a bit underneath where it gets sweaty. And all these little skin tags have grown there as well.

Thank God I finally found a book that said this was perfectly normal.

Sports crop-tops seemed the best, but now they feel like elastic-bandage boob-tubes three sizes too small. If I'm sitting around at home I don't wear a bra at all. No doubt this means I'll end up having bosoms shaped like tube socks that I can tie in a knot behind my neck when they get in the way. Don't care. Those areas around my nipples I can never pronounce have started to go brown and are getting bumps on them.

Farewell, my strawberries-and-cream nipples, my horizontal, pointy bosoms! Will you now both be called South forever? Why don't I have a photo of you?! Was my youth so misspent that I never even posed for nude photographs? What was I thinking!

I'm feeling very annoyed with myself for not being a supple, lithe, yoga-frenzied woman.

The bath in the new house is of such a ludicrous design by some kind of deranged handyman that before I can get in it I have to crawl over about half a metre of tiles or take a huge, dangerous step on one leg. (Well, obviously, otherwise it would be a jump, not a step. I'm losing my mind.) And given that there isn't enough room in the bathroom to swing a cat – actually there isn't even enough room to *shout* at a cat – it won't do. The whole thing is a disaster waiting to happen for a woman whose centre of gravity is changing every day.

I call Wayne the plumber to come and fix it. (All sensible handymen types are called Wayne, just as all sensible women are called Lorraine.) Wayne, of course, finds that the bathroom floor is practically rotted through as well and that there's some other piping-style disaster, which means the job turns out to be five times bigger.

One of the reasons I feel like I'm going mad is sleep deprivation. It never occurred to me this would happen BEFORE the little tacker arrived. One of the books says this is because I'm sleeping like a baby – not much deep sleep but plenty of REM sleep. That stands for Rapidly Enraged Mother-to-be.

Call me dense, but it's only just hit me I'm not one person who's pregnant – I mean, I am – but I'm also two people. No. I'm not two people but there are two people – a big one and a little one – sharing the same body. Well. That's a bit spooky.

Des is reading bits of a book for wannabe fathers, which argues that men shouldn't be expected to be at the birth because they can't fix the pain, and if they prefer, they can plant a tree or invent a new dance instead, to celebrate the birth. I'm afraid Des is the sort of bloke who thinks this is a load of old cobblers, and the way that book is being hurled about it won't last the evening. I don't think he's the making-up-a-dance type.

Pregnancy diary, week 23

Just ate entire block of chocolate. Feel sick. This won't stop me from having lunch, mind you. By this stage I find I am in need of some even more simply enormous underpants. They are the kind of thing you could wave if you were surrendering. Later I might recycle a pair as a doona cover. I find it is infinitely more soothing not to think about the size of my bum. I also picked up a bargain – a free pair of socks with every pair of maternity tights! Some bargain – the whole package was $20 and the tights laddered when I looked at them sternly.

Boy, do I have this Nesting Thing really bad. All afternoon I daydream about moving the furniture. Why can't I live in a minimalist house like the ones in *Elle Decoration* magazine? Pout for a while. I collect more boxes to put things in and cut out magazine articles that introduce a new verb, 'de-cluttering'.

Thank God I am removed from the house by the necessity to travel interstate for a day or so and do a bit of promotion for the new fashion range. Realistic sizes are flavour of the month, but you watch – by summer every other fashion house will be back to toddler-sized persons jigging about in grown-ups' clothes. I have to do an interview at ABC Classic FM, where it's so posh that as I'm eating a muffin out of a paper bag while I'm waiting to go in, somebody comes and gives me a plate so I won't 'have to be a savage'.

I'm supposed to say in the interview why I've chosen these bits of classical music – and I don't even know what they are. I got them all off this relaxing CD that my beautician plays while I'm having a facial. So the interviewer's going, 'And why is this passage by Debussy a favourite of yours?', and I just take a punt and say, 'Look, it's got a lot of piano, and if you're in the bath you can go underwater to wash off the shampoo, come back up and not feel like you've missed anything.'

And then the interviewer says: 'And you're pregnant. We had another pregnant lady in a while ago – or maybe she was breastfeeding, I can't remember.'

I say, 'Well, did you see her bare bosoms? If you saw her bare bosoms, she probably had passed the pregnancy stage.'

Being in a huge city is really no fun in this condition. The queue for a taxi at the airport is 200 long and full of business people who look at you as if you're an alien pregnant person and never offer to help with your luggage.

And seven times out of ten when you *do* get in a taxi you're totally at the driver's mercy. Either they will not speak to you at all. You say, 'I'd like to go to Kings Cross, please.' Silence. 'Do you know where it is?' Silence. 'Do you have a pulse?' Silence. So you just sit back and relax, wondering if your family will ever hear from you again.

OR you get the ones where you say 'Kings Cross, please', and they say, 'How was your day? I'm just listening to the radio. I'll turn it up in the back. I'll tell you what's wrong with this country today. The Immigrant Devil makes work for Andy Pandy and yea through the valley of the Beelzebub the spawn of life will be transcended. The Prime Minister is a communist and will burn dripping in hell for all eternity for his permissive Y-frontery. You know that, don't you?' And that's when you say: 'Couldn't agree more! Just let me out at the next corner, thanks!'

Meanwhile, a local mall owner has banned public breastfeeding in the foodcourt because it's 'just exhibitionism'. Hear, hear. I am sick of these mothers pushing their prams around the streets in string bikinis, removing their nipple tassels and just flaunting themselves generally. I mean, it's too much. There are many people who don't know what a breast looks like, and when confronted with one in the street, for a split second before a bub wraps its gob round the pointy bit, people could lose their reason!

And everybody knows that when a woman is breastfeeding, it is impossible not to be reminded of such classic films as *Debbie Does Dubbo*, *Swedish Knockers Akimbo* and of course any *Carry On* film starring Barbara Windsor. In fact, breastfeeding is such a salacious and provocative act, I'm surprised it isn't banned altogether.

Obviously a lot of nursing mothers will pretend that they just want to feed their child to stop it from shrieking – but I think we all really know that it's just an excuse to behave like a strumpet and give all the blokes in the vicinity a bit of a saucy come-on. Apparently when you're getting twenty minutes of sleep a day and you spend your life cleaning up somebody else's poo and you haven't had time to wash your hair for three weeks, all you really want to do is have sex with strange men in public places. Can't help yourself.

All the newspapers have gone wild with letters, including one from a member of the Breast Police who has managed to insult *everyone* by saying she finds mothers who *bottlefeed* their baby in public to be offensive because everyone must breastfeed. She's alienated all those mums who would love to breastfeed but can't. I hope her nipples rotate at night like propellers and keep her awake.

Frankenboob

SARAH DARMODY

Riddle me this, David Attenborough. What is the name of a furry animal without breasts who still lactates? Who lactates *remotely*? Who lactates (without a drop of milk in sight) quite comfortably while watching *Buffy* repeats, kissing her boyfriend in slow-mo, selecting asparagus at the supermarket, or playing crazy-chasings with her cats? Who manages, without breasts, to lactate unseen during important meetings in front of men in dark suits, and at spring picnics while wearing sheer frocks? *Mammalius Freakus? Mammalius . . . moi?*

Would you believe it, Mr Attenborough? I wouldn't have. It's strange news to digest, and especially awkward at the breakfast table.

This breakfast begins at six a.m. in the posh old part of Melbourne. An intensely hot wind is already blowing. Dried, hand-sized leaves fall off trees and blow into each other, then crackle and burst into dust. From a distance I can see swathes of pink fabric outside a building, like a field of soft flowers in bloom.

Approaching the pink fabric, I see that these flowers are women being whooshed through the doors of a smart hotel, dressed in the full spectrum of breast-cancer-certified pink. The shades range from I-Scratched-My-Leg-Through-Nude-Pantyhose, to Just-Caught-Kissing-Cheeks to Hey-It's-Almost-Red-Does-That-Still-Count? Grown women dressed in a riot of colour usually reserved for small girls or 1980s telemovies can be hard to take seriously at first glance. But I'm one of these women. I take my place in the group. The pink is just to get your attention. Yeah, we'd try cleavage, but most of us haven't got any – that's the *point*.

A year ago I didn't own the bright-pink floral vintage frock I'm wearing. A year ago it wouldn't have struck me as macabre that there are tables laden with jugs of creamy, fresh cow's milk, dollops of butter originating from big bovine teats, and countless unfertilised ovum harvested and then lightly cooked and served with precision-cut slices of dark-pink meat. I'm no vegetarian. I'm just a bit sensitive about breast milk and eggs and surgical-looking flesh first thing in the morning. It's like holding a meeting of the chronic bed-wetters' association at the waterfall restaurant in Crown Casino. Someone would *think*, surely.

Seated, I push the wilted spinach around my plate and try to wake up. A woman in a beige pantsuit leans across the table to speak to the man next to me. 'Marcus is going to be bloody late. He had to rush out to Greensborough at first light to get that sample.'

'Was that today? God, did he get it?' The man looks concerned.

She shakes her head. 'Don't know, haven't heard. Fingers crossed, this'll be a good one.'

My throat closes up. It shocks me how often grief can still ambush me. These must be cancer researchers. In my brief experience, rushing to get a sample means the worst has happened. My dad's beautiful little sister Danni, the reason I'm here this morning, had some blood removed for breast-cancer research just hours before she died. The heat from outside swells my face. I abandon the spinach. 'Are you collecting blood?' I ask.

The woman is distracted. 'Mmm, testing material, yes. Sometimes it's a bit of a race – it usually happens early in the morning, you know, so you have to be quick!' She winks, laughs a little and makes a speeding car motion with her hands. She checks her watch and rolls her eyes at the time of day. She smiles a big sunshiny smile and smooths her hair. 'Phew,' she says, breaking a gobby egg yolk open and stabbing a hunk of glistening meat.

I suddenly wish I looked scarier in pink. I itch to pinch her. I use my silver hotel-knife as an angry extension of my finger. My voice wobbles. 'So that means someone's just died then, right now, right when we're all happy having breakfast, tra la la.' I raise my eyebrows and point at my croissant. *J'accuse.*

The woman and her colleague look at me in horror. She spits yolk on me in her rush to explain. 'Oh my god no, *no*. Sorry. We collect breast tissue from women who donate it during surgery – elective surgery – and doctors like to operate at the crack of dawn, so we're always on alert . . . it's far too precious a gift to waste.'

The three of us laugh together then, that kind of ice-breaking, body-relaxing, 'You thought – ha ha, but when she said – ah ha ha ha.'

'Ahhh. Hmm. Well . . .' I begin polite chat. 'Are you speaking today?' I ask pantsuit woman, indicating the podium.

She nods. 'We're involved in some really exciting research. It involves the BRCA gene, or rather the mutant variations of this gene that are known to cause breast and ovarian cancer.' My eyes light up and they both see it.

'So,' says the guy, 'you're familiar with our work?'

I lean way back in my chair and deploy the heavy silver knife again. 'Perhaps,' I say, using the blunt end of it to prod my firm bosom, 'you're familiar with *mine*?'

'Oh!' says shoe woman, gazing with delight at my chest,

while the man begins speaking to my forehead, bless him, even though it turns out he's a breast specialist.

'You've donated tissue?' he asks.

'Yes!' I say. 'All of it! Every scrap! This is so cool. I kind of thought the whole donation thing might be a myth to help keep our spirits up. You know, to stop us picturing our breasts in an incinerator —'

'Oh, no!' says the woman. 'It's incredible what we've been able to achieve. I'd love to show you —'

'Er,' interrupts the guy, 'we should tell you it's impossible for us to know we are handling your, ah, specific tissue. There are no names assigned to the, er —'

'Where does the tissue go, though?' I ask. 'Slides? Would you still have any frozen or anything?'

The woman claps her hands together and shakes her head vigorously. 'The most amazing part is —'

There's an unsubtle kick from somewhere under the table. She falls quiet.

'What?' I say.

'Nothing,' says the man. The universal answer for something.

'Is it gross? I can handle gross.'

Silence.

'I like biology. And I didn't puke when they pulled my drainage tubes out, and there were four of those, filled with blood and fat like veiny, chickeny, gutsy . . .'

They still don't say anything.

'Worse than that?'

'No . . .' They look at each other. The event hall has filled around us. I can sense the lull into which the speeches will come.

'Please just tell me,' I say. 'I don't care what it is, promise.'

At this point you might be wondering about all the lactating that is going on. But I need to go back to the real beginning, because the end is strange enough for me that I need to be relaxed into it like a lobster in a pot of cool water. I'll straighten out the facts first.

Not so long ago I was diagnosed with a mutant variation of the BRCA gene (BR for breast, CA for cancer. Inventive, no?), and with that, a buggeringly high chance of developing breast and ovarian cancer. It took roughly the same time as fresh-cupcake resistance lasts before I decided to have my healthy breasts removed as a pre-emptive strike against the c-bomb.

Young women having prophylactic mastectomies are depicted in the media as brave and steely creatures, and it's assumed that we require great gumption to carve up our perfect, healthy bodies. But the truth is that hereditary cancer patients are *shit scared*. We go through the pain because other things make radical surgery sound like a really sweet, fun option. Like death! Nothing takes

the fluff out of your pancake quite like the realisation
that you are, in fact, mortal. Patients with the gene for
breast cancer know what death is. We know what cancer does. We've seen enough of it in our families, and
had our nearest and dearest physically mangled or completely destroyed – which is why we've been tested for
the gene in the first place.

I've watched a young woman's cancer battle played
out over five years from diagnosis to death. Let me tell
you, if cancer were chasing me, demanding body parts,
I'd be flinging them off in its direction as fast as I could.
No bravery here. No 'Ha HA! Chase me and *lose*! I am
young! I am strong!' Not even a wobble. Just a 'Yes, *yes*,
anything you want, take it all! And my little dog too! I
have tic tacs, look, do you want tic tacs? ChapStick?'

There are things about death anyone can imagine –
physical pain, the tragedy of watching your family suffer,
the fear of leaving your loved ones behind without the
care only you can give them. But there's other stuff that
only people who have seen real death from the sidelines
can know. I have seen death. I know just what to be afraid
of, and knowing its shape makes me the exact opposite of
brave. It absolutely curdles my bowels to know for sure
that when you die, everything truly does go on without
you. The huge and beautiful story continues, but you
never get to find out what happens next.

There's a difference between being brave and being

hopelessly in love with life, and I'm in the second category. Once you know that about yourself, losing your breasts, losing any bits for that matter, is as plain a choice as breathe or don't. It's just everything else afterwards that gets complicated.

No one prepares you for the fact that all things cancer-related are tedious and very time-consuming. It's like taking a second job. Preparing for cancer is *boring*. It grates to be forced into something so yawny and predictable. I have been diagnosed with the genetic propensity for the medical equivalent of Homy Ped shoes. Beige, bland, suggestive of pain, and most of all – inevitable.

In my first waiting room, I wonder if anyone else feels the same way. I look across at an attractive woman wearing a terry-towelling turban. Is she thinking, 'I can't believe I'm having *chemo*. It's so overdone! So passé! So daytime TV! Let me out of this crap role, please!'?

Even these waiting rooms suck with unbelievable regularity and sameness: out-of-date gossip magazines; plastic plants; pink, puce and lilac Formica; grey chairs upholstered with caravan-park curtain fabric. Laminated payment information and ceilings made from weird, pock-marked cement-sheet panels. And the literature assigned to us is the supporting cast-member in this twee cancer drama. I flick through leaflets with snappy titles

such as 'Information for Women Considering Preventative Mastectomy Because of a Strong Family History
of Breast Cancer', replete with pictures of women in
perfect make-up wearing hospital gowns and looking
at partially obscured surgeons, both parties radiating
intelligent interest and concern. What a creepy model-
ling assignment that would be, I think. What would the
photo shoot be like? I imagine the photographer saying
to the model, 'That's it, Jessica. Hands on lap, no slump-
ing . . . Remember, you might have cancer, but you need
good posture too! Okay, not sooo cheerful . . . Thaaaat's
it, work that paper gown now . . .' Eww. Worse is the dis-
turbing propensity to put flowers on anything to do with
female cancers. I now have a range of pastel-coloured
pamphlets, all with gently opening tulips, frosted orchids
and brave little daisies. What do they put on prostate and
testicular cancer material, I wonder? Droopy little trucks
all in blue? Slightly deflated sports equipment?

I kick at the floor a bit to register a protest. I look
around the room. If anyone in here is as bothered by all
this as me, it's not immediately evident. Then again, I
suppose I have my game-face on too. We're all women
in here, naked except for our knickers under voluminous
hospital gowns. I'm the youngest by a long shot. This
group missed nirvana in the sixties and Nirvana in the
nineties. One woman keeps peering at me over her knit-
ting bag, decorated with a transfer of a photo of her pet

Shih-tzu. She sniffs, her eyes flicking from my pink toe-nails to my ponytail. I'm a hysteric, she's decided. Not one of the club, that's for sure.

I'm too busy checking out her tits to care. Everyone's tits, actually. Free from their regular stays and trappings, I'm finally beginning to understand the giant flesh-coloured bras labelled with consonants in the mid-range of the alphabet. Most of the boobs in here simply could not swing unleashed down the city streets. These are impressive orbs of flesh without any kind of bones to support them. Jugs. Boulders. Bazookas. Missiles. I look down the gaping collar of my robe. I can't compete. I'm packing tiny grenades. Perhaps small landmines. For kittens.

A week after my first mammogram, I receive the message that my 'pictures are in'. Like holiday snaps. Inside the surgeon's office, I'm shown the pics, then given the opportunity to choose my own scars. It's curious business. Dr Efe draws on a bold black-and-white photocopy of perfect C-cup breasts, doodling the scars that belong to different varieties of breast operation.

'Oooh, that one! That one's nice,' I say, tapping on the paper like a hopeful bride at a dressmaker's.

'Yes, isn't it?'

'Mmm, kind of veiny and organic,' I gush.

'Yes, when you face a mirror front-on it's barely visible,' she says.

I have images of crab-like side-to-side viewing and lovemaking for the rest of my life. Some of the operations produce scars that run right across the woman's chest. The photos of these reconstructions look like magazine pages of porn folded heavily in the middle. Another option for me involves ellipses of skin like two half-ovals around the nipple, making a scar that looks like an eye, like an Egyptian hieroglyphic eye. I don't want a humorous scar. Find me a woman who wants her breasts to be humorous.

The next time I see him, I tell my regular GP about my decision to have the prophylactic mastectomy.

'So will you, er, you'll, ah, have breast implants then?' he asks.

'No!' I roar automatically. But he's right. Of course I'll have implants. Why am I so mortified about the whole thing?

'I mean, yes, I will, but not like that!' I correct myself. 'I'm having a *reconstruction*.'

'Yes,' he says. 'With implants?'

Even admitting to a man that I'm going to get breast implants makes me feel cheap. Traitorous to the sisterhood. But what else can I do? Would I otherwise have loose skinfolds where the boobs used to live, like the flaps on ex-*Biggest Loser* contestants? Or should I get the excess skin trimmed away, leaving nipples pulled down tight, pointing east and west to each corresponding roll-on deodorant mark? Or would it be better to be a nipple-less nothing, a genderless, alien expanse of flesh? Polished smooth and cancer-free?

Flicking through magazines and watching women on TV, I find myself drawn almost exclusively to their breasts. What will my new boobs look like? What cup size is she? When shopping for clothes, I wonder, will my new boobs look good in this? Will I be able to move them like I can now – you know, a bit of squash up or down depending on a hidden zipper or a tricky neckline? Will the round tops of my fake breasts tickle my throat like the boobs of porn stars and B-grade actresses do? What shape should I get? What shape am I now? What shapes are there? I'm terrified I'll pick a rack that's in fashion now and end up with the future equivalent of what magazines now call 'eighties boobs'.

When I was sixteen I got a lesson in forever-fashion. I decided I wanted a tattoo. Nothing stupid, not a dolphin or a broken heart or anything, but something really fresh and individual. You know, like a *Chinese character*. Something that said luck or prosperity or kung-pao chicken.

I waited until Dad was relaxed and comfortable on the couch with a family block of Cadbury Almond and announced, 'Dad, I'm getting a tattoo.'

'Mmm hmm.' He unwrapped more silver paper from the block.

'I'm sixteen, I'm in charge of my own life and my body, and there are places in the city that don't even check ID.'

'Okay,' he said.

'Amanda's got one on her foot.'

'Mmm.'

'It's wicked cool.'

'I'll bet.' He snapped off a finger-sized wedge of chocolate and leaned back, crossing his feet over each other on the ottoman.

'So,' I said, 'you don't care if I get one?'

'Um mmm,' he said, concentrating on the chocolate. 'You bring me the bill afterwards and I'll even pay for it.'

I stared at him. There was something afoot. This was the man who for most of my childhood pretended Santa Claus had forgotten us because we'd moved house, or the Easter Bunny hadn't had time to deliver our treats, before pulling the big reveal just as our tiny chins started to wobble.

'I'll pay whatever it costs,' he said, 'but you have to get what I say.'

'What?'

'Mmm hmm. You have to get what design I tell you to get.' He crunched an almond and sighed with pleasure.

'Derr,' I said, because that was actually a word in the early nineties. 'You want me to get "I love Dad" or something. I'm being serious!'

'So am I,' he said. 'Very serious. It's a very serious business, a tattoo. Lasts a very long time. If you're lucky.'

I huffed and flopped around in the chair a bit. 'What do you want me to get then?'

As if all fathers of teenage daughters predict this day will come and arrange some kind of back-pocket plan, he didn't miss a beat.

'A My Little Pony.'

'A WHAT?'

'My Little Pony. You remember them?'

'Derrr, *I* remember them. Why would *you* remember them?'

'Little plastic horse? Pictures on its bum? Colourful hair? Goes in the bath? What's not to love?'

'Daaaad!'

'That's what you have to get,' he said, polishing off another hunk of Cadbury. 'A My Little Pony.'

We sat in silence for a few minutes before he stood up and dusted choc crumbs off his jeans.

'Go on then,' he said. 'Need a lift to town?'

'I don't want a My Little Pony,' I mumbled. 'They're gaybees.' This was another word from the early nineties or perhaps just at my gaybee high school, I can't be sure.

'Ohh,' said Dad, bending down to kiss my hair. 'But didn't you love them? Loved them all. Tucked them in. Got one every birthday. Called one Windy the Brave. I remember Windy.'

And then he was gone, the Zen Choc Master, whose words have left my skin ink-free for over a decade since.

Forget tattoos – imagine choosing breasts! It's a far more dangerous business. I have been an accidental shopper before. This usually happens when an airline sends your luggage to Peru instead of Christchurch, or when you pack for winter when you're travelling to an unexpectedly warm climate and you actually *have* to go shopping. Looking at reconstructed breasts on the internet produces a similar sense of hedonistic, wasteful delight, but my fantasies of guilt-free *Baywatch* boobies are shattered within seconds of the first Google image search. This is not *Baywatch*. This is Frankenscience.

And there are other things to consider. After eight years with The Boy, they're his boobs as well as mine. He spends more time looking at them than I do. He must really love me too, because these are not mighty jugs we're talking about here. Men have never been caught talking to my A-cup chest. I don't own a sports bra. In fact, we've mostly stayed out of each other's way, my boobs and me, but now that they're doomed, I feel a desperate longing for them, balanced by a guilt so great I can't bear to look them in the eye in case they guess what I'm up to.

'How would you feel about fake boobs?' I ask The Boy.

He rubs his chin. 'They're not fake if I can touch 'em,' he says, with a certain tree-falling-in-the-forest consideration. 'If you can touch them, they're real.'

'Yeah, but these are weird-looking, babe,' I explain, pointing at the computer screen. 'They could end up less Barbie, more . . . roadkill. What if you aren't, you know, into me any more after the operation?'

He pulls me close and rubs my worried cheek.

'Well, I know for sure I'm not into necrophilia.'

Pictures of fake boobs online are so universally horrible that I contemplate not getting any at all, and having my front match my back. While I'm sure my insurance company would also like this idea, the time has come to get off the internet and go breast-shopping in the real world. Dad, who now lives in the USA, wants me to consider having the operation near his town in Florida. I think that apart from wanting to be near me when I'm recovering, he has the idea that American healthcare, by virtue of costing thousands of dollars, and being regularly serialised on TV, is somehow more real, more effective, more serious and more . . . medical. I try to point out that south-west Florida isn't exactly Boston or New York.

'If I lived in the US and you lived in Australia, you wouldn't insist I travel to Cairns for life-changing surgery, right? Just because it's the US doesn't make it the Mayo Clinic, Dad.'

When I mention to friends that surgery in the US is an option, I'm surprised by how many people nod solemnly as if this is a logical choice. I live five minutes away from an inner-city healthcare Riviera of some of Australia's best and most renowned surgeons, but regional Florida is still considered a sound choice by many people.

'It's tits,' says my best friend Renee. 'You think America, you think tits. It's like a major export. They've been refining fake tits for decades.'

'But they look fake!' I squeal. 'That's how we know! And I don't want *fake* tits!'

'I dunno, dude,' she says. 'You should seriously check it out. You don't have to go all Anna-Nicole or anything, but I think the States are where it's at.'

'Two words,' I say. 'Tori Spelling.'

Renee's eyes widen. 'No way,' she says. 'Her boobs are reeeal, Darmody. Her breast implants are like an *E!* "True-Hollywood" story.' She pauses. 'It's only her nose that's confirmed.'

With such a strong vote of confidence for the American medical community, I decide to combine a pre-planned family trip to the USA with a round of visits to plastic surgeons and oncologists in Florida. We are taking my cousin Sally to Disney World, on our first proper family gathering since her mother Danni died of breast cancer. Sally is eight. If I need a reminder that this surgery is necessary, all I have to do is look at her little face.

My first port of call is a doctor specialising in breasts and oncology. Familiar with my genetic condition, she explains that I should have my ovaries taken out first. As she describes the procedure, I wonder at her pronunciation of what I am sure must be an 'ovariectomy'. The way she keeps saying it sounds very chic and French. Later, reading some more of those crap cancer pamphlets, I discover that the operation being offered to me is actually called an 'oophorectomy'. Ooph! It's like a Monty Python sketch.

I like this doctor; she's bright and articulate and has lovely earrings to distract me. She's patient and kind while she talks to me and my family, and thorough in explaining my options. (I have come to hate the word *options*. I wince when I hear it. Try it out yourself – when someone offers you an option, it usually means your flight has been cancelled, your phone company has just thought of a new way to screw you over, or your office is relocating to the other side of town. That's if you've got off lightly. Options are bad luck sautéed in menace.) She also hits my dad up for nearly 800 bucks for this single consultation. I say 'my dad', because Lord knows I don't have that kind of money. What average girl in her twenties can lay out six weeks' rent on a visit to the doctor? I begin to realise there's a problem with choosing surgery in the USA when the 'financial considerations' of my 'options' must be considered before some of the physical and mental ones.

Perhaps the dollar-madness explains the oddly cynical marketing of health 'care' in America, beginning in the waiting room among the bold tropical plants and gilt-edged tat. In this same doctor's office, like each one I visit in the States, hangs a largish portrait of said doctor in the place a president or figure of royalty might traditionally feature in another land. The doctors are always young and toothy. One looks to be winking. Another has an airbrushed shine on her peachy lips. Is this what we're paying for? Who cares what the doctor looks like, for chrissakes?

Well, it turns out *I* do. I'm moved to cancel one appointment with a doctor based on his pretty face alone. He has sent me some 'Advance Information for New Patients', which turns out to be an extended infomercial for Dr William S. Wittenborn III. His tight, bright polo-shirt, downy chin and laser-white smile – with what looks to be an actual *twinkle* added via Photoshop – instantly worry me. He has blond lifeguard hair and a smattering of freckles. I peer closer. I think I saw him do a keg stand at a party once. Maybe he's a genius, I reason. Maybe he's freaking Doogie Howser and went through med school at the age of twelve, but they don't give car insurance to guys his age because they're too reckless and have short attention spans! Maybe I'm ageist, or perhaps I'm just young enough to want the grown-ups in charge of the big stuff, but the only way the smiling Dr Wittenborn III will get to feel my breasts is if he picks me up after eight p.m. with a good reservation and a bottle of pinot noir.

The last plastic surgeon on the list has misshapen eyebrows like fat tadpoles, one stuck much higher and further back from her face than the other. She squints at me beneath these brows like I'm a medical curiosity. Standing a metre away from me, she listens to my story with her mouth open before telling me what I'm 'going to want'. She says 'surgery' like *sor-jor-ry*, and pokes at my breasts cautiously through the half-open gown, as though she's nudging a rotten apple that may or may not have a cockroach hiding underneath it. 'Mmm,' she says. 'Mmm.'

'You know,' she says, 'your breasts will have to heal with incredible alignment, okay, with precision timing, okay, for them to end up with your nipples in the same position. You're going to want everything to be even, but the chances of two areas of tissue healing in exactly the same way are small, okay, you understand that?' She nudges again, purses her lips. I resist the urge to tell her that my breasts are lovely, healthy, cancer-free, fungus-resistant, and now – thanks to Florida – lightly tanned, and I would appreciate it if they were allowed to shine a moment. I wonder why she isn't gazing at their current state of perfection, marvelling at their alignment. *Your eyebrows aren't even in alignment, lady*, I think, because fear can make you small and petty. I look down. My nipples are pink and healthy. When I push my breasts with my own finger they feel firm and when I move them with my palm, there's a distinct weightiness as they shift back down a centimetre. They are very small, but soft and good and just right.

'May I see what they look like, please?' I say.

'What?'

'The types of implants. The difference.'

She looks at the attending nurse. 'Get her the *difference*,' she commands.

The nurse returns with two perfectly round pads of super-thin plastic, as big as hamburger patties, and sealed with a visible seam around the circumference. One is pumped full of water with an air bubble like a snow dome, the other of silicone, which is viscous and much heavier. They are horrific.

'Okay,' she says, 'Saline is salt and water, okay? And when your implants leak —'

'*When* they leak?'

'They last between ten and twenty-five years, okay? Then they leak,' she confirms. 'So the silicone, it feels much more natural, and you're gonna want that, okay, but when it leaks it's much harder to tell, and it can form hard lumps. We call those granulomas.'

'Why do they leak?' I ask. Is this not the country that put a man on the moon? In the *sixties*?

'The new ones are better,' she says, shrugging, 'so you might get a sturdier model. Less likely to burst.'

I drive back to Dad's house furious and wobbly all at

once, loud radio-singalong crying interspersed with silent rage and disbelief. When I come up the stairs, my dad's wife, Caroline, and my two aunts are all in the kitchen cooking dinner and drinking holiday drinks while my little cousin Sally holds court. The beautiful Florida sun is setting outside the bay windows, and it looks just like it did yesterday, before I knew what breast implants looked like. But now I do, and it's all wrong. I don't feel 'fixable' any more. Someone hands me a beer and the taste is exquisite. I sense a bender coming on.

'How did it go?' Liz asks.

'Pretty much like this,' I say, reaching for a plastic shopping bag. I blast some tap water into it and, with a cowgirl flick of the wrist, tie a knot. I hold it against my chest.

'This,' I say. 'This, with some leftover skin the thickness of a pair of old jeans to cover it.' I wiggle a fraction. The sloshing is audible. Everyone starts talking at once.

'Farkin' hell.'

'Oh, jeez! Maybe they have something better in Australia —'

'Should we make another appointment?'

'Have you thought about just getting rid of it all?'

Sally looks up from her Disney World postcards, hand curled around the pencil, and says, 'What's that?'

The chatter stops and suddenly we are four grown women in a kitchen, staring at a dripping plastic bag held high in my fist.

'Uh, it's a w-water bomb,' I stammer. 'Not a good one though.' I prod it. 'Too floppy. Not enough . . . bursting.'

Sally shrugs. 'Looks like it would burst to me.' She turns away. She's not included, and she knows it's for all the usual crap reasons. You're not old enough, not a grown-up, not a woman, your mother is dead so we have to be careful, so careful, with what we say to you.

'Bloody water bombs, eh?' says Bee, whose laugh is as regular and staccato as a sprinkler system. She hates her own water bombs, which are huge and give her trouble. I dump the bag in the sink where it deflates and the water gurgles away. Caroline squeezes my shoulder. 'I'm so sorry, Sar,' she says, and suddenly it's quite nice. To share this thing. Four odd women with so much but so little in common. We all have boobs, at least. We're all childless, but our breasts connect us in the way I imagine mothers must bond. Universally.

It's a small epiphany, the first of many; the surprise treats that will turn up like daisies near dung all the time in the months ahead. 'Hey,' I shrug. 'It's not so bad.'

And in the end, it wasn't.

Back at the breakfast, I push meaningfully at my new bosom. It's made out of a burst-proof gummi-bear-like substance, covered in safe, washable plastic just like a Barbie doll.

'Come on,' I ask again. 'Please tell me.'

The senior researcher tucks her hair behind her ear and leans in. 'Okay,' she says, exhaling in a long sigh. 'We grow the tissue.'

'You grow it?'

'Mice do.'

'Mice?'

'Special mice.'

'Special mice?' I'm beginning to sound like a learn-a-foreign-language tape.

The researcher explains that my breasts, those lumps of flesh that were the focus of so much fear, sadness, desire, hope, longing and finally life-changing surgery, have gone off to live a life of their own, without me. On the bodies of special mice. Not only that, but my mutant-self now has mutant family.

Somewhere in this city, my breasts are lined up, no longer in a modest line of two, but in two lines of three. Six boobs, grown on nude, hairless mice. They have no immune systems to speak of, so they can accept body grafts from just about anything. I'm assured that there are very strict rules dictating the use of these mice in sci-entific research. I imagine this is to prevent people from grafting them in orangutan fur to check its suitability for the next season's Louis Vuitton.

Some of these mice have had their prepubescent breast tissue removed and replaced with mine. The research scientists then initiate pregnancy and stand back as the mice grow six healthy breasts each, genetically stamped human: Sarah J. Darmody. At some point, the mice begin to lactate.

The researchers look at me for signs of imminent vomiting or collapse. There are tears welling, but not from shock. 'I work!' I tell them. 'I *work*.' My breasts have not been a waste. They're still out there, not dead and discarded, but living and growing, multiplying, warm and plump, full of the human milk I never made myself. Lactating.

For a year now people have told me that I'm a lucky girl: lucky to have the information; lucky to have such a choice to make. But not until this moment did I truly feel lucky. To have on board a fairly rare and ugly genetic mutation that has been around for hundreds or thousands of years – pretty unlucky, if you want the bare truth. Nope. Don't much like that at all. But realising that I've been born at the precise moment in history when the research could catch up to me, tap me on the shoulder and say, 'Hi! We're here to help' – that's lucky. That's a shot in a billion.

I picture the mice. My sisters? Surely – like twins who have the same DNA, we must be sisters in some way. In my mind's eye they mill around the water dripper like rats in a Gary Larson cartoon, trading gossip and hanging out. *Nice rack, Shirl. Oh these? Down half a cup size, but just so perky, y'know. These humans – so selfless. One day I just know they're gonna cure mouse cancer once and for all.*

My head is swimming. My throat is dry.

'Sarah?' It's time for my speech.

I nod, dizzy, wondering what on earth I'm going to say. In front of me in the sea of pink are faces young and old, tired but hopeful. This is the breast cancer RSL, and for once I'm proud to face the audience feeling like I've brought my troops home safely after all.

'Are you okay?' asks the researcher. 'How do you feel?'

Honestly? 'Like an accidental astronaut.'

'Is that . . . good?'

'No,' I say. 'It's fantastic. Thank you.'

That's all I needed to say up on stage, and I'll never be able to say it enough. Thank you.

In Recognition
of Fifteen Years'
Service

JESSICA DETTMANN

Dear Breasts,

According to our records, this year marks the fifteenth anniversary of your joining Jessica Pty Ltd. In recognition of this milestone, we here at head office would like to take this opportunity to thank you for your dedicated service.

You have been a valued member of the Jessica family since beginning with us as a work-experience student when the company was a mere twelve years old, after which time we happily accepted you as a trainee. Of course, those early years were not without their trials, but we celebrated your graduation as a fully fledged member of the business when Jessica was fifteen.

The company wishes to acknowledge your hardworking and uncomplaining nature in those early years. Not all breasts would have been so accepting of such indignities as undergoing the assessment method known as the Pencil Test, in which you were not deemed worthy of support until a single pencil could be held unassisted between you and the chest. Recent developments in testing have rendered this method obsolete, you will be pleased to hear (as was the company stationery budget: a full set of Derwents would be required these days if this test were to be repeated).

The way you worked in conjunction with our nervous system to force Jessica to muster up the courage to ask her mother to take her to buy her first bra was, as our adrenal gland can attest, a difficult and frightening task. Far be it for us to belittle our fears at the time, but in hindsight the company has downgraded this event from Traumatic to No Worse Than Asking for a Payrise on the Jessica Fear Scale (one of our on-going bugbears here at Jessica Pty Ltd, and one which we are constantly working to keep appropriately calibrated, it having a tendency to give readings at the upper end of the scale if not constantly fine-tuned).

When Jessica elected to participate in rhythmic gymnastics at school, your exemplary behaviour was immediately noticed by management. We were impressed with the way you rose above the indignity of being shrouded in a black and gold high-necked, long-sleeved leotard to provide a steady platform for the black plastic ball apparatus to roll down one arm, across the chest and back up the other arm in one continuous flowing movement. Your performance stands out in stark contrast to that of Jessica's bottom, a known troublemaker, who, in cahoots with her swayback, was known to behave in an entirely unruly fashion during rhythmics routines, wiggling and carrying on and generally calling undue attention to the hindquarter area, which we are sure cost us points and quite possibly the 1994 All-Schools Rhythmic Gymnastics Championship.

While we try to keep your interests front of mind, we apologise for instances where we have plainly forgotten about you. For example, we are very sorry for occasionally telling the story of Brigid, the Irish backpacker we used to work with. You know, the one about the time she was shaving her underarms in the shower, when she was still a little bit pissed, and she accidentally took a few layers of skin off her nipple when she didn't lift the razor up enough when coming in for landing? We know that story makes you wince, and makes your nipples want to go concave. While we truly can't promise never to tell it again, we'll try not to do it often, or when you're feeling particularly sensitive.

Several working groups within the Brain department here at Jessica would like to thank you for the enormous contribution you have made to the material available to them, not least the amygdala – or Worry Central, as we like to call it. Senior staffers at Worry Central have informed us that without you, Breasts, they would not have had nearly such elevated output figures over the past fifteen years. They tell us that career concerns, boy worries and suchlike have accounted for a relatively small part of their workload in comparison to panic relating to you, Jessica's Breasts.

Major projects that you have contributed to at Worry Central range in scale from constant low-grade fear of breast cancer, assisted by your own – and here we quote our doctor – 'lumpiness', to stabs of embarrassment when we realise we have sat up straight and pulled our shoulders back while wearing a blouse that buttons up the front, thereby causing buttons to ricochet off and ping around the room, endangering the eyes of passers-by and leaving you exposed.

Of these worries, the most profitable has certainly been the breast cancer fear, which has worked in synchronicity with so many other fears that staffers at Worry Central have been, and we quote, 'awestruck by the scope, scale and persistence of the worrying we have been able to do about the Breasts'.

We would like to thank you for giving Jessica an excuse not to run very often. We were never a good runner, even as a flat-chested child, so having you working front and centre has allowed us to blame you, even though we are aware that there are such things as sports bras. We just think we all look a bit silly when we run together. We are also grateful to you for providing a shelf for our wineglass when we are in the bath or reclining on the sofa.

Many thanks, too, for your contribution to all the good service we have received over the years. You have played a major part in getting us served before other people at bars, and your work on our recent trip to Italy was sterling. The free coffee, desserts and directions with which we were plied by swarthy men were all thanks to you. Perhaps next time we shall wear higher necklines to avoid being offered so many shots of grappa, since no one here actually likes it and it has led to a steady stream of complaints from the throat. None of these complaints were expressed particularly eloquently – generally just variations of a whispery croak of 'It burns, it burns' – but we do need to take all such feedback seriously, no matter how much it makes us giggle because we sound like Marlon Brando.

Remember our days as a barmaid? You certainly proved yourselves worthy team members for those few months. To start with, if our Bartending Skills Department wanted to dispute the role you played in securing the job in the first place, they would be hard pushed, as that department is non-existent. Working closely with the Department of Chatting Up, Jessica went from recently unemployed bookseller to barmaid in the time it took to drink a gin and tonic with the manager of the pub.

Please be aware that, like you, we are also hurt when our male friends make comments about breast size to the effect of 'more than a handful's a waste'. While they have never spoken directly about you that way, this comment has been made in your presence. It's usually made to smaller-busted girls who are complaining about how tiny their boobs are and threatening to have them enlarged. These are the kind of girls we envy. In fact we confess we've often just been fantasising about having breasts the size of theirs – the size that would mean we could wear anything we wanted, shoestring straps or none at all, and damn the consequences – when men have made the 'handful' comment. Here at the head office of Jessica, we pride ourself on never (or rarely) stooping to this level to elicit compliments. You will never (or rarely) catch us whingeing about your size in order to get people to say 'less than a large pudding-basinful's a waste'.

To be honest, you know as well as we do that most of the comments you elicit are along the lines of 'did you pick those up at Pamela Anderson's garage sale when she downsized?' We've worked hard to become accomplished at laughing such remarks off.

We are aware that the Department of Courage has on occasion failed to provide the backup you need. Please be advised that we are working with that department to increase its productivity. That department has asked us to convey its sincerest apologies for the incident last summer when Jessica nearly drowned in a Vermont lake.

As you know, this occurred after a wholly uncourageous attempt at skinny-dipping with three friends – two men and one woman – in which rather than being brave enough to strip off and rush shrieking down the shore into the water, the four of us dived in wearing our bathers, swam into the middle of the lake, formed a Square of Cowardice approximately 50 metres wide. Only then did we get naked and wave our clothes in the air as evidence that our submerged bodies were unclad. As our top was the string variety that ties at the back and at the nape of the neck, we then had great trouble getting it on again while treading water. The others all reached the shore and looked on curiously as we flailed around, looking as though we were attempting a game of full-body Cat's Cradle. As our energy flagged and our panic levels rose, we realised that if only we were brave enough to expose you, our naked breasts, to our friends, we could float on our back and quite easily and calmly untangle the bikini top and put it back on the right way up. But we were too shy.

So we struggled on and eventually, out of breath and having swallowed too many mouthfuls of parasite-ridden lake water, we hauled ourself back onto dry land, with our swimsuit covering you just enough to satisfy the Department of Extreme Prudery. Following this incident, top-level discussions have led to the decision to close the Department of Extreme Prudery altogether, and management consultants have been enlisted to help the Department of Courage meet accepted industry standards.

We've had some laughs with you, Breasts. We will never forget when we were at a wedding, and while standing with our dad, the father of the bride asked us if Jessica Pty Ltd was married. When we said no, he leered (there is no other word for it) at you and said (in a leery American accent): 'Well, you should have no trouble finding a husband with *those* "natural assets".' We've never been sure how he verbally put air quotes around 'natural assets', but he somehow managed.

Once we and our father stopped rolling on the ground with laughter, our dad turned to us and said, 'If I was a better father I probably would have punched him.' And we thought how glad we are to have a father who laughs with us about such things instead of punching people. We are even gladder that he is not the sort of man who leers at guests' breasts at weddings.

At the insistence of our HR department, we come to a rather delicate topic: sexual harassment. While we at the head office of Jessica are fairly confident that we have no internal issues of sexual harassment, we are responsible for you outside the company too, and so it is with some hesitation that we ask if you are comfortable with the amount you have been, shall we say, manhandled in your time with us. Realistically, if you feel we have allowed too many people to cop a feel (such an uncouth turn of phrase but it's what we mean), there is little we can do. Similarly, if you are unhappy with management decisions of exactly who has been permitted in your unclad vicinity, there is little to do except put it down to experience. I'm sure we all agree that if we had our time again, one or two unworthy suitors would not be allowed to touch you with a 10-foot pole. Not that anyone has ever touched you with a 10-foot pole – as you know, that's one of the rules we have.

If by any chance you feel that not enough manhandling has gone on, then that is another story entirely and we suggest you take it up with the Department of Morals.

Regarding arousal, after fifteen years we are reasonably confident that we have figured out what sorts of things make your nipples tingle, but if you would like to add anything to the list that includes very cold weather, unexpected kisses, and men on the television with Scottish accents, please fill out the appropriate form and submit it to HR.

We understand that at times you've had run-ins with our Department of Style. Style has, we realise, often been influenced by the external fashion world to the extent of forgetting your existence. We have repeatedly attempted to explain to the Department of Style that there is no such thing as plausible deniability when it comes to your existence, and that the department would benefit from working with you, not against you, but you know what bitches they can be up there. We haven't exactly been working in the most amenable of sartorial climates, either. For the last two or three years Jessica has been fighting a losing battle against the tide of faux-maternity fashion.

First came the empire waist, and one need only look at dramatisations of Jane Austen's novels for evidence of why it's a bad idea to push one's boobs up so high they are indistinguishable from a quadruple chin. Then we had to deal with the smock dress, and now apparently the shift is back, both doing their damnedest to make Jessica look like the mascot for a brickworks. When it comes to dressing we are all in agreement that when dealing with your presence the fabric must *in some way* follow the contours of the body or we risk looking like a monolith Christo has draped and forgotten to finish wrapping.

Of course, following the contours of the body can also be interpreted as 'wearing tight tops to show off your tits'. Quite frankly, here at the head office of Jessica we are beyond caring. This argument has gone on long enough. If we wear something loose over you we look like the front of a cruise ship of the magnitude that causes traffic jams when it docks in Sydney; wear something tight and we risk looking like the husband-stealing neighbour character from an American midday telemovie. As of now, the company has no official dress code. We'll wear whatever the hell we like.

As we look to the future, we hope to maintain Jessica as a working environment where you would like to remain. New human-resources initiatives have recently focused on what we can do to achieve this, and after much discussion, development objectives for you have been decided on. We look forward to retraining you in the coming years to take on increased responsibility. These plans include, but are not limited to, the feeding of our children and playing a key role in laying the groundwork for a breast fixation in any sons we have.

Such roles will necessarily lead to some changes in your departmental structure: as we have seen in other, more established companies, you may become somewhat bottom-heavy and your morale may suffer. Here at the head office of Jessica we will endeavour to help meet your new needs with an increased budget for supportive underwear, for we are well aware that bras are one of those things, like cling wrap and condoms, in which there is a clear and documented correlation between price and quality. We will also attempt to help enforce the No Cat Standing on the Chest rule.

We thank you sincerely for your first fifteen years with us, and we anticipate a great future for you here with Jessica. If you'll indulge the pun: 'Grow old with us; the breast is yet to come.'

A Full Fitting with Irene

MERRIDY EASTMAN

Setting

A busy department-store fitting room with six cubicles.

Characters

IRENE: a well-groomed bra-fitter and chatterbox in her mid-fifties
NARELLE: her gormless young assistant who remains offstage
MOTHER: a well-dressed woman, possibly a former beauty queen
DAUGHTER: her sullen, awkward teenage daughter

IRENE is lecturing her colleague, who remains offstage.

IRENE Don't you come back here shaking your head at me with that sorry look on your face, Narelle. Get back out there. There must be one Magenta Suddenly Shapely in a 36C on the floor somewhere. And where's my Tawny Lustrous Plunging 38D? Get a wriggle on! *(To the audience)* Honestly, you'd think she had an allergy to elastin.

IRENE enters cubicle one.

Knock knock, it's the Mormons again. How are we going with the Miracle Worker? Oh dear, you'd get more support if you wore it backwards, wouldn't you? It'd be a miracle if anyone bought one at all, frankly. Now cheer up. I've sent smaller women than you home with cleavage and I haven't had to use the staple gun yet. *(Barking out)* NARELLE!

A hand from offstage offers IRENE various bras.

Oh, there you are. Just pop back out on the floor and see if we've got any pink Elle Corantos or Promise push-ups in 34B, will you? No, she's already tried a Miracle and it didn't work.

IRENE enters cubicle two.

Now, how's my neutral Triumph Everyday Sport Supporter holding up? Well it's supposed to feel firm, you silly nong. Breasts can bounce by up to sixteen and a half centimetres during exercise. A well-endowed lass like you jogging all over the place with the wrong bra could end up with squashed lymph nodes, damaged nerves, breast pain, unsightly shoulder grooves, numbness in your fingers, neck, upper back and a sluggish immune system. I know one large-breasted lady who actually broke her collarbone during vigorous exercise because of a badly chosen bra. I'm serious. One minute she was doing Tae Bo, next minute – bang! Everyone hit the deck. Thought it was a sniper.

(To audience, between cubicles) See? If I wasn't here, off she'd go, bouncing round Centennial Park in a Chantilly Duchess hidden-wire half-cup. She'd never get beyond the duckpond. *(Sighs)* An unacknowledged, undervalued breed, your professional bra-fitter. Some people think we're just interfering old women with latent lesbian tendencies, but your qualified bra-fitter can mean the difference between life and death. It's no laughing matter, sir. *(Eyeballs man in audience)* I've seen happy marriages crumble due to the wrong-shaped underwire. Just last week we had three cases of strap trauma. There are women out there on the verge of nervous breakdowns, all because they're walking around in deficient underbands.

IRENE accepts bras from an offstage hand.

Thanks, Narelle. And *Narelle*! *(Suddenly hissing)* What are you thinking, letting that big lass in cubicle five try on a zebra-print push-up and panties? I don't care, Narelle, use your noggin. If someone *that size* asks for something from the Kylie Safari range, just tell her we've sold out. Tell her there was a fire at the warehouse. Tell her anything. Poor creature looks like a bomb went off in a zoo.

IRENE pops her head into cubicle three.

Well, my goodness, it's not called the Balconette for nothing, is it? Now isn't that a flattering bra? Is it for a special occasion? A wedding anniversary! We had our silver last month, me an' Roy. Now you see how the stretch microfibre gracefully flatters the cleavage without taking away any of the support? And don't you love the pearl detailing with that adorable little bow? You don't? What – the bow, or the whole shebang? Oh. *(Immediately drops her voice)* Oh. Would you? I don't know. You mean a Peephole? No, no . . . we just don't get much demand for them, not since Mardi Gras. I'll ask Narelle to have a peep. I mean, a look.

IRENE steps outside the cubicle and shouts.

(Shouting) NARELLE!

(Dropping voice) Just hop up the ladder in the stockroom and see if we still have any of those Eros open-tip bras left, will you? Open-tip, Narelle. Peepholes. The ones with holes around the nipples. Just stop pulling silly faces and do it, you silly girl. *(To audience)* Honestly, you'd think she'd been raised by nuns.

IRENE whips open the curtains on cubicle four.

(To MOTHER) Sorry to have kept you waiting. It's the full fitting, is it?

MOTHER That's right.

IRENE turns to DAUGHTER

IRENE Oh, hello there! Can I get you a colouring-in book or something while Mum has a fitting, petal? *(To MOTHER)* Santa's visiting on Level Four if you think she'd find her way back.

MOTHER Well, actually —

IRENE And apparently this one's safe. *(Lowers her voice)* After last year, they've started doing full checks, even on the elves.

MOTHER Well it's Daphne, actually, my daughter, who's having a fitting. Not me.

IRENE turns and smiles at DAUGHTER instead.

IRENE And here she is.

Pause.

MOTHER I think it's time she began wearing a bra.

IRENE I can see it's time she began wearing a bra!

IRENE maintains a sunny smile as she lowers her gaze to DAUGHTER's flat chest, and up again.

Yes indeedy!

After an uncomfortable pause for all three, IRENE swings into action with her tape measure.

Arms up!

While deftly measuring every single distance on the girl's upper torso, including the circumference of her head, IRENE continues chatting.

Your first bra, how exciting! I remember my first bra. Aunty Nell took me to Mark Foy's on a Saturday morning – arms out – where two miserable old biddies stuck their cold hands all over me – arms down – before fastening me inside what felt like a surgical vest. I was so upset – 23 centimetres – Aunty Nell took me for a milkshake at Town Hall station – turn around – threw it up on the platform soon as we got off at Punchbowl . . . *(Calling out the curtains)* NARELLE! *(Quickly back to MOTHER)* And were we thinking underwire or elasticised, full cup or three-quarter, front clasp or back, two hooks or one, padded or non-padded, cotton, microfibre, nylon, lace, plain or print, with or without a bow?

MOTHER I think we'll go for the padded, full cup, double hook, clasp at the back, nothing too lacy, with a bow, thanks.

IRENE Colour?

DAUGHTER Black.

MOTHER Pink.

IRENE *(Yelling through the curtains)* NARE—! Oh there you are. Just pop over to Miss Teen and pick up a Princess

Trixie padded training bra without wire and a Brittany Beginner 32AA in pink, will you?

DAUGHTER *(sullen)* I don't want padding, Mum.

MOTHER Well what else are you going to put in there, Daphne? I can't help it if you take more after your Aunty Vonnie than me! *(To IRENE)* At her age I didn't need padding, I was bouncing all over the place.

IRENE Oh, me too. I had to give up netball and join the choir.

MOTHER I had to give up guitar and take up the flute.

They share a naughty laugh.

IRENE They used to call me Norks Norton.

MOTHER They used to call me Babs McBoob.

They laugh again.

IRENE I couldn't see my feet!

MOTHER I couldn't see my dinner!

The two women roar laughing as DAUGHTER looks on miserably.

IRENE Ah, well Narelle will be with you shortly . . . if she hasn't found another half-eaten Snickers bar somewhere.

IRENE knocks on cubicle five and enters.

Knock knock. How are you going with the Perla, pet? Don't be shy. You've seen two, you've seen them all.

Now how am I supposed to know what's going on under that big floppy jumper? That's the girl, off it comes . . . and just bend over for me – you're nowhere near filling those cups. My daughter Debbie-Lea hides her figure in those oversized tents all the time – you in? Got used to them while she was expecting and hasn't been able to shed the weight since – upsy-daisy – completely backfires if you ask me. Makes her look like she's hiding a yak or something. Now see how the wider band's giving you good base support and a lovely profile at the same time? I like to call this one the sheep dog, know why? – arms up – 'cause it rounds them up and points them in the right direction – and arms down.

IRENE comes out and talks to audience.

Well you've got to have a joke or two up your sleeve when the poor things are standing half-naked in front of you, haven't you? Maureen taught me that, bless her heart. She was a funny bugger. Used to say bras don't just come in different sizes, but also religions. The Catholic bra supports the masses, the Salvation Army bra lifts the fallen, and the Baptist makes mountains out of molehills . . . dear old Maureen. Worked till she dropped. One minute she was adjusting a convertible halterneck, the next we found her standing in the stockroom, face down in the silicone push-ups. She looked so peaceful it seemed a shame to move her.

IRENE re-enters same cubicle.

How you going, yak smuggler? Oh, I'm sorry, pet! Why didn't you say so? Not expecting a yak I hope! Oh love, what haven't we got? We've got maternity bras designed by medical engineers to adjust to the increasing breast throughout pregnancy, and nursing bras with direct nipple access via clasping flaps over the cup. But whip that underwire off right now. Underwires can constrict the breast and cause blocked ducts and mastitis. Our Debbie-Lea had mastitis and sat crying in her backyard for two weeks with cabbage leaves stuck to her boobs. Cabbage leaves, I'm not making it up – she read it in a book somewhere.

IRENE comes out and shouts after her colleague.

Narelle! Never mind the lacy Miranda latex. Sprint over to Maternity and bring us a So Lovable seamless soft cup, a Berlei Babe with the padded slings, a Triumph Nursing Mum and a snap-front Big Sister in a double D. Or, Narelle, anything with clasping flaps!

IRENE pokes her head through curtains of cubicle six.

And how are we going with the Lady Chatterley, love? Oh, dear! Not so much a lady as a nasty little tramp. Well, hand it back and give us a hoi when you've got the Veronica on.

IRENE closes curtains behind her, and tiptoes towards audience.

(Conspiratorially) In this job, you get to see all sizes . . . big, small, pert, retired, and then *(lowers voice)* there's the ones that have had a bit of help. *(Points to cubicle six)* Oh yes, I may not know much about beetox, but after thirty-seven years' service on the floor, I know an implant when I see one.

It's not that I'm against implants. I'm all for a bit of breast enhancement if it makes you happy, ladies, but let's learn from Pamela Anderson's mistakes, shall we? Rule number one: when choosing a new breast size, never go bigger than your own head.

The lights slowly fade on the cubicles, leaving only the area around IRENE illuminated.

(To audience) I'm not convinced Narelle's heart's in this job at all. As I told Bronwyn in Personnel, I think she'd be happier in Accessories. I said to Narelle in the canteen today – Narelle, I said, make friends with the breast. You can't be a good bra-fitter unless you're prepared to shake the breast by the hand and look it in the eye. It's not going to bite you, Narelle, I said. The breast deserves our attention. It's a living, breathing, beautiful part of the body, deserving love, respect and a good home. Of course Narelle just sat there, next to that dingbat Donna from Stationery, giggling until tea came out her nose. *(Sighs)* As I said, better off in gloves and handbags.

IRENE continues picking up bras.

Ah, well. Another day, another seventy-three breasts all looking for new homes, some of them with extensions, balconies, and even *(picking up a peephole bra)* portholes.

IRENE bends down and picks up a single padded prosthesis.

And three recovering mastectomies today. Sometimes, I swear we're in the midst of an epidemic. Needless to say, Narelle doesn't cope too well with prostheses or mastectomy bras. So I had a little chat with her in the storeroom. I told her how much courage it takes these women to walk into a lingerie department again. God knows, they've been through enough already. They need to be greeted by warm, caring staff, happy to be a part of their healing process . . . not a tall gaping idiot having a panic attack at the first glimpse of a silicone nipple!

I never wanted a reconstruction. When the woman in the bed next to me at St Vinnie's came back after seven hours in surgery with three operation sites, one where her left breast used to be, one on her back where they'd extracted the spare tissue, and one under her arm where they'd taken out the lymph nodes, I knew I just couldn't go through with all of that. Doctor MacNeil still tells me it's not too late . . . which is nice to know, just in case I decide to go back to wearing a bikini this summer . . . But, honestly, I'm so used to my prosthesis, I just couldn't imagine life any other way. Specially since I upgraded to a contact prosthesis. You know those kiddies' toys you throw at the wall and they stick? A contact prosthesis is a bit like that. Not that I stand against the wall half-naked every morning and let Roy practise his overarm spin . . . I just wet it with a special cleaning fluid in the shower and it sticks for days. Besides, Roy couldn't hit a bull in the bum with a banjo.

IRENE stoops to pick up one last bra from the floor.

(Sighs) Oh, but it's nice to get old and make friends with your mammaries again, isn't it, ladies? Whatever state they're in . . . When they no longer have to jump through hoops, feed hungry mouths, or turn into some bloke's theme park twice a week. Yes, it's nice to have them to yourself at last and just accept them for what they are. *(Calling off)* NARELLE!

Be nice to your breasts, ladies. Be nice to them now. Whatever size, shape or colour they are, whatever traumas they've survived, and whatever challenges may lie ahead, for goodness sake, invest in some good underwear and experience true happiness. Come and see me for a fitting, and I'll send you home in a flattering bra that doesn't make your eyes water. And keep getting them checked whatever you do. Don't be scared to find something. It's missing something you gotta worry about. *(Shouting out)* NARE— ! Oh for goodness' sake.

IRENE pokes her head inside a cubicle.

I've told you before, Narelle. You're too broad in the back for the Balconette. Come on now. Put your top back on, finish your Snickers bar, and I'll walk with you to the station.

IRENE closes the curtains and turns to audience.

Or Garden Supplies. Perhaps she'd be happier in Garden Supplies. I'll have a word to Bronwyn.

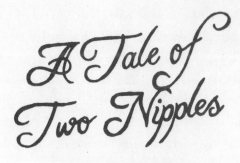

MIA FREEDMAN

Saturday, 9:30 p.m.

I'm sitting on the couch playing with my nipples. My husband glances over at me, rolls his eyes, then resumes watching the stupid DVD he rented – the DVD that made me shove both hands down my top in anger. I fume and fiddle silently. But a few minutes later, I'm forced to speak. 'Um, babe?' I venture. 'I think I've fucked up.'

It had seemed like a good idea at the time. I was almost nine months pregnant and *over* it. I adore being pregnant, but not at the end. The last four weeks are always heinous. To say I lose my sense of humour is an understatement. I become a monster.

I was hot, huge, grumpy, puffy, snarky, bloaty and uncomfy – the seven nightmare dwarves of late pregnancy. Jason had made the horrific mistake of renting a DVD I didn't like and my considered response was to explode like a fat, angry hand grenade.

'I'm pregnant and I'm bored and I'm over it and you can't even rent a decent DVD!' I had railed attractively. 'Is it too much to ask you to find something in the video store – SOMETHING – that would be interesting to me and doesn't have guns in it? Something in which nobody DIES? Where nobody gets their FACE whacked in? Something with Jennifer Aniston in it, maybe? Or Gwyneth bloody PALTROW? Is that too much to ask when I'm carrying your child and I'm SUFFERING?'

From there, inducing my own labour was the logical next step. That's where the nipples came in. I remembered reading somewhere that nipple stimulation can trigger contractions. Pissed off about the DVD, and about being so damn pregnant, I thought I'd give it a whirl. What I didn't expect is that it would work.

Within two minutes, I feel a slight twinge. I immediately dismiss this as a coincidence. With a few more nipple twiddles, the twinge becomes a contraction. Not massive. Not unbearable. Not even painful really. But a contraction nonetheless. I stop twiddling and reach for another handful of Smarties. A few minutes later, another unmistakable contraction. Time to confess to Jason.

'You're kidding me,' he replies, slightly surprised, but also not. The man has lived with me for more than ten years and is used to my ability to create unwanted, unnecessary and unpleasant drama out of a perfectly nice evening. 'You're an idiot,' he adds, shaking his head as I nod mutely in agreement.

As impatient as I was to hurry this pregnancy along to the birth part, late on a Saturday night was not the ideal time to go into labour. Particularly because my beloved obstetrician, Dr Bob, did not deliver babies between ten p.m. and six a.m.

Plus, it was bedtime and I wanted to go to sleep. I hadn't slept properly in weeks and I was exhausted. Our eight-year-old son, Luca, was already crashed out, blissfully enjoying his last hours as an only child. Another contraction. And was that another? Yes. Another. Oh dear. This was not the plan. This was most definitely not the plan . . .

Saturday, 10 p.m.

I decide to ignore the contractions. Maybe they're not contractions, just Braxton Hicks, those practice ones. Fine. Except Braxton Hicks are painless and these ones aren't.

We'd already been to the hospital that morning for a false alarm. I'd woken up feeling a bit damp in the knickers and thought it might be a trickle of my waters breaking. I'd had no experience of this before. With Luca, the midwife had broken my waters for me with some kind of giant hook thing while I was lying down being examined mid-labour. Despite what you see in movies and sitcoms, waters rarely break all over the shoes of horrified strangers in supermarkets. Although the thought of gushing litres of warm liquid all over the ground at Luca's school or the fruit shop was quite mortifying, it was also slightly appealing. I love a bit of drama.

When my knickers felt suspicious that morning, I wondered if it could be some sort of amniotic leakage. I rang the hospital. Explained about my knickers. 'If the sac had broken you'd know about it.' Oh. Okay. 'But there could be a tear. Come in if you want to, or you can wait at home and see what happens.' A combination of boredom, nerves and impatience made me keen to get it checked out. Hospital it would be.

After breakfast, we'd left Luca with my parents and driven calmly to the maternity ward. Laughing and joking, we made our way to the reception desk where a man looked up, a flicker of surprise crossing his face. He wasn't used to seeing women arriving at the labour ward in such high spirits or capable of speaking in sentences. By the time most women get to hospital, they're usually in great pain.

'Um, I think my waters may have broken a little bit but I'm not really sure. My knickers are a bit damp and, well, I was wondering if someone could check me out?'

Too much information for the guy on the front desk. He was just in charge of the computer.

Ignoring my knicker reference, he located my details in the system and picked up the phone. 'Hi, Gwen. I have a patient here, full term, thinks she may have broken her waters and would like to see someone.' Pause. 'Okay, thanks, I'll send her through.'

He directed us through the big doors into the delivery ward. 'Keep going to the desk and someone will look after you.' It was quiet in the hall. No screaming or moaning. Or maybe the delivery suites were just well soundproofed. A nurse took a few more details and showed us through to an examining room.

This was when I started to feel a bit funny. I clambered awkwardly onto the bed. It was narrow. I was not. Suddenly I felt faint and hot and I couldn't sit up any more. I fell back on the pillow and Jason jumped up. 'Shit, you've gone white.'

Torn between staying with me and calling for help, he stayed. The room spun a bit. I didn't remember reading about this in the pregnancy books. A minute or two passed and a guy walked in. He was around thirty-five, no white coat, could have been a janitor or a doctor, hard to tell.

'Hi, I'm Simon. Tell me what's going on?' I made a snap judgement that he was indeed some kind of medical professional and automatically started to take off my underwear while Jason quickly explained that I'd almost fainted.

'Pretty normal. It's a blood-pressure thing. Roll onto your side for a moment. That should help.'

It did. I felt better. Better enough to fill him in on the possible breaking-of-waters situation.

'Well, let's take a look,' he said chirpily, reaching into the cupboard near the bed for . . . a very large torch. Like the ones that used to be on the ads with dolphins bouncing them off their noses. I blanched ever so slightly.

'Hmmm, that's interesting,' I said, falling into polite small talk like I always do when I feel uncomfortable. 'A torch! Goodness!'

'Yes,' he nodded, waving it around a bit to demonstrate its usefulness.

This is how I came to be lying on my back half-nude while a nice man wearing gloves and glasses shone a giant torch between my legs. As he peered into my illuminated lady parts, which were now lit up like a night-time cricket match, a young female intern looked intently over his shoulder.

The verdict was swift. 'Hmm, no, I can't see any sign of a membrane tear. The cervix looks nice and ripe but it isn't dilated. Perhaps it was urine you felt?'

'Oh, perhaps,' I mumbled, 'you know, maybe.' As he hooked me up to a monitor to check my blood pressure and the baby's heart rate (both fine), I felt faintly ridiculous but reminded myself that the actual birth bit would be far worse. Far worse than chatting about whether I'd accidentally weed my pants while a stranger looked up my clacker with a torch. At least he wasn't wearing a miner's hat.

An hour later we were home. Still pregnant. Possibly incontinent. Definitely over it. Who knew we'd be doing it for real within hours? I blame the DVD. And the nipples.

Sunday, 2 a.m.

The pain wakes me. I lie in bed for a while, trying to go back to sleep, but the ten-minute windows between contractions aren't enough to slip through. So I get up and waddle to the lounge room, back to the scene of the nipple crime. I take my watch – so I can monitor the gap between contractions. In denial about what's to come, I mindlessly flick TV channels and ignore the fact that I've brought this on with my nipple twiddling. Who knew nipples have such power?

Sunday, 3 a.m.

The contractions are already five minutes apart and getting ouchy. Could this be it? Apparently so. This is definitely not a false-alarm wee issue. Dry knickers. Sore tummy. I call the hospital to report my progress and ask when we should come in.

'How far apart are the contractions?' asks the midwife.

'About five minutes.'

'And can you talk comfortably during them?'

'Um, well, not really, no. Sort of. Not very comfortably. No.'

Her tone strikes a fine balance between concern and boredom. 'Well, you can stay home a bit longer or you can come in. It's up to you.'

'I think we'll come in. You know, to be safe.'

I waddle back to the bedroom and touch Jason on the shoulder, shaking him lightly.

'Babe, we're on.'

He reacts quickly, rolling over and blinking while he tries to remember who I am and what I'm doing next to his bed.

'What? Oh, right. Yes. Okay.'

And then he closes his eyes again. Just when I think he's gone back to sleep, he sits bolt upright, startled, blinking madly, trying to focus his eyes in the dark. 'How are you? What's happening?'

'Contractions are five minutes apart. I've been up for a while. I think it's time to get going.'

Because it gives you a false sense of control in the unpredictable journey of pregnancy, for months we'd discussed What We Would Do when the time came. My only birth plan was 'Get To the Hospital and Get Drugs'. I knew enough to recognise that birth plans are mostly useless. But I was happy to plan the getting to the hospital part. I'd gone into labour with Luca in the middle of the night too so this wasn't entirely new territory for us.

But the process had been far slower the first time and I'd laboured at home from four a.m. to three p.m., before we'd gone to the hospital. Eight years later, we had a son who liked to plan ahead. We'd discussed it many times. We were ready.

There was some added excitement about it all going down at three a.m. and, taking after his mother in so many ways, Luca would have been disappointed with any less dramatic option, except perhaps me giving birth on the kitchen floor. That would have been *cooooool*. Jason goes to wake him up and, according to The Plan, call my parents who will come and collect him.

Out of habit, I hit the shower to wash and blow-dry my hair. As if to prepare for a night out. Or a meeting. More control. And vanity. I'd conveniently forgotten how fast I'd tossed away my vanity the last time I went through labour.

So here I am again, eight years later, preparing to look attractive while giving birth, huge and naked in front of the mirror with a blowdryer in my hand.

Last week I'd dragged my bits – which I hadn't seen for months – to the waxer for my regular Brazilian, an experience even more undignified than usual due to my size, heft and inability to lie on my back without suffocating.

'Get on all fours,' commanded the waxer, before calling for backup.

'Hi. I'm Angie,' came a perky voice from behind my bottom, which was pointed elegantly at the door.

'Hi. I'm pregnant,' I snapped.

Choosing an outfit to wear to the maternity ward is actually harder than it sounds. Well, it is if you're vain and stupid. Tick, tick. You need something that will make internal examinations quick and practical. Something you can hike up to your armpits every time someone new comes into the room to rummage between your legs. Which is often.

Being December and hot, the weather is on my side. Much harder to dress a whale when it's cold. Layers are hard. So between contractions, I peruse the very small section of my wardrobe containing things that still fit. I find a knee-length silk dress that's loose, light and comfy. Come on down.

Luca wanders into the room.

'So, it's happening?' he says, seeking confirmation.

'Yep,' I grunt, trying not to lose my balance and fall into the bath. 'Happening. Got a bag packed?'

'Yes. I've got my Game Boy and a book and pyjamas and two changes of clothes.'

That's my boy. I should have put him in charge of choosing my outfit.

I hear my dad's car pull into the driveway. It's 3.30 a.m. Not feeling up for a chat, I stay in the bedroom. But first, I give Luca a huge hug with the vague sadness of knowing that the next time I see him, our intense only-child bond will be different. Then another contraction comes along to blow away any sentimentality. All I can think is: 'BLOODY OUCH.'

I peer out the window and see Jason standing beside the car, talking to Dad while Luca hops in the passenger seat. Uninvited but sensing an opportunity, the dog jumps in after him.

Good idea, probably. Who knows when we'll be home.

It's all still fairly unreal. Like watching a documentary about someone else being in labour. Big moments in life – well, in my life – are often like that. They're almost too big to comprehend at the time. I go into autopilot – I'm a helicopter hovering over the action, watching it unfold.

But the contractions bring me back to reality. They're getting stronger, and I'm getting antsy about getting to hospital.

Luca safely away, my dress on, my hair dry and straight – a quick GHD to smooth down those stray flyaways – and Havaianas on my puffy feet. Time to go.

'Jason, we need to go NOW.' I do this a lot – take my own sweet time to get ready but as soon as I am, demand everyone be standing at the door like sprinters waiting for the starting gun. I am the gun.

Although it wasn't funny at the time, our drive to the hospital for Luca's birth has become a running joke. The route Jason chose eight years ago has the most speed bumps of any road in Australia. Every 15 metres, another bump.

If you have ever been in labour, witnessed someone in labour or even just know what labour MEANS, you will understand that a contraction and a speed bump are not natural allies. The only thing more painful than having a contraction is sawing your own arm off, or having a contraction while going over a speed bump.

To make things worse – yes! Possible! – Jason was on the phone to the hospital at the time, informing them of our approach.

JASON Um, hello. I called earlier about my partner, who's in labour.

(bump)

ME *(in hoarse whisper)* FUCK. FUCK FUCK FUCK.

JASON What? Yes, her name is Mia. Freedman. F-R-E—

(bump)

ME *(trying to stuff my fist into my mouth)* IDIOT. FUCK. I HATE YOU, JASON!! FUCK FUCK. OW FUCK. HATE!!!!

JASON Hang on. Sorry. Yes, that's it. Um, yes, we're about ten —

(bump)

ME (trying to punch him while grabbing phone) HANG UP, FUCK, SHIT. HOW COULD YOU TAKE THIS —

(bump)

ME ROAD! FUCKING FUCK!

In the end it was totally worth it – I've been able to use the story against him ever since.

This time, my labour clearly isn't that advanced. As we get in the car and Jason starts taking a different route, I say, 'Wait, what about the speed bumps?'

'Right,' he replies, doing a U-turn and heading towards Speed Bump Boulevard. But within fifteen seconds, another contraction hits and instantly deletes my sense of humour.

'Do you want me to turn back again?' Jason asks, my fingers digging into his arm.

'No,' I gasp valiantly, still keen to maintain a silly

tradition. I love a silly tradition.

Moments later, he's easing the car over the bumps and I'm gritting my teeth, neither swearing at him nor able to rustle a smile. 'I'm an idiot,' I mutter, for the second time tonight. 'This isn't funny any more.'

We spend the rest of the drive in silence. My contractions are getting longer and stronger. We pull into the car park and I grimly trudge the 20 metres to the entrance. No chitchat with the person on the front desk this time. I want a bed and some drugs. Drugs first. Gimme.

My paperwork is waiting and we're ushered into an examining room. Jason helps me up onto the bed where I lay down on my side, holding my belly. Every so often, the baby kicks.

A youngish midwife comes in to examine me. 'Hi, I'm Amy,' she says, in an English accent. Soon I will hate Amy, but not yet. At this point our relationship is still a blank page and I want her to like me in the way I always want people to like me. Especially when they're people who control my access to pain relief.

'How frequent are your contractions?'

'Five minutes apart, started last night about 9.30 but didn't get bad until about two a.m.'

'Let's time one,' she suggests, and we wait. Three minutes later, I say 'Now' and ride the pain wave while she looks at the second hand on the nurse's watch pinned to her shirt.

'Okay, finished.' I grimace.

'About fifty seconds,' she pronounces. 'Now let's see how dilated you are.'

This is the big moment. Well, one of them. Every woman in labour imagines herself to be more dilated than she actually is because this means you're closer to the end. And it's like a tangible measure of the distance you've travelled on the Pain Bus. Are we there yet? Huh? Huh? Are we? Are we? It's also worth nothing that the further you journey on the Pain Bus, the faster you lose your vanity, your dignity and your inhibitions. And sometimes, your mind.

As I hike up my pretty silk dress and wriggle awkwardly out of my knickers, I decide on the spot I'm done with them. I know that Amy will be the first in a conga line of strangers to get up close and personal with my bits so really, what's the point? Bye-bye, inhibition. We're well on our way.

The silence stretches as I wait for her verdict. Based on the intensity of the contractions, I figure I'm a little further gone than I was when I arrived at hospital the first time I gave birth. Then it was 3 centimetres. So I'm guessing at least 4 centimetres, but hoping for more. If it was 5 or 6 centimetres, I wouldn't be surprised. It hurts that much.

'One point five centimetres,' Amy announces briskly. My heart falls through the floor. It's not possible.

'Really?' I manage to spit out, as another contraction hits.

'Yes, really.' I instantly detect a note of condescension in her voice. I begin to dislike Amy. She has decided I'm a drama queen. Which, sometimes, I am. But definitely not at this moment.

'You know, Mia, you may not even be in labour,' she singsongs. 'This may be pre-labour. The baby might not come for another few days yet. When's your actual due date?'

This is a trick question. The hate intensifies. 'The seventeenth,' I mumble petulantly. Five days away. She's delighted with this answer.

'You see,' she declares smugly. 'It could still be days away!'

Then, just as I'm thinking about how I'd like Amy to die, she delivers the killer punch. 'So, we can't take you to a delivery suite yet. You might want to go home and rest there where you feel more comfortable.'

Comfortable? COMFORTABLE? What part of having the pain equivalent of a rocking chair shoved up your arse might be COMFORTABLE, AMY?

Out loud, I say, 'Amy, there is no way we can go home. I'm staying here. I'm in too much pain.'

She thinks for a moment. 'Well, you could go outside and walk around the car park.'

The car park? Is this *Candid* Fucking *Camera*?

'Moving around can help get the labour going,' she adds helpfully.

'What about the pain?'

'Here. If you like, I can give you two Panadol.'

It's official. Amy is on fucking crack and I've never hated anyone more.

This is how Jason and I come to be staggering slowly around a hospital car park at 4.30 on a warm Sunday morning in December. Of course, the two lovely Panadol have taken away all my pain so I'm feeling fantastic. No, wait. The Panadol doesn't even touch the sides because I AM IN LABOUR AND PANADOL IS FOR PISSY LITTLE HEAD-ACHES. She may as well have given me Tic Tacs.

Every few minutes, when a contraction comes, I lean forward and brace myself against Jason or a car. And I'm starting to make noise during my contractions, which is a new thing for me.

With Luca, I was quiet, which in itself had been a surprise. I'd seen the documentaries and the movies and the TV shows where real people and fake people give birth. It was uniformly a noisy affair. Much panting and groaning, shrieking, yelling, crying and grunting. But when it was my turn, I discovered that making any noise required me to use my stomach muscles, which were otherwise occupied during a contraction. Noise of any kind seemed to make the pain worse so I stayed as silent as a Scientologist.

But this time? Tom Cruise would not be impressed. In another inhibition-losing milestone on my road to birth, I care not a hoot about passers-by. Fortunately my shape and proximity to the labour ward tell the back-story pretty effectively, so no one calls the police. And hey, Amy the Sadist probably sends all her patients to do laps outside. A gigantic woman doubled over in pain and wailing among parked cars is no doubt standard around here.

After about half an hour of this, I can't take it any more. 'We have to go inside,' I pant to Jason and he slowly steers me back to the exam room. Surely I must be 8 centimetres by now. My nemesis Amy returns.

'Amy, Mia can't keep walking around the car park,' Jason says, frustration creeping into his voice. 'When can we be admitted?'

'Well, it's only been half an hour since I examined her so it's still too early to go to a delivery suite. You can go into the waiting room if you like.'

Fucking great. But I'm in no position to argue. That would require words and a functioning brain. 'There's a shower in there she can use,' she adds brightly. 'Sometimes that helps.'

Amy leads us a few metres down the hall into a small poo-brown-carpeted room with some ugly art posters on the wall and eight Formica chairs dotted around. 'The shower's in there,' she says, gesturing to a door directly opposite the chairs. And then she walks out.

Through the haze of pain, I try to feel grateful for small things. Like the fact there's no one else in the ugly waiting room. And that it's not a car park. 'Shower,' I grunt, and Jason helps me into the bathroom. It's slightly larger than your average public toilet. There's a sink, a toilet with handrails and a shower nozzle attached to the wall. No discernable shower area. Just a tiled floor under the nozzle where I am soon standing, naked and moaning.

Jason aims the hot water towards my back as I brace myself against the wall. The sounds I'm making mildly surprise me, although in my head I'm already somewhere else, the pain transporting me somewhere above my body.

Time falls away. I have no idea how long I've been standing in the shower or if, in fact, I will ever be anywhere else. Later, Jason tells me we were there for about forty-five minutes. At some stage, blood starts to appear on the tiles. Bright-red blood. If I was in control of my mind, this would worry me, but I'm detached, just focused on surviving between contractions.

Every so often, Jase says something like, 'I'm going to try and find someone, will you be okay for a minute?' I know he can't help me. He doesn't have an epidural needle or know what to do with it, so frankly, I don't care where he is or what he does.

Eventually, he drags a midwife back to my shower prison to prove that I am indeed worthy of a delivery suite. The bathroom door is now wide open. I'm past caring. I look up from under the shower, my hair plastered to my head, my body wet and the floor red with my blood to see a grey-haired lady quickly taking in the scene. 'Right. I think we can take you through now.'

You RECKON?!

Jason wraps a towel around me and helps me walk around the corner to a delivery room. Finally. 'Epidural,' I moan. 'I neeeeeed drugs now.' In the relative comfort of a non-public place, my body decides it's time to kick things up a notch. Or five.

There's a new midwife. I vaguely register that she's in her forties, Nordic-looking. An accent. Not Amy. Seems kind.

'Hi, Mia. My name's Bianca and I'm the midwife who's going to look after you. Let's just hop up here on the bed and we'll check the baby's heart rate. Jason, is it? Jason, why don't you go and run a bath for Mia? The heat might help as those contractions build.' Build? BUILD? 'And we'll just check how dilated you are, okay?'

'Okay,' I wail quietly, like a petulant child. The baby's heart rate is good and Bianca waits for my next contraction to subside before checking my cervix.

'Five centimetres. Very good.'

My thoughts turn to Amy. 'Amy tried to send me home,'

I wail. 'She. Tried. To. Send. Me. HOOOOOOOME.'

At this moment, more than anything else, maybe even more than drugs, I need everyone to agree this was an injustice. A grave error of judgement on her part. A travesty.

Bianca pats my arm noncommittally. 'Yes, dear. Well, Amy has been called upstairs for a Caesarean so she won't be looking after you any more.' It's not nearly enough, but it's a start.

'Good!' I shout. 'Because Amy TRIED TO SEND ME HOME.' Drugs. Back to the drugs. 'I REEEALLY need an epidural. Where's the anaesthetist?'

'He's upstairs for the Caesarean too but I'm sure he'll be here soon, dear.'

How do all those women do that active birth stuff? All that moving about with fit balls. All I want to do is lie down and die. Regularly, new people come into the room. 'Are you the anaesthetist?' I beg every time.

'No, dear, but I'm sure he'll be here soon.' Liars.

If you've not been in labour before, here's what you need to know about contractions:

1. They are the most pain you will ever know.
2. It's not just the physical pain but the mental head-fuck of knowing there's another one right behind it. And another one right behind that. Like if you got run over by a bus and were lying on the road

knowing there was a line of buses stretching into infinity, waiting to run you down again and again and again. And again.

Jason is conspicuously quiet. I find out later this is because each time someone promises me that the anaesthetist is coming, the midwife catches Jason's eye and silently shakes her head. They know with near certainty the drugs aren't coming but no one has the heart to tell me. This is probably a good thing because it is the one tiny bit of hope I cling to.

My waters break. A sudden gush all over the bed. Whatever. The noises are getting louder. At one point, I hear a terrible wailing and wonder, who the hell is that? Oh, wait, it's me. I sound like a barnyard animal.

When I do manage to form words instead of animal noises, it's to moan one of the following two sentences:

1. 'Amy tried to send me HOME!' I am still finding it hard to move past this. Everyone now just ignores all mentions of Amy.
2. 'I want to DIIIIIE. Just take me outside and run me over with the CAR.' Thankfully, Jason ignores this too. The ravings of a mad woman.

The next time Bianca examines me, I am 8 centimetres. My response to this happy news is naturally to raise the subject of Amy. Jason reacts with slightly more sense and ducks outside to call my parents and his, and summon them to the hospital with Luca. At least I think he does, because soon after, I hear him saying, 'Luca and your parents are here.' Whatever. Unless they've brought a big needle to stick in my back, I don't care.

Sunday, 8 a.m.

We've been at the hospital for what feels like three weeks but has actually been three and a half hours. Approximately one hundred years later, a new man walks into the room. Even in my out-there state, I can feel the energy in the room change immediately.

'Epidural?' I whimper, forever hopeful.

'Good morning, Mia. I'm Stephen. Remember me?'

It's the locum doctor. I've only met him once; at the time I was nervous about the prospect of him delivering the baby. Dr Bob makes me feel safe and knows my history. But right now? I want to roll off the bed and kiss Stephen's feet. His voice is commanding and confident.

'Hi, Stephen,' I wail pathetically. 'Thanks for coming.' Now I'm polite? As he examines me, between animal noises, I share with him my thoughts on Amy, the lack of epidural, wanting to die and the general injustice of life. He is focused and yet unmoved.

While I'm still begging, whingeing and ranting, he comes over to the side of the bed, takes hold of my arm and puts his face quite close to mine to get my attention. He speaks firmly.

'Mia, there is no epidural. There's no time. We're having this baby right now.'

This takes a moment to sink in but I'm swept up in his confidence. I love to be bossed when I'm feeling out of control. This is good. Had he suggested it, I would have agreed to adjourn to the car park to give birth there.

'Okaaaay,' I nod in my now signature singsong wail. 'Thanks for coming, Stephen.' This becomes my new refrain. It's finally dawned that no one is going to engage with me about Amy. And Stephen is the first person to actually do anything constructive, like suggest I give birth now. My gratitude must be expressed, oh, every fifteen seconds or so.

As I begin to follow his instructions about pushing and stopping and breathing and panting, it all feels very . . . organic. Simple. Unadorned. With Luca there had been so many people in the room, and I'd been hooked up to so many machines. But now it's just me, Bianca over one shoulder, Jason over the other and Stephen in a shirt and chinos gently and carefully easing the baby's head out of me.

Stephen looks up. 'The head's out. Lots of hair! Do you want to see?'

I glance down and see a head protruding from my body. Somewhere in my brain this registers as odd. A few more pushes and Stephen asks casually, 'Do you want to pull the baby out?'

Really? I reach forward and he helps me hook my fingers under the baby's armpits.

'Now pull.' And I do. My baby slides out of me, as slippery as a tiny seal, and I instinctively pull it onto my stomach. Stephen helps turn it over. 'A girl!'

A girl. My girl. My girl with two teeny, tiny nipples of her own. Which, maybe one day, she will twiddle in frustration as she sits on the couch waiting for her own baby to come into the world.

She's taken from me quite quickly to be wrapped and weighed and I lie there in a happy, stunned daze until she's returned to me, snuffling. I put her onto my breast, onto the nipple that began us on this journey eleven long hours ago. She sucks hungrily and I look down at her perfect little face, her funny dark Mohawk, her tiny fingers.

'We made a girl,' I marvel to Jason, who has squeezed onto the bed, his arms around both of us. 'My nipples worked!'

5318008

MARIEKE HARDY

I was mad about her. The entirety of Year Seven was.

Her name was Harriet Fisher, and she was the most self-assuredly magnificent blonde with braces in the history of time. Everyone wanted to be her friend, even when she was behaving like an overtired child with ADHD. If you didn't, then you were either the retarded kid who sat up the front of the bus trying to eat your seatbelt, or just plain mental.

Harriet Fisher had a pool, proper brogues with tartan laces, and custard-yellow hair that somehow worked even though it frizzed out of the sides of her head like it was trying to escape. She had a loud, warm laugh, and the undying affections of resident almond-eyed heartthrob Tony Macafee. Her fluid running style on interschool athletics days instantly brought to mind a wild elk sprinting through an African landscape.

Very quickly there was a jostling sense of competition among the entirety of the form over who was to take pole position as Harriet Fisher's right-hand gal. Miranda Black – a milk-fed dumpling from Ferntree Gully with small, serious marbles of eyes and a sense of humour that could strip paint – made her shameless bid early in the term, and was duly rewarded with linked arms and deliciously whispered conversations in the corner of the quadrangle while the rest of us simmered on the four-square court. The magnificently monikered, ice-cool Eliza Georgiou pitched with equally measured competence and soon completed their trio. As the three of them sashayed around the playground like an impenetrable force, the remainder were left to argue amongst themselves; bargain-basement friends merely killing time in each other's company before the coveted invitation to escape.

Us rejects made stilted, uneasy conversation – the sort of dispirited half-talk partygoers make when there's someone more interesting across the room entertaining enviably glamorous people – and maintained a poisonous atmosphere of distrust. We didn't much like each other for the sole reason that Harriet Fisher had failed to recognise worthwhile qualities in any of us, and we hated the sharp stab of recognition when we witnessed the desperate hopefulness in each other's eyes. Worst of all, we knew that when Harriet Fisher and her bull terriers turned their viciousness upon a member of the underclass it would undoubtedly be one of us in the firing line. So, displaying a complete lack of comradeship, we shoved each other into the spotlight like panicked birds. If it wasn't my show-offy child-actor tendencies Harriet and her entourage were tearing apart, it was Charlotte Schroeder's rough, eczema-addled skin or Cathy Bodey's trusting, doe-eyed placidity. One after another we took a beating, hapless victims on a lazy susan of torment.

But some Monday mornings, after a weekend's brief respite, you'd feel a palpable sense of relief upon discovering that far from icing you, Harriet Fisher and friends would be girlishly gathering you into their confidences and urging you to hock a loogie into Charlotte's schoolbag when she wasn't looking. And, pushing aside the feeling of appalled self-loathing, you'd comply – secretly thrilled that for once you'd escaped the hangman's noose and were instead breaking bread with the blood-spattered executioners.

That was the thing: you could never be sure when it might be your turn. You might have a run of two blissful, sunny weeks; a fortnight of exhalation where you'd be greeted with open, conspiratorial smiles when alighting from the bus, and saved seats in art class. I once spent an entire get-out-of-jail-free month enveloped in the bosom of the elite and thought I would die with happiness. There were slumber parties and group science projects and invitations to float about in Harriet Fisher's pool on burnt-concrete Saturday afternoons. These events flowed with such easy continuity that I assumed the worst of the abuse was over. I ceased waiting for the other shoe to drop; stopped worrying that I would open my locker and find a note loftily informing me my services as timid giggler and fawning support network were no longer required and p.s. I had stupid hair. The note never came. I had what seemed to be a permanent slot up the back of the bus, and even Eliza Georgiou cracked her princess veneer when I repeatedly performed my crowd-pleasing impression of Marty Monster being kicked in the nuts by a kangaroo. Charlotte and Cathy had been on the outer for so long they could barely muster the energy to try again. I had passed the audition, and three had become four. All was well with the universe. There were only two things I needed to be afraid of. They were blossoming on my chest and showing the world, to my abject mortification, that I was growing up.

One minute they were nothing: darling buds of May adorning a lazy brown streak of a body. Then overnight – their horrified owner waking as if from a bad dream – there they were: surly, sullen, swollen, *awkward*. Worse, they didn't appear to be going anywhere and no amount of coaxing, rain dancing, elastic bandaging (yes really), cauldron stirring or simple shaking of fists at the cursed gods of adolescence would budge them. I'd go to sleep with my arms tightly folded against my chest in the vain hope that in the morning I'd have worn them down to pleasingly low-maintenance nubs. God knows what actually happened during those nocturnal hours while I lay dreaming of chaste picnicking encounters with Michael J. Fox, though given the apparent speed the fucking things grew at, presumably I sleep-phoned some sort of mysterious augmentation team of specialists who sped in under cover of darkness and stuck a bike pump in my nipples. And this was in the days long before Stilnox. These things *grew*. They were like Sea-Monkeys of the flesh. Just add water and they'd be swimming around in castles wearing tiaras. My mother thought they were wonderful and I loathed them.

I'm not sure if I presumed myself to be some master of disguise or if I was simply unaware of the fact that Harriet Fisher and cohorts were in possession of two functioning eyes each, but for a brief time after The Swelling began (it was very similar to *The Shining* except without the axe and corridors of blood), I carried on living as though this sudden and startling apparition of rounded flesh-pots adorning my person basically didn't exist. I gambolled, I hijinked, I made merry. I rudely talked smack about the physical defects of fellow classmates and guilelessly poked barefaced fun at those tortured souls suffering the blanket effects of puberty. It was only after a week or so that I noticed the slight distancing of Harriet Fisher, and her accompanying sly, hooded smirking. Not long after that the seats stopped being saved and the bus rides ceased being fun.

Even less time after that, they started to call me 'Knockers'.

At first it was semi-privately guffawed about in the sport change rooms or whispered when I walked past in class (to settle miserably and obediently once again with the ever-patient and ever-forgiving Cathy and Charlotte; blessed and unrecognised saints of the late 1980s), but after a while even Harriet and friends grew bored with the lack of result and cut out the middle man. They just marched up and called me Knockers to my face. There was also a dance to accompany the jaunty nickname, and it involved a not uncomplicated process of jumping up and down on the spot with one's fists jammed beneath one's shirt, giving the impression that any second now a pair of untamed bosoms would leap forth and attack a crowd of startled onlookers. Harriet and pals performed it when I walked through the school gates, when I was queuing up to buy lunch at the canteen, and out the back of the toilets if I had the misfortune of running into one of them. The dance was particularly effective in getting the message across, and I was duly mortified. My blossoming had been spotted. I had been exposed to the elements, and these girls seemed to loathe me solely for the fact I was growing up.

Naturally, my response was swift and brutal. In floods of tears, I demanded that my mother allow me to leave school to take up a career as a professional suicide bomber. Failing that, I wanted to be injected with a course of anti-tit injections that reversed the process of puberty. As a last and final resort I felt it reasonable to request that she stab me directly in the heart. She seemed bewildered by all this.

'But, darling,' said my mother as she stood outside my bedroom door, yet again negotiating the wrath of a distraught adolescent. 'Why don't you just wear a *bra*?'

It was a perfectly reasonable question. But for some reason the mere thought of strapping my irksome orbs into an adorable apricot-coloured boulder holder made me want to vomit blood. Even looking at pictures of bras in magazines terrified me. To this day I have absolutely no idea why. I had reached an impasse – I could no longer function in the real world without the assistance of chest support, yet my mother had about as much chance of dragging me in for a cup fitting as she would've had asking me to grow a penis from my forehead and name it Gregory. She begged, she pleaded, she pointed out (most reasonably) that the most efficient way of getting Harriet Fisher's axis of evil off my back was to remove all residual movement from my torso and stride about strapped up like something out of Tutankhamen's tomb. I wasn't having a bar of it. Instead, I took what would go down in Hardy folklore as 'the quirky option'. I began wearing a lycra one-piece swimming costume beneath my clothes. Constantly. Problem solved. The crones from Macbeth would have to find fresh meat.

Then, as quickly as my breasts had appeared, my family moved away. To Echuca. When I was five years old my parents had taken me to live in this sun-smoked border town – population: eighty-three ruddy riverboat drivers and a cattledog named Stuart – while they did important grown-up-type things on the set of a television miniseries. While they plotted and produced and planned, I was allowed to race around the dry bushland and make friends with lizards and other such wholesome Blinky Bill activities. I had a simply marvellous time. Seven years later the Hardy family returned to the area – this was a time when Australian television could afford to make sequels – and by then I was a gangly, lilywhite, angular bracket of a twelve-year-old with a couple of over-ripe peaches smack bang in the firing line of my torso, and a swimming costume over the top.

Being taken from school and back to Echuca should have been a blessing, and in a way it was – I was freed from the viciousness of Harriet Fisher's next attack. But her constant putdowns and poking and hideousness had done its work, and I was now unbelievably ashamed of my body.

Despite the turgid, baking heat I roamed the streets dressed in my trademark outfit of head-to-toe fabric, with the swimming costume holding everything firmly in place beneath the surface. I might as well have been wearing a burqa. I was permanently pink in the cheeks, perspired freely, and occasionally livened up a family outing by fainting from heat exhaustion. My mother continued cajoling me gently to get a bra, but I was a particularly odd child and had somehow convinced myself that I had cannily beaten the system at its own game by bypassing the need for breast support entirely. A curse on all those twits who had bought the urban myth about young ladies requiring foundation garments to support and enhance breast shape during everyday activities. I WAS LIVING IN THE COUNTRY WEARING SWIMMERS AND A KNOWING MONA LISA-ESQUE SMILE AND I HAD QUITE CLEARLY WON THE BATTLE AGAINST PUBERTY.

My mother – of course, of course, as mothers do – saw it differently.

She couldn't understand my seething aversion to brassieres, nor why I curled up like a slater whenever she poked at me and said, 'For fuck's sake, take those ridiculous bathers off or you'll catch thrush.' She would despair about me openly in mixed company, and call up my aunties and wonder aloud exactly what she'd done to deserve a teenage daughter who almost ripped out her thorax when she suggested a trip to the Berlei factory might be in order if she didn't want a pair of black eyes when next going wing attack on a netball court.

'I'd understand if she thought it was some kind of feminist *statement*,' she'd say on the phone to Melbourne. 'But the kid still wants to be Punky Brewster when she grows up. There's something mentally wrong with her.'

Eventually, after watching me horseriding one afternoon, my mother took the only course of action left: she lied and told me she was buying me a fishing rod, then crash-tackled me before I could reach the bait counter. When I realised what she was doing I put up the sort of hair-pulling, flesh-scratching fight one does when you're on the way to the electric chair for a crime you didn't commit. But the woman was determined.

Being fitted for your first bra at any stage is generally a cause for discomfort and slight embarrassment. Being fitted for your first bra in a cubicle that smells like wee in the middle of an overlit Echuca department store by a myopic pudding of a woman stabbing at you with pins, while your mother stands outside demanding you show her the options 'like a fashion parade', is tantamount to torture. God knows why I didn't just scream for police assistance and have myself shunted off to a foster home.

I certainly felt like it at the time. If memory serves, I refused to speak to my mother for the better part of a month. She copped it on the chin. After all, she'd won. I was wearing a bra. The chickens were back in the coop.

Considering the eccentric course of action I'd taken with the whole chaste-Muslim-above-Esther-Williams-beneath sartorial choices, it should have come as no surprise to anyone that once I'd been fitted with a bra and worked out how to use it I wouldn't take it off. As in, ever. I wore it around the house, I ate in it, I slept in it. I possibly even showered in it. My mother was right – there was definitely something mentally wrong with me. It was as though a Magic Eye picture I'd been staring at for a long time had finally become clear. I was comfortable, and contained, and no longer had to dress as though fearing condemnation from a team of stitched-up wowsers from 1933. It was the beginning of a slow acceptance of the changes in my body and it only took months of pleading and a world war to shift. God knows what I would have done if Mama Hardy hadn't been such a feisty dame. I'd probably be polishing my shoes with my nipples every time I took a neighbourhood stroll. I owe the woman my social life.

When eventually back at school in Melbourne I had stopped jiggling, but Harriet Fisher had moved on to some poor unfortunate soul with a harelip and a limp or something equally as colourful, and had ceased caring about my chest. As the term progressed I realised I gave less than two-thirds of a flying fuck about her opinions and was far more interested in what nestled between the thighs of Clinton Bown and how I could get it to go stiff using only my fingers. My circle of friends widened, I fell in love with an older boy, and before long shed that haunted, desperate need to be liked by a trio of girls I wasn't actually all that sure deep down were very nice people.

In the intervening decades I've made peace with those once-irritable fatty deposits adorning my torso and have spent many happy years revelling in their exist-ence – often in the company of my mother, who has a habit of grabbing at them in public and announcing proudly to anyone in earshot, 'I MADE THESE.' She's a wonder woman and tolerated a thousand transgressions during those twisted, inept years of adolescence, and I'm sorry for her that I was such a terrified little insect. Every now and then she'll wonder aloud whatever happened to Harriet Fisher and those other girls from my childhood, though I tell her I'd rather not discuss it if it's all the same to her – too many painful mammaries.

Under Wraps

KATE HOLDEN

A young Englishman in Paris is obliged to amuse himself. The Sphinx, the most famous bordello in town, was full of officers and the talk of war, and the girls had taken on a frettish manner that set my own nerves on edge. Cafés, studios, bookshops – yes, my friends and I haunted Shakespeare & Company in rue de l'Odéon, like any craven group of hopefuls – and the *demi-monde* dives of the city had kept me busy, and there were always the boulevards to lose oneself in. That winter, in my flannel trousers and blue cravat, I traipsed the stark streets of Paris as dutifully and as pensively as any real artist.

So I tried a few of the smaller places in the 4th, and went home to London for a week after a telegram arrived. But now I found myself back at La Jolie, where I had always found things as I liked them. As I pressed the small brass button beneath the discreet name plaque, its art nouveau facade made me smile.

Opening the great dark wooden door, Madame gave me an inscrutable look and smoothed her hair. 'The girls have missed you so.'

'I'm sure they have been bereft,' I said, walking into the foyer. 'Languishing.' My French came more or less naturally, unlike when I had first arrived last year. It was always, it seemed, evening inside La Jolie, though outside the day still froze with grey light. Lamps made glorious little discs of gold on the lacquered tables, and soft fabrics muzzled all sharp edges. From another room came the sound of laughter; the scent of cigarillos.

'We have some new beauties,' she continued. 'Of many types. Perhaps you would like Odette – almost the same name, and the same type as your former *petite*, very slender —'

'Thank you.' I lit a cigarette. 'As you see, I am a month more aged; a month more mature. My tastes have changed. An inevitable and very useful phenomenon.'

'Young man, your sentimental education progresses,' she said, taking a seat and smoothing her hair. 'One moment.' She picked up a small crystal bell and rang it shrilly.

The girls came trailing in, pale and dreamlike in their lace and silk and the soft light. Some I knew. Some I had taken before. We nodded at each other, if they bothered to catch my eye.

'*Tu*,' I said, looking at a woman who had walked in last. She might have been in her forties, the opposite of lissom Odile. 'Tell me what you do.'

'As you please,' she said. Her broad face lifted and she glanced at me, then let it lower again. It was a heavy face in the cheeks, but it had a fine, tightly made set of features, a superb line to the brows where they were plucked very thin. All the girls showed their flesh, but there was something especially of the slattern in her costume: blue, watery, silk, stained at the hem.

I put out my cigarette and turned to Madame. 'Yes,' I said.

'Natasha, one hour with Monsieur.' The other girls turned away and filed out of the room. Natasha slouched over and took my hand.

'*Enchantée*,' she said.

Her chamber was one of the smaller ones. She had not been here long enough to warrant a more beautiful room. With her age and her heaviness, I doubted she ever would ever get one; this world was severe in its economies, its logic. Pleasure was not the premium, but satisfaction was; at the same time, the deferral of satisfaction, the sustaining of promise, the *jeu* that would keep the patrons returning, held the highest remittance. Those who could manage this fine balance – to deliver, and yet draw on – might be rewarded. And yet those who simply gave could gain much too. A man will pay a lot to be relieved of himself.

'Monsieur, as you please,' Natasha said. It was slow, her accent. I guessed she was a White Russian. I'd met so many of them in these places. They were all tired.

She had barely looked at me, but posed herself on the bed. Her thighs were wide, muscular where they broadened into her buttocks.

'Take my shoes off,' I said. She sighed and rose. The small hands untied my shoes, eased them from my heels. As she knelt I pushed my hand roughly into her blonde hair. It was full of pins to keep the braids in place; I let them loosen. She reached for my trouser fastening.

As she stood again, she put her hand on my arm. 'You are nervous?'

'No.'

'Shivering?'

It was the cold outside, I told her. We went to the bed, sat on its edge. 'You kiss?' I asked.

'Yes.' She leant forward, opening her mouth with closed eyes. I turned my face away.

'No. I simply inquired. You allow the mouth on your sex?' She nodded. 'The arse?' Nod. 'The paddle? Restraints?'

'Monsieur, I am at your disposal. I will oblige you. If you have made arrangements with Madame.'

'Madame knows me.' I examined her. Beautiful skin, for a woman of her years, though in the dim light I caught sight of a scar on her strong jaw. Her arms, legs and décolletage were naked, very smooth and firmly plump. She made no move to undress, so I turned her onto her knees, lifted the hem of her negligee to bare her buttocks; lifted it to under the arms. Underneath the slip she wore no underwear, but a kind of bandeau around her bosom, a wide black satin wrap. My blood was heating. 'Let us start simply.'

I had her skin sweating soon enough. She was indeed obliging. For a heavy woman she moved quickly, turning from position to position with deftness, cleverly simulating pleasure with grace notes of ragged breathing, creased brow, trembling limb. As we performed I began to sense that she was conducting me as much as I her. And yet always the impression of docility. I had met this cleverness in such women before. I gripped the soft flesh of her upper arm more tightly.

She met my eyes, our faces near. Closed her eyes again. Her lip curled and then she clenched around me and I was lost.

'I will see Natasha again,' I remarked to Madame as I left. 'She is quiet.'

Madame raised her eyebrows, and closed the door behind me.

It was a week later that I returned. An icy night, this time, late. The brass door-knocker, the warm air, the lamplight. Natasha greeted me with no smile but recognition.

Her room smelt of semen. She cast a red silk cloth over the lamp. A gramophone was playing in a room down the corridor.

'We will take more care, this time,' I told her. 'Now, I know, my dear, that to you I am simply a task. But I don't care to be "a task".' I was a little drunk. Garcia had kept me at the café for hours talking about *Sons and Lovers*, and the freezing air had sent the wine to my head. 'I should like us to know each other.'

She looked at me. 'Very well.' I had the uncomfortable sensation that she already knew me. She had met me a hundred times before. She would have no sincere questions to ask.

I got up and stood with my back to the door. 'Where are you from?'

'Russia.'

'Where in Russia?'

'Kalinin.'

'Exile?'

She nodded.

'The scar?' I pointed to her jawline.

A shrug.

'A long way to Paris.'

'I was in Shanghai,' she said. 'Shanghai, then the Japanese came, and then a boat to Europe.' She raised an eyebrow, smoothed it with her finger, looked away wearily into a corner.

'That is a long way. And here you are. Children?'

She lifted her eyes to me, pale blue and this evening, after so many men, smudged with mascara paint. Dark and light together. 'Monsieur, what should you like me to do for you tonight?'

She was a stupid woman. I strode forward suddenly and shoved her backwards on the bed. She bounced a little on the mattress, but showed no shock. Grabbing her hips I hauled her over briskly, and raised her negligee.

She let me slip out of her once, just as I was nearing my crisis. I paused, and she settled herself in position again. She bowed her head, but her spine in front of me stayed very straight.

'Next time,' I said as I tied my shoes, 'I expect you to remember to undress.'

'You will have to remember to allow me.' She held a match to a little cigarette. 'You are too hurried. Like most men.'

'I should take time to learn your ways,' I smiled, but held her gaze. 'All your tricks.'

'No tricks,' she said.

'Of course not.' I threw a few coins on the bureau and walked out.

I saw Natasha several times in the next month. There was a sense I took from her of an ample indifference, one that seemed to put me at ease after all the talk in the cafés and my self-conscious, solitary walks along the boulevards. Paris was tensing as news came in of the Führer's activities, and the dull rainy days that had come seemed not to soften the atmosphere, but bloat it to tautness.

Natasha's body was solid and the blood was close to her white skin. She had a way of inviting me to push her face aside; to fasten my palm around her upper arm or thrust her thick thighs apart, which amused me. She would never acknowledge her complicity; it suited her to act humbly. It suited me to enjoy her humility. I came to believe that she enjoyed our encounters. Certainly there were times when there came a raw flush of blood across her brow, and the skin of her chest, above where the bandage hid her breasts.

It was strange, the bandage wrapped so cruelly tight about her ribs. She had, clearly, an adequate bosom, and there seemed no gap or tumour in the flesh she confined. I had attempted more than once to prise the satin away from the skin but she had quickly twisted her big body and presented me with her legs craning over my shoulders and the more lascivious spectacle of her damp sex. Some girls were slovenly with their hygiene, but Natasha's bandeau at least always seemed clean, and I was, in any case, well occupied with the range of negligent invitations she offered. The inside of her body, whichever part of it I rummaged in, took whatever I could give it, and softened and swelled afterwards; it was always snug the next time I returned.

I connived to get her conversation. Sullen, she refused to ask me any questions. It was as if she had heard so many confidences that, replete, she had no space left for more. She smoked, and stared into a corner of the room as I spoke. I admonished her for her glumness, and goaded her until she raised her eyes and replied. My inquiries as to her travels in the East and the history of her arrival in the bordello got short shrift, but I learned that she had had a husband and a child many years ago in Kalinin; that her husband had remained in Shanghai to unaccountable fate, apparently of no great regret to her. There was no mention of the child's whereabouts; the only response was her pale stare and hitched shoulder and a hint, only a hint, of eyelids still able to grow hot with feeling.

We grew used to each other. She kept her slip on, knowing that I liked to reproachfully remove it from her and run my hand down her haunch; I learned that a certain droll glare on my face would make her wrap her legs more closely around my hips; we came to talk, after our exercise, with my head resting on the cool black satin cushion of her bosom while we both smoked and listened to the gramophone rustling melodically in that other room. In our imperfect French we spoke together more and more easily.

'Do you like giving your body?' I asked once. 'To use your body to make pleasure?'

'My body?' she murmured. 'This old donkey thing?' She was quiet. Then, 'I do not mind to give it. The things one does with one's body, what do they matter? In any case, I do not sell my body, I lend it, and it comes back to me. You see,' and she pinched her belly flesh fiercely with small, pink fingers. 'No mark.'

'That is just as well,' I said. 'I've met women like you who are angry.'

I heard her breathing, steady and shallow. I nuzzled my head into a more comfortable angle on her breast.

'Oh, I am angry,' she said eventually. 'All women are angry.'

'Surely not,' I said. 'Women are so gentle.' I felt, not heard, her scoff. I smiled against her, so she should know I had been joking. 'I think I was right, that you have tricks.'

'Maybe some.'

'I dare say we all do,' I said, yawning.

'I'll tell you one of mine,' she said. I felt her exhale a puff of smoke, saw it a moment later above our bodies, where it disappeared in the hazy golden shadows of the room. She took my hand, and put it on the black satin.

'What's that?'

'My secret. I keep one thing. One has to always keep one thing. And when your body is lent and a man can see everything and turn you one way or another, you have to hide your secret somewhere.'

'But I can see it,' I mumbled. I was growing drowsy. I had taken her hard.

Another exhale, another drift of smoke. 'That's the best kind of secret. A trick, as you say.'

We lay there in quietness. Her skin was hot and damp under my hand on her belly. I felt something unlatch inside me, some clasp loosen, like a door in an empty house with boards settling. She put the cigarette out and settled back. The gramophone record finished. A woman's voice cried out down the hall, then silence. I supposed she was falling asleep.

'What do you do about being angry, Natasha?'

'What do *you* do?' she asked with sudden weariness, and rose so I was jostled rudely from my rest.

I came to La Jolie late one night, after another session with Garcia and Marcel. They were both drunk and taking themselves too seriously, and in the midst of a discussion about Greek tragedy I decided that I couldn't bear another moment of such fatuousness; my throat was full. Marcel stank of decay, and Garcia had spittle at the corners of his lips. A woman walked past the bar and I caught her perfume: an old-fashioned scent I knew, in my mind the colour of peonies, mixing horribly with the reek from Marcel's coat. A terrible thing. The room was too loud, the cloud of smoke too acrid. I made my excuses, ignoring their gibes about 'old Tiresias here', and arrived at the tall heavy door to find myself almost panting with urgency, and clammy under my suit. The smell of the dark street, the cobblestones and the iron-work of the balconies, was all metallic. The wet on the stone was like sweat. A car went past, heavy on its wheels in the slick, and a face stared at me from its window. I felt suddenly near tears.

Madame opened the door. '*Bonsoir*. I am very sorry. Natasha is ill.'

'Ill!'

'She will be better tomorrow. Another girl, *chèr monsieur*?'

'No. No. I'll come back.' I stumbled away, home to my room, a bottle of cheap cognac and a panic I couldn't name, a desolation I couldn't expel.

I returned to La Jolie early the next evening. Natasha greeted me without expression, as usual, and took me to her room. The red silk over the lampshade, the gramophone. I felt as if I had recovered a dream.

Holding her hips in my hands I took her, driving in firmly, concentrating on her flesh and the muscles of her body shifting and tensing beneath me, the heat of her; fixing my eyes on the black line where the bandage crossed her back, the fringe of hair at the nape of her neck, the sound of her breathing as I thrust. She seemed the only real thing in the world. I followed myself into her body until the world was eclipsed, until thought was obliterated and I was blood rising, strength held taut.

Bent over the round of her haunches I emptied, pushing my face between her shoulders, clutching at her helplessly, the groans of my pleasure giving way to a sob.

She crept out from under me, turned and put a hand on my neck as I crouched there on my haunches. The grief grew, surging through my throat; I couldn't breathe; I heard myself making sounds I did not recognise. It hurt.

'So.' The word, in her accent, came out like a sigh. *Alors*. It sounded like 'hello'.

I held my breath, gathered the crushed bones of my ribs, pressed myself together, and straightened a little. 'So.'

She moved her hand from my neck to my hair, cupped my skull. It was a very gentle touch. 'I don't believe I mentioned,' I whispered, my head still lowered. 'My mother . . .'

'No, you didn't mention,' she said.

'Two months ago. I haven't told anyone. My father was killed when I was a baby, in the war. I had only her.'

'I see.'

'I don't mean to be wet,' I said, more loudly. 'I'm sorry. One mustn't be wet.'

'But one can be sorry. Not for being . . . wet.'

'Yes.'

'One can share a secret.'

'Yes.' I wiped my face with my fingers. We knelt there; I stared at the golden quilted bedspread.

'Shall I show you my secret, *chèri?*'

I felt tired as a child. I sagged a little, groped for my tin of cigarettes, pushed it away. 'If you wish.' How humiliating, to have blubbed like an infant.

There was a silence and a stillness. I glimpsed her elbows rising; a repetitive movement. My head felt as heavy as a bag of water as I raised it. I thought, for a moment, that I caught my mother's scent of peonies.

Natasha unwrapped her bandeau. A long cool slither of black satin was put into my hand. I looked up.

She had the most perfect breasts I had ever seen. On her thick, pale body they were the breasts of a young girl. Sweet, full curves, sweet, kind nipples, bare to the light, so delicate and smooth and naked, the most naked things, with a faint crease running above and below from where the bandage had pressed. She ran one hand over them, hesitantly. They were white as milk, restful as water.

After a silence I said, 'But there's nothing wrong with them.'

'Did you think there should be?'

'You cover them. I've never met a whore who covered her breasts, I thought perhaps some disfigurement —'

She gave a short laugh. '*Only* a whore might have need

to cover her breasts. Why not? They are mine to cover, after all, whatever you might think.' But her voice was still soft. 'I show them to *you*, because —'

My face was damp; I wiped it with the red silk cloth hanging over the lampshade. In the new, white glare, the room was brighter.

'Because I might need them?'

She shrugged, smiling, gently cupping one of the smooth globes so it plumped, smoothing it affectionately. 'I thought . . .' She reached forward, cupped my skull to draw my head towards her chest, a shy beckoning.

I jerked my head back and stared at her. I was hot and hard and whole again. 'You're not my mother.'

I stood up. 'You are not my mother, to take me to your tit and make it all better. You . . .' I breathed. 'I need a woman to be fucked, and to keep her mouth shut.'

Her hand clutched at one breast.

'Shut your mouth. Shut it.' I shoved a palm blindly at her face. She flinched. I pushed again at her face, but she let me push her, stayed kneeling, and opened her eyes.

'Don't you know,' she whispered, 'don't you know, that if you can see the secret someone is carrying, then it's not really their greatest secret? You should know.' She snatched the ribbon from my hand, and began winding it around her. 'I've seen more of people's tricks than you can imagine. It's my business. And I could see yours the first time you came here. You thought I was so stupid and ugly. The stupid old woman. Lucky to have you. And so lucky to have your pain, now, eh?'

Her hair was undone; the blood hot at the skin. Her body, as she turned the cloth around it, showed all its vigour, the strong tendons of her limbs, the flush of sweat on the surface of her.

'You want to hurt me with your words?' She laughed. 'You try. You just try.' Abruptly she wrenched the half-wrapped bandage down once more. There they were again, these perfect young breasts, like a miracle. Like an old painting. She leant forward into the clean white light of the lamp so they gleamed palely.

And now I could see, slashed around the areolas, something whiter even than the light or the skin of those breasts, knitted in lines, more than I could count, shining against the soft skin: scars. An invisible ink pattern of scars.

They were almost beautiful.

I reached out a hand, and passed it over them. Very lightly.

'Someone . . .' I whispered. 'When you escaped?'

She shrugged once more, mockingly; shook her head. 'The world will hurt you enough. But nothing hurts as much as the hurts you make for yourself. That's the kind of thing only you can own, that real kind of pain. The kind of pain that feels like "sorry", like "I have lost". Even when you have nothing else to hurt, you always have yourself.'

It occurred to me that these breasts couldn't have suckled a baby.

She raised her chin. 'So go and fuck some other whore. Come back to me when you've learnt how to be a man, how to hurt yourself before you try it on others. Or don't come back, don't come back at all! Don't come back at all!'

My fingers lingered on that soft, soft, forgiving flesh. It was only when I shut the door of the brothel behind me and in the glossy wet street found the night already come that I realised that the season was, after all, starting to turn.

I still felt her breasts, but my hands were empty. I shoved them into my pockets and turned away.

Becoming a Woman

JIN XING

My father is a traditional man, a military officer to his very fingertips. We have never been close, and now that he and Mother have separated we've grown even further apart. I shudder to recall our walks in Shenyang, when he would march ahead, stiff-necked and with his arms crossed behind his back, while my sister and I lagged behind, so intimidated that we barely dared talk to him. But as I lie in hospital after my breast-enhancement surgery, I decide I need to tell him about my new incarnation. I brush my hand against my nipples under the hospital sheet: my first womanly gesture. Mother thinks I shouldn't tell him. Why bother? It doesn't matter whether he knows or not. But he is my father. He must be told. I have been wanting to call him for a few days now. Not only to share the news with him that his only son – the only male in an entire generation of our extended family (his brothers and sisters only have daughters), the one whose sole duty it is to pass on the family name – is about to become a woman, but also because I need his help. Now that Mother has moved to Beijing, he is the only one in the family who still lives in Shenyang, where I am officially resident, and the only one who can help me change my identity card.

If I do not change the gender on my identity card, I will not legally be a woman – and that's out of the question. At this stage, the silicone breasts can still be removed: take them off and I'll be flat as a pancake again. But it will be a different case once the major operation has taken place – they're not going to reattach a penis! I want things to be clear and official before I take the final plunge.

At first Father does not understand what I am doing in the plastic surgery hospital. Did I suffer some burns? I don't say anything. I am wearing a big, shapeless sweater over my hospital pyjamas. He sits on the couch across from the bed and pulls a cigarette out of its case. I wait until he lights up, and then I dive in.

'I have something important to tell you.'

He exhales the smoke through his nostrils in two long columns and waits for me to go on.

'Your son is going to become your daughter . . .'

'What?'

'. . . Father, I am going to have an operation to change sex.'

His face, not particularly expressive at the best of times, freezes in surprise.

'Why?'

'Because I want to become a woman.'

He smokes in silence. I watch him from my bed, my hands flat on the sheet. There's no way he can see my chest under the big sweater. He drags on the cigarette once or twice without saying anything and shakes his head a few times.

'Wow!' is what he eventually manages. 'That's big. When did you decide to do this?'

'I've been thinking about it for a long time.'

'Did the idea come from someone in the West?'

'No, it's my own idea; I've been thinking about it ever since I was little. And since I've come back to China I've been sure.'

Last toke. Last spiral of smoke. Fag-end squashed in the ashtray.

'You will finally be in tune with yourself.'

'What do you mean?'

'When you were a little boy, I never understood what was going on. I had a boy, but he acted like a girl. And now you've found yourself. Congratulations! What can I do for you?'

I had imagined many reactions, but not that one. I am staggered; maybe he's not as uptight as I had always thought. Or else he knows that once I've made a decision, nothing and nobody will make me change my mind. And I think he respects that. He agrees to help me change my identity card. As a military officer, he's right in with the Shenyang police and they all do favours for one another.

Consider the Adam's apple. It doesn't look like much – a bump on the neck that you would think could be planed as easily as a knot on a piece of wood – but it touches the vocal cords and if the ablation is not handled exactly right, there's a risk the voice will be damaged. Dr Yang gives me a local anaesthetic and starts to cut through the cartilage. To make sure she doesn't remove too much, she makes me cry out at regular intervals. It's a strange sensation, but not really painful. I visualise my neck slender and smooth, like a woman's. I will have a husky voice, but a feminine neck. My voice must stay as it is: I don't want to be shrill like a Chinese woman. That's not me.

Right after the surgery on my Adam's apple comes the procedure to remove my facial hair. I have the two operations back to back. The depilation will be done without anaesthetic and Dr Yang has already warned me that it will hurt. For some reason, though, I am not afraid. I almost relish the idea of suffering, as if that will be the sacrifice I must offer in exchange for this enormous gift I am to receive. Why should I expect not to have to make a pay-off for this privilege? While the nurses prepare the needles, Dr Yang explains the procedure again. Each hair follicle must be individually removed with a needle. The area around the mouth is especially sensitive and so, if anaesthetic is used, there's a risk that the lips may swell and the stitches might be wrongly positioned as a result. Therefore, it's better to operate without. She doesn't need to convince me.

'Go ahead. No anaesthetic.'

My God, what horrible pain! First, the incisions around the lips; then torture by needle as it is repeatedly jabbed into the dermis to remove each follicle. Unfortunately, for a Chinese man I am very hairy. For a wannabe woman, that is the ultimate bad luck. Somebody – I don't know who, a friend, or a nurse, I am so out of it I can't even tell – gently strokes my hand. I focus on the soothing feeling. When it comes to the stitches, I almost faint. One of the camera crew passes out. I hear the others fussing around him, trying to bring him round. This never-ending pain reminds me of the stretching sessions in the barracks, our bellowing like cows in a slaughterhouse. Still I bear it, chiefly for Dr Yang's sake. I don't want to upset her: she has got to keep it together and the nurses are not helping – from the corner of my eye I see two of them nattering near the instrument tray. They are so distracted that they pass a blunt scalpel to the doctor, who angrily rejects it. I could cry, not from the pain, but out of rage at those couldn't-give-a-damn nurses.

After four or five hours – though it could have lasted ten hours and I wouldn't have noticed, my sense of time is so shot – the torture ends. By the time they get to the final stitches I can hardly feel anything; my body must be used to the pain. A nurse leans over to admire the end result. 'Dr Yang has performed a real craftsman's job,' she says. My face looks like a piece of hand-stitched embroidery.

The photo I send to my father for my new identity card shows a pretty woman with fine features, a smooth chin, a pulpy mouth and long hair parted down the middle and falling to her shoulders. No make-up. I won't allow myself any make-up until I become a complete woman. But I am happy with the result. The photo will look good on my new ID card. When he comes back from Shenyang, my father recounts his interview with the police officer.

'Mr Xing, what can I do for you?'

'It's for my son. He can't come. He is in Beijing.'

'Okay. Does he need to renew his ID card?'

'Well, in a manner of speaking, yes. But it's a little more complicated. My son, you see, well, to tell you the truth, he has become my daughter.'

'Really? We've never had a case like that. In the whole history of Shenyang police headquarters, never!'

'It's a first then. Look, here is her picture.'

'She's quite a looker, your daughter.'

We laugh about it together. I am relieved. My big operation is set for April: a spring date for my rebirth. There are still a few more weeks to wait and for the time being the trees outside my hospital window remain stripped of leaves, the winter sky still the colour of lead.

Chicken Fillets and Plus Sizes

MARIAN KEYES

The following is an extract from This Charming Man. *The material has been condensed and edited for the purposes of this extract and differs from the original edition.*

Friday, 26 September 22.12
Lenihan's, Miltown Malbay

Noel from Dole was sitting in alcove, pointy knee crossed over other pointy knee, pointy elbows resting on table. He looked around and gave me full 180 of his pointy foxy features. If toppled on top of him, could sustain quite nasty puncture wound.

He leapt up, summoned me into alcove and whispered, 'Did anyone see you come in?'

'I don't know. You didn't tell me to sneak in.'

'Yes, I know, but this is highly confidential.'

I waited.

'It's about your job,' he said. 'Being a stylist. You ever help people track down clothes in difficult-to-find sizes?'

That was it?

'Certainly,' I said. 'Actually my speciality. Worked for wife of investment banker who had to go to unmerciful number of gala dinners, but, unusually for wife of investment banker, was a size fourteen. Rarely come in such a large size.'

'What about accessories?'

'I do everything. Shoes, handbags, jewellery, underwear.'

'I have this friend, you see,' he said. He sounded nervous. Suddenly he declared, almost in anguish, 'Look, I'm married! And I have a friend.'

'A lady-friend?'

He nodded.

Married *and* with a girlfriend? Just goes to show, looks aren't everything. Perhaps he is very good at telling jokes.

'My girlfriend. I like to buy her nice things. But she has trouble getting nice shoes in her size. Can you help?'

'I'm sure I can. What size feet has she?'

After perplexingly long pause, he said, 'Eleven.'

Eleven! Eleven is HUGE. Most men aren't even size eleven.

'. . . Is quite large size, but will see what can do . . .'

'How about some clothes for her?'

'What size is she?'

He stared. Stared and stared and stared.

'Wha – at?' I asked. He was beginning to scare me.

He exhaled with abnormal heaviness, as if he'd made decision, then said, 'Lookit.' Expression of intense distress. 'Can you keep a secret?'

Monday, 20 October 18.33

Car parked outside front door, practically beside front door. Almost no room for Noel from Dole to open car door without banging into house door. He emerged. Did furtive running-crouch from car to house. Keen not to be seen. Once in house, straightened up and handed over bottle of wine. Unexpected. Nice thought, even if it is rosé.

'Lola, is beautiful boa you are wearing. What is it . . . ostrich feather? Oh is gorgeous.' Taken aback. Not used to him being pleasant. 'So where are they? Where are my babies?'

'Here.' Indicated box.

He alighted upon it and reverently unwrapped pair of leopard-skin stilettos in size eleven. Cradled them to him, like newborn lambs. Rubbed them against his foxy face.

I watched anxiously. Had almost irresistible urge to cover eyes. Feared he was going to do some sex act, like wank into them.

As if he read my mind, he said – angrily – 'Am not pervert. All I want to do is wear them.'

He whipped off trainers and socks and rolled trouser legs up to knees. Removed tie and wrapped it around hairline, like scarf thespian lady would wear.

'And for record,' he added. 'Am not gay. Am straight as Colin Farrell.' Second mention of Colin Farrell in one day. What can it mean? 'I have fine-looking wife, who has no complaints, if you get me.'

Gak! Do not like to think of foxy Noel in that way.

Slowly, respectfully, he placed shoes on floor. Sensuously slid one foot into them, then the other. 'They fit! They fit!' Cinderella moment.

Paraded back and forth across slate floor. 'Love the sound the heels make,' he said happily. Further clattering ensued.

'Oh there's my bus! Wait! Don't go without me!' he squealed, breaking into ludicrous 'run', kicking up heels behind him, as high as his bum. 'Oh thank you, Mr Driver, for waiting for me.' Hand placed at throat in coquettish fashion. 'You've made this lady very happy.'

Cripes.

'Where can I change?' he demanded, back to his man's voice.

Change?

'Change into my dress.'

Dress?

'Yes, my dress!' Tapped his briefcase in exasperated fashion.

Oh God. 'You have trannie clothes in briefcase?'

'Cross-dressing, cross-dressing, I am sick telling you.'

Didn't want him to change into dress. Wanted him to leave. But couldn't say that because feared he would think was judging him.

But not judging him for being trannie. Simply didn't like him.

'Change in kitchen.' Didn't want him going upstairs. Boundaries already shot to hell.

19.07

He disappeared into kitchen, coyly shutting door. I sat on couch and waited. Quite miserable. Had got self into tight spot. Not sure how it happened.

Had all started when he said to me that night in pub in Miltown Malbay, 'Can you keep a secret?'

I had answered, 'No. Cannot keep mouth shut. Am famous for lack of discretion.'

Not true. Simply didn't want to keep *his* secret. Whatever it was, it would bind me to him in some heinous fashion.

But he didn't care. He needed confessor. 'I like wear ladies' clothes.'

Hadn't known quite what to say. Settled for, 'I like wear ladies' clothes too.'

'Yes, but you are lady.'

'So you are trannie?'

'Cross-dresser.'

Trannie, cross-dresser, is all the one, no?

'You don't really have girlfriend?' I asked.

'No.'

'Those size eleven shoes for you?'

'Yes.'

(Had *known* he couldn't have both wife and girlfriend. Lucky to have even one woman.)

Over course of next hour, got his life story. Had lusted after women's clothes since late teens. When he had house to himself – only happened rarely – he tried on wife's make-up and underwear. But not her clothing – 'too dowdy'.

Over the years he had assembled one outfit of his own – dress, accessories, wig, make-up but no shoes – was making do with opentoed slingbacks in size 8, biggest he could get, but toes and heels stuck out over edges and were painful to walk in. He kept outfit in bag in boot of his car. Lived in terror of wife finding it.

Then watershed: went to Amsterdam for stag weekend. Slipped away from companions. Found trannie shop. Had time of life trying on shoes that fitted him, wide choice underwear, negligees, frocks. 'Never knew it could feel so wonderful!' Bought large quantity of merchandise, but after leaving shop, lost his nerve. Feared airport customs man might do random search on his bag – in front of all his pals. Shame would kill him. Decided dispose of stuff. Walked around Amsterdam for hours. Eventually threw purchases into canal – littering. When got back to hotel, mates demanded know where he'd been. He had to lie and say he had gone with prostitute. Mates scandalized. Atmosphere strained for remainder of weekend.

Back home, Noel couldn't settle. Friends giving him wide berth for prostitute offence. But far worse, couldn't shake memory of how he had felt while twirling before mirror in trannie shop. 'For that short time I was my true self. Awoke something in me. Tried bury it, but couldn't. And then you walk into office and say you are stylist!'

'. . . Er . . . yes . . . but you don't need me. I'm sure you can get trannie clothing on internet.'

'*Can't* get it on internet. Can't look at sites at work. They could check. Even if erase, it stays on hard drive. And even if could look at sites in anonymous internet café far from Ennistymon hinterland, cannot have stuff delivered to home. Wife would see. Would open parcels.'

'Even though addressed to you?' His wife has nerve.

'Well, maybe she wouldn't open, but she would drive me up wall, asking what was in parcel, who was it for, could she see it . . . She would break me down.'

I had sudden thought. 'Would it be so bad if she knew?'

'Jesus!' He buried fizzog in hands. 'Don't even want to

think about it! No one must know! I have three young children. I am respected in community. I am taking massive risk telling you all this.'

'All right, keep pants on.'

Then thought, Pants. Wonder what kind he's wearing right now. Gak! Gakgakgak!

Somehow ended up agreeing to order trannie catalogues for him. When first one arrived – for specialist shoes – he got me to order pair leopard-skin stilettos. 'Cannot put it on my credit card. Dervla will notice.'

Dervla (wife) sounded like absolute harridan.

Had to pay with my credit card – frankly, lucky it didn't get declined, considering state of finances – and delivery address was Uncle Tom's cabin. In fairness to Noel from Dole, he reimbursed me in cash on the spot.

(Hard thing to admit, but not keen on transvestism. Don't want to stop them doing it, not at all, but find it a bit . . . Put it this way, wouldn't have liked if Paddy did it. The thought of him in women's underwear and lipstick, trying to be alluring . . . He'd look . . . Actually feel sick thinking about it . . . Oh no. Now am trannie-hater as well as racist. Am learning all kinds of unpleasant things about self since came to Knockavoy.)

19.22

'Da-dah!' Proudly and shyly Noel emerged from kitchen, wearing short, stretchy, orange and black leopard-skin dress, elbow-length leopardskin evening gloves and – of course – the leopard-skin shoes. By look of things, he likes leopard skin. (Have often found that redheads do.) Fishnet tights, Tina Turner wig, badly applied make-up. His look quite trashy. All a little obvious. Less is more, often find. But say nothing. He has his look, is working it.

Also do not want to engage with him and prolong his presence here.

'I'm Natasha,' he said, in 'lady' voice. 'Do you have my new catalogues?'

'. . . Er . . . yes . . . here.'

'Let's have little drinky. Little tipple.'

Stared at him. Did not want to have little drinky. Apart from being poisoned after weekend, this was veering further and further into realm of nightmare.

'The wine I brought,' he said impatiently. 'Open the wine.'

Oh. Was not gift for me. Was for him. Well, for *Natasha*.

Opened bottle. Poured him glass. He sipped at wine and perused new catalogues in leisurely fashion, legs crossed, as if at hairdresser's. Shapely pins. Long, slender, not very hairy and what hairs there were, were pale ginger-coloured. Many a woman would be proud.

I watched. Anxious. How much longer was he going stay? I had plans for evening. (Sea wall, Mrs Butterly, etc.)

He looked up. 'Have you any snacks?'

'Snacks? Like what?'

'Cheese straws.'

'*Cheese straws?* Where would get cheese straws in Knockavoy?'

'Okay. Any crisps? Peanuts?'

'Probably not.'

'Check.'

Grumpily went to kitchen. Located half-bag of greasy peanuts in back of press.

'Found peanuts, but God knows how long they've been – '

'Put them in bowl – nice bowl – and offer them to me.'

Muttering to self, 'What your last slave die of ?' returned to kitchen and tipped them into dish, but not very nice one, just out of spite.

'Peanut, Noel?'

'Natasha.'

'Peanut, Natasha?'

'Oh cannot! Watching figure!'

'But you just asked for them!'

Then understood. Was fiction. Obliged to join in. 'But you have gorgeous figure, Natasha. You did not have dessert all week and you did Bums, Tums and Thighs class this morning.' Getting carried away. Feeling mildly hysterical. 'Be naughty girl. Have peanut. And another little drinky!'

Sloshed more rosé into his glass.

'Oh! You are very bold! Will have another drink if you will join me.' Wicked twinkle in his eye – so much blue eye shadow! 'Go on, Lola, one little drinky won't kill you.'

Is this way girls behave? Is this what he sees?

Accepted little drinky. Quite grateful for it at this stage.

'Okay, Lola, can you order me these two sexy frocks – I have ticked them. Also baby-doll negligee, in black and in pink.'

Heart sank. Relationship not at an end. Also, he has such terrible taste.

'Can leave my new shoes here?' he asked. 'Too good to throw into boot of car.'

'But what is use of them if they live here?' Anxiety ratcheting up!

'I can visit them. We could arrange regular time. Like every Friday evening. Wife thinks I go out for few jars after work. Could come here instead.'

Officially in grip of paralysing fear. Do not want regular arrangement with Noel from Dole! 'But this is not my house! And I could return to Dublin at any moment!'

He frowned. Not happy with that. 'You will have to report change of address immediately. As soon as leave jurisdiction, no more payments from County Clare.'

'Yes, know all that.' Had been explained to me until was blue in face.

'Anyway you don't look sane enough to return Dublin yet. Look at cut of you.'

Yes. Favourite outfit. Pyjamas, wellingtons, feather boa.

Regretted feather boa. Feather boa gives people wrong idea. Feather boa is badge of true eccentric.

'From now on, Friday night is girly night!' he decreed. 'Okay, Lola?'

'Will have to square it with Tom Twoomey, owner of this house.'

'Square what? You are simply having friend over for drink.'

'Yes, but . . .'

'Simply having friend over for drink,' he repeated. 'Okay, Lola? We agreed about that?'

Miserably nodded head. No choice. Looks like relationship with Noel from Dole set to run for some time. Unhappy. Really don't like him.

But – as already observed – he has expedited welfare payments with unprecedented speed. He owns me.

Friday, 24 October 16.35

Phone rang. Noel from Dole. Why was he calling? Could only be to cancel!

'Will be over around seven,' he said. Not cancelling! 'Don't forget snacks. Set up mirror in kitchen and put my new clothes in there. And I have little surprise. Am bringing friend.'

'Friend?'

'Yes, found him in internet chat room. He lives only nine miles away. Told him about you and the safe house – '

Safe house!

'Noel, you cannot bring other trannie!'

'Why not?'

Spluttered, '*Why not?* This isn't even my house.'

'Is your address for welfare purposes. Anyway doing nothing wrong. Just friends calling round for little drinky. See you at seven.'

Paced. Actually paced. Very distressed. Would have wrung hands if I knew how. Wondered if this was actually illegal? Do you need licence to have gathering of trannies?

19.03

Noel whipped past me, pulling other man into the kitchen. Brief impression of rough-hewn mortification, then the door slammed shut. Much chat and giggling from behind the door.

19.19

Noel emerged looking pretty slinky in his new finery – black spandex tube dress – but other bloke – Blanche – could *never* pass for woman: a big, solid lump with mile-wide face; mouth a red gash; thick swipes of foundation; visible stubble; Margaret Thatcher wig; old-fashioned mauve tweed suit (at front of skirt, his man-bump clearly visible) and pale pink blouse – exact colour of band-aid – with pussy-bow tied crookedly, just underneath super-sized Adam's apple.

Shook hands with me – his paws enormous and rough as sandpaper. Some sort of manual worker?

'Am grateful to be welcomed into your home,' he muttered, with shy smile and thick, thick culchie accent.

'Not actually my home,' I said quickly.

'Is for moment,' Noel threw over his spandex-covered shoulder, lady-walking back to kitchen to open wine. 'Is where dole money sent.'

Rubbing nose in it constantly!

'Take seat, please.' Indicated couch to Blanche. 'Snack?'

'No,' he whispered to the floor. He sat with legs wide apart, shovel-sized hands hanging over his knees.

Felt uncomfortable. Blurted out, 'Where you get your suit?'

'Me mother's, God be good to her.'

'Is gorgeous . . . um . . . colour.' I mean, had to say *something*.

'Time for little drinky!' Noel dispensed glasses of rosé. Couldn't help but notice mine had far less than theirs. Was not worthy of full drink because was not trannie.

'Cheers, m'dear,' Noel said, clinking glasses with Blanche. 'Bottoms up, girls.'

Bad, burny feeling. Felt like telling Natasha that no woman I know would ever say, 'Bottoms up.'

'That's a mighty frock you're wearing, Lola,' Blanche said shyly. '. . . Is it Dior?'

Actually was! Vintage, of course, could never afford first-hand price, but impressed. 'Is Dior!'

''Tis a work of art,' he muttered. 'A work of art.'

'Mint dress,' Natasha agreed, trying to muscle in.

'How you know it's Dior?' I asked.

'Just knew,' Natasha said.

'Not you!' Couldn't hide irritation. 'Blanche.'

'Read a lot of books about style. In secret, of course.'

'Really? And have you been . . . dressing . . . in ladies' clothes . . . for long?'

'All me life, Lola, all me life. Since I was a gorsoon.' ('Gorsoon' culchie word, means 'little boy'.)

Fascinating. 'And did your parents know?'

'Oh yes. Every time they caught me, my father'd belt me black and blue.' Curiously upbeat delivery. 'But couldn't help meself, Lola. Tried a million and one times to stop. Have suffered desperate shame.'

Chattier than he'd originally seemed.

'And what are your current circumstances . . . er . . . Blanche? Married?'

'I am indeed.'

'And does your wife know?'

Heavy pause. 'I tried telling her. She thought I was trying to tell her I was homosexual. She reared up on me. 'Twas easier to leave it be . . . But it's been hard. I've been living a lie, Lola, living a lie. Then Natasha told me I could come here. 'Twas a lifeline, nothing less than a lifeline. I was thinking I couldn't go on. I was thinking of putting a rope around me neck.'

'You mean . . . you were going to kill yourself ?'

He shrugged. 'I'm terrible lonely.'

Oh cripes! Feared I might cry.

'I love beautiful things,' he said. 'Sometimes I want to wear them. Does that make me a beast?' (Pronounced 'bayshte'.)

'No. No, not at all!'

'I'm not a . . . pervert, a . . . a . . . deviant. It's nothing at all to do with sex. I'd be happy enough just watching telly in my outfits.'

'Of course!'

'Natasha says you'll help me order clothes and shoes from catalogues?'

Cripes. Swallowed spasm of terror. But I felt for this poor man. I wanted to help. I *could* help.

19.37–20.18

Noel modelled his new clothes, including pink baby-doll nightie and matching knickers.

Difficult to endure.

20.19–20.40

Enthusiastic discussion of gorgeous frocks on *Strictly*

Come Dancing. Had not seen it due to lack of telly so could not join in.

20.41–22.10

Noel noisily flicked through *Vogue* and criticized all the models, calling them 'fat bitches'.

Blanche scoured trannie catalogues. Dismissed most dresses as 'too racy' but stabbed a horny finger at navy shift dress and dignified lambswool cardigan. 'Classic.'

'Yes,' I agreed. 'Streamlined. Would be nice on you.' Had sudden idea! 'Could I perhaps make suggestion . . . ? You won't be offended? If you wore pearl choker around neck would cover Adam's apple.'

'Not offended in slightest.'

'And maybe navy pumps with little bit of heel?'

'Yes.'

'And . . . again, hope you won't be offended . . . but special underwear to preserve your modesty?' Meant, To tuck in your man-bits so they won't be poking out through your navy dress. He understood. No offence taken. Pleased, in fact.

When selection finalized, he produced pencil, licked it, totted up cost, shoved pencil behind ear, opened antediluvian handbag, took out huge dirty-looking wedge of fifty-euro notes, peeled off several and slapped them into my hand as if he had just bought prize bullock from me.

'You've given me too much money,' I said.

'For your trouble.'

Noel looked up, flint-eyed, from magazine. 'You have to declare all income,' he said sharply.

'Isn't income,' Blanche said. 'Is present.'

Felt uncomfortable. Many worries. Was Blanche bribing me to be nice to him? Was I running business from Uncle Tom's cabin? Where would it all end?

22.15

Evening drew to a close. Blanche had to leave. Is dairy farmer. Has sixty head of cattle and has to get up at 5 a.m. to milk them. Blanche is man of means.

'Can I come again next Friday?' he asked.

'Yes, and every Friday,' Noel replied.

'You are decent woman,' Blanche said to me. 'I've felt so alone.'

Friday, 31 October 18.59

And here they come. Punctual creatures, trannies.

They dived straight into kitchen where new purchases were laid out.

'Blanche,' I called through shut door, 'if you need help getting into your new underwear, please call me.'

Did not relish thought of having to wrestle Blanche's manhood into submission, but am a professional.

'Also do not apply make-up. Have special stuff for you both.'

Have to say, had unexpectedly pleasant evening. Blanche amenable to my suggestions. Permitted me to dress her in beautiful new clothes, paint her fingernails, demonstrate how to apply a discreet maquillage and give lesson in deportment.

'I'm feeling Jackie Kennedy, in the White House,' I said. 'I'm feeling Jack in the Oval Office, Jackie at his shoulder, wearing simple classic shift dress and single string of unfarmed pearls. I'm feeling perfect hair, low-key lips, super-soft cashmere cardigan.' (Sort of thing you have to say as stylist. Is expected of you.)

Blanche thrilled with my monologue. Quite a different woman by time I finished my work. In fact, she might actually get away with being large-boned, mannish woman. (In light shed by 30-watt bulb.)

We shared bottle of wine, ate one mini-roll between us and waxed lyrical about Audrey Hepburn.

Now and again Noel jumped to his feet and danced around in his trashy party-girl outfit, peevishly saying he wished he could go to a disco. But each to their own.

Wednesday, 5 November 16.17

Had to get up and go home. Had responsibilities, to wit: deliveries of trannie clothing. Over last couple of days hadn't cared, not a jot, that Niall the DHL man might be calling with boxes of chicken-fillet bra fillers and glittery sandals in size eleven. Wild and carefree and having such a wonderful time, hadn't given a damn.

Friday. 14 November 20.13

Knock on door.

We froze. Air electric with fear. If we were animals, our fur would have stood on end.

'Upstairs, upstairs,' I hissed at the three men. 'Quietly.'

When they had vamoosed (that strange word again) I composed self. Cleared throat. Opened door. Beautiful woman standing there.

'Is this party invite-only?' she asked in sexy, husky voice. 'Or can any girl join in?'

I was struck dumb. Like automaton, I opened door wide in invitation to join us. This creature was dazzling. Tall, elegant, glossy dark hair, black satin cocktail dress, elbow gloves, taffeta wrap and Swarovskilike choker.

Not exactly sure when I realized she was a man. Perhaps slight ungainliness in narrow, high heels gave game away. But that realization was simply subsumed in all the other dazzlement.

'I'm Chloe,' she said, smiling winning smile, navy-blue eyes sparkling. Her eyeliner perfect! Better than when I do own! She flicked quick glance at television. 'I knew that wasn't a microwave!'

Excuse me . . . ?

'I hope you don't mind me arriving like this.'

'No, no, more the merrier.' Didn't mean it. Noel had gone too far this time. 'I'll just get the others for you. Girls, you can come down now!'

Chloe put the others to shame. Beside her groomed beauty, they looked like brickies in lopsided wigs.

'I'm Chloe.' Chloe extended elegant arm.

'Natasha,' Noel grunted shyly.

'Blanche.' Poor Blanche couldn't even make eye contact. Osama pulled her burka tighter and hung back on fringes of little group.

'Lola, a word.' Noel grabbed my arm, moved me short distance and in small, angry voice said, without moving his jaw, 'You didn't say other lady would be joining us tonight.'

'Wha—? What you mean? *I* didn't invite her. You mean, you don't know each other?'

Much shaking of heads. Sudden and extreme fear in me. How did this Chloe get here? Where did she come from? Is Uncle Tom's cabin on trannie ley line? Will more and more trannies start making their way here every Friday night, impelled by forces greater than themselves? Where will they all fit?

'Please! Let me explain,' Chloe said.

'Yes, would be obliged if you would!'

'Saw the girls getting changed in the kitchen. Have seen it for past few weeks. Wanted to be sure before showing up.'

'But how did you see?' The kitchen is at back of the house. Chosen for its hiddenness.

'From over there.' She tipped elegant head towards Rossa Considine's house.

'You know Rossa Considine?'

Long pause.

'Lola,' said very, very gently, 'I am Rossa Considine.'

20.27

Extreme shock. Had to repeat words to self a few times before I understood.

Peered at beautiful woman and once I knew what was looking for, could definitely see Rossa Considine under there somewhere.

'Oh my God! You are girl in Vera Wang wedding dress!'

'Only a copy, not actual Vera Wang, but yes! I thought you knew all along I was cross-dresser!'

'Why? How would I know?'

'Whenever meet you, you are sarcastic.'

Am I? No, am not. Am not sarcastic person at all. Except, actually, had to admit something about Rossa Considine did trigger sarcastic impulse . . .

'And you caught me burning clothes.'

'What was that all about?' I asked.

'The purge.'

Noel and Blanche nodded and repeated, 'The purge.' Rueful laughs.

'What on earth is the purge?' I asked.

'When we decide we are giving up cross-dressing for good and burn all lady belongings.'

'A regular thing?'

'Oh yes!' Laughter all round. 'Always regret it!' Further group laughter. 'But can't help it. Self-hate. Resolution to never lapse again. Always do.'

'Then I saw the girls getting ready in the kitchen every Friday and was like all my dreams had come true.' Sudden look of mortification crossed her face. 'Apologies! Should have waited for official invitation before landing on top of you. Got carried away.'

'But you have a girlfriend,' I accused.

She smiled. 'Yes, have a girlfriend.'

'And you go potholing. Have seen you with ropes and stuff.'

'Am a man.' Another smile. 'And sometimes I like to do manly things.'

'Oooo-kaaaay.' My mind being opened.

'And sometimes I like to wear beautiful things.'

'Give me example.'

'You like Alexander McQueen?'

'Yes!'

Fell into passionate chat. Discovered I had much, much in common with Chloe – admiration for Alexander McQueen, Thai food, Smythson's passport covers, Nurofen Extra, sycamore trees, *Law and Order* –

' – *Law and Order*! I LOVE *Law and Order*,' I said. 'Is best show on telly.'

'Yes! "These are their stories" – '

'Duh-duh!' we both exclaimed. (Duh-duh is gavel noise at start of each episode. Very pleased that Chloe knew to say it. Not some dilettante *Law and Order* fan, but the real thing.)

'Only a true believer would know that noise,' I say.

'That's because I AM a true believer.'

'Tell me what is happening in it,' I beseeched. 'Haven't seen it since September.'

'Why not? What is the true situation with your microwave-telly?'

'Only plays DVDs.'

'But you must come to me to watch *Law and Order*! Is not right that a true believer should miss a single episode. Thursday nights, ten p.m. It's a date!'

'To you, Chloe – or to you, Rossa Considine?'

Pause. 'To me, Rossa Considine. Am not usually Chloe during the week. Too much work.'

'Hmmm.'

'Problem?'

Might as well admit it. She had alluded to it earlier. 'Perhaps. When you are Rossa, we . . .' What were the right words? 'We seem to rub each other up the wrong way.'

Chloe considered the matter. Didn't deny it. Admired her honesty and maturity. 'Let us consider it an experiment.

If it doesn't work, notice can be given on either side.'

'Very well. Thursday ten p.m. it is.'

Other trannies were clamouring for a 'go' of Chloe, wanting to hear her stories so turned her loose onto them.

You know what? Had a fantastic night. Enthusiastic discussions of clothing. Only sad note: Osama didn't seem to enjoy self. He tried hard to hear film – much shushing from him – over racket of the rest of us making whooping noises.

Friday, 12 December 19.27

Had noticed interesting phenomenon over last few weeks – evenings didn't really get going until Chloe arrived.

Natasha, Blanche and Sue the new girl were getting changed in kitchen, but I felt as if were hanging around, killing time.

Sue was bachelor smallholder from 'out the road'. (Seemed to function as actual postal address.) His real name was Spuds Conlon. Presumed his real real name was not actually 'Spuds' but refrained from asking why called 'Spuds'. Presumed it was because he

a) ate spuds

b) grew spuds

c) . . . erm . . .

He was scrawny, bow-legged man, missing many, many teeth. Took lot of persuasion to get him to remove his flat cap. Reminded me of chicken from third world (sorry, developing world) country, the sort you would see pecking on dirt road, as you whizz past in your airconditioned jeep. Nothing like plump Irish chickens, all top-heavy with breast, but bird where you would have to do much poking with your fork in order to find any bit of meat at all.

'Where's Chloe?' Noel yelled from kitchen. 'Need her to do my nails.'

'Any minute now . . .'

Then in came Chloe with sparkling eyes, smiling mouth, pleasant comments, and readiness to help the other girls. Very, very likeable. If she really was woman, would have wanted to befriend her.

'Love your hair, Chloe.'

Long, dark wig she usually wore, but backcombed slightly and pinned on top.

'Was feeling Jacqueline Susann,' she said.

Now that Chloe mentioned it, Jacqueline Susann was exactly what I was feeling too. (Unsettling to be stylist, i.e. a person who makes their living from anticipating and enacting fashion trends, to be overtaken by trannie-man.)

Unlike my other trannies who had their look and stuck to it (Natasha, leopard-skin, Blanche, tailored classics, etc.), Chloe arrived in different look every week. This week, black leggings, shiny, pewter-coloured ballet flats and excellent metallic off-one-shoulder sweater-dress, also in pewter colour.

She probably really could pass for a woman. Tall, yes, and not skinny, definitely not skinny – but not like brick shithouse either (unlike, say, poor Blanche).

Shapely legs – perhaps little too muscular around the calves and thighs, if you wanted to be critical, but didn't want to be critical – and really lovely face. Very pretty dark eyes, enhanced by expert make-up and lush dark lashes.

Clamour came from kitchen. 'Chloe's here? Chloe's here! Chloe, come in, need you to help me with my monobrow . . .'

Chloe flitted about helping the other girls. She had much specialist information because had done year of eco-swot training in Seattle, city with 'sizeable' cross-dressing population. She knew about 'male' foundation, a thick, wet-cement-style unguent which filled in gaps and entirely covered evidence of beard on face and set into naturallooking, attractive finish. She advised on waxing of chests, shaving of backs of hands, helping affix false nails, etc.

But despite giving freely of her knowledge, she looked like princess and the best others could manage beside her were Ugly Sisters from panto.

Plan for the evening – we would watch film, *The Devil Wears Prada* (delivery of new stock at Kelly and Brandon's) – then have 'deportment lessons', where we would practise walking like ladies. (Had got book on subject.)

19.57
'Ready for film?' My hand poised over remote.

'Just need to do little tinkle . . .'

'Better refresh my lipstick . . .'

'Must look in handbag for my glasses . . .'

Girlish clamour eventually died down. I hit play, song started – then four slow heavy raps on front door!

Jake? And if not Jake, then who? Not another bloody trannie?

'Girls, anyone got any friends they've invited and not told me about?'

Fearful shaking of heads.

'You sure? Because if I open that door and find trannie outside looking for sanctuary, will be very cross.'

'No. Promise.'

'Then hide,' I urged. 'All of you.'

They scampered away upstairs and I opened front door. Large, intimidating-looking policeman, in navy serge uniform and brass buttons, standing there.

Game was up.

Mixed emotions. Undeniable relief that Friday nights had come to end, the responsibility had been heavy one.

But also sadness on behalf of trannies. Feared they'd get into trouble, that their names would be published in the *Clare Champion* and they would be laughing stock throughout county.

'Am Guard Lyons, can I come in?' deep voice boomed from beneath peak of cap.

'Why?'

'Believe you hold cross-dressing events here on Friday nights.' Was almost blinded by shininess of his enormous polished black boots.

'Is not illegal.' My voice wobbling. 'Doing nothing wrong. Tom Twoomey knows and doesn't mind.'

(Had continued to check with Tom every time a new girl joined. His unvarying response was that so long as no one broke the toaster again, he didn't care what we did.)

'No one said it was illegal. Can I come in?'

'No.' Sudden defiance. 'Trannies inside. Nervous dispositions. Need to protect their identities.'

'Look.' Sudden drop in decibel of voice. 'Would like to join in.'

Oh for the love of God! Cannot believe this. Simply cannot believe this. Who knew there were so many trannies in County Clare? In Ireland, for that matter?

'You are trannie, Guard Lyons?'

'Not gay. But, yes, like to dress up in ladies' clothing.'

Heart heavy in chest. 'You'd better come in, then.'

20.03

Ran up the stairs. Trannies clustered in my bedroom, their little fizzogs bruised with anxiety.

'There is policeman here.'

'No!' Noel began moaning. 'No, no, no, no, no, no, no! It's over, am sunk, am ruined, am – '

'Stop it! He is one of us. You. He is cross-dresser.'

Lipsticked mouths fell open. Pancaked jaws swung with surprise.

They clattered downstairs in their high heels and suspiciously circled Guard Lyons, like pack of mascaraed hyenas. I effected introductions.

'How you know about us?' Noel asked with some defiance.

'Happenstance, Natasha, happenstance.'

Guard Lyons had slow, ponderous way of speaking, as if giving evidence in petty larceny case.

'Please explain.' Noel sounded positively bitchy.

Guard Lyons cleared his throat and got to his feet. 'On the morning of Tuesday, December the second, a housewife, to be known from hereon as Mrs X, domiciled in the townland of Kilfenora, North Clare, mistakenly took delivery of a parcel from An Post.'

'Please sit down,' I murmured. 'Is not court of law. Rest of you, also sit down, enjoy your little drinkies. Yes, thank you, Guard Lyons, continue.'

'Mrs X, a busy woman, the mother of three children

under the age of four, neglected to notice that said parcel was not addressed to herself but to one Lola Daly of Knockavoy – '

'Nosy bitch,' Noel said.

' – and had it opened "before she knew what she was doing". Direct quote.'

'Nosy bitch.'

'On divesting the box of its packaging, the housewife discovered strange undergarments within, to the sum of four. "Pervy" was the word she used to describe them. In considerable distress she summoned the parish priest, who blessed the garments with holy water and advised bringing in the local constabulary. Who happened to be none other than my good self.'

(Had half noticed that consignment of underwear had failed to reach me. But so many deliveries of clothing arrived on almost-daily basis, had never fully focused on missing order.)

'On account of my specialist interest in the subject,' Guard Lyons said, 'I recognized the items for what they were – merely reinforced jocks. Nothing at all "pervy" about them. Did not explain this to the woman. Simply removed the items and the box addressed to Miss Daly for safe keeping and swore Mrs X to secrecy – '

'How?' Noel demanded. 'How you know she'll keep her mouth shut?'

'Because I have something on her. Everyone has their

secrets, Natasha. Mrs X will keep her mouth shut.'

'Oh. Well, good. Good.'

'I then proceeded to make enquiries about Miss Lola Daly and discovered that gatherings were held at her Knockavoy address at seven o'clock every Friday night. I "put two and two together" and concluded that the Friday-night gatherings and the reinforced jocks were linked. My conclusion was correct.'

'Nothing short of amazing!' Noel had changed his tune considerably. 'That's three of us who have come to you, Lola, by accident. Me. Chloe. And now . . . ?'

'Dolores,' Guard Lyons said. 'My name Dolores.'

'Welcome, Dolores! Yes, welcome, welcome.'

'That's all very well,' I said. 'But what about my delivery of reinforced jocks?'

'Impounded. Write them off. Blame it on An Post.'

20.32

Dolores Lyons very tall. Six three or thereabouts. Large-framed and actually extremely overweight but carried it well. Unbuttoned thick serge jacket, releasing enormous stomach harnessed to super-sized ribcage, and I thought, My biggest challenge yet.

An Ode to the Barbie Doll on her 40th Birthday

KATHY LETTE

It all began with Barbie. The Breast Yearning, that is. Ever since I was a little girl, I wanted to grow those two pneumatic melons that adorned my favourite plaything. The blonde locks, long legs and small hips would come as accessories, of course; but it was the *breasts* I really coveted.

Looking back, it seems bizarre that I wanted to grow up to look like my dolly; do little boys grow up wanting to look like a piece of Lego? And, girls, let's face it. There are logical drawbacks to a Barbie role model; a bit of moulded plastic between the legs for starters. (Barbie manufacturers seem to think a 'clitoris' is a beach in Crete.)

Well, needless to say, puberty dawned to find my mousy brown hair ... still mousy brown (the reason

blondes have more fun, by the way, is because we bru-
nettes are too busy waxing, shaving, electrolysizing and
Nair Hair Removing). The legs? Still stunted. The hips:
two fleshy sidecars that rode pillion with me everywhere.
And the breasts – an undernourished 32A.

My cup did *not* runneth over.

My mother's solution to my mammary-angst was
a 'trainer bra' . . . But what exactly would it train my
breasts to do? Fetch slippers? Heel when called? And if
anatomy could be trained, why, I wondered, were there
no trainer jockstraps? (For men like Mike Tyson perhaps;
men who need to be taught that there are times when a
penis should roll over and play dead.)

Training gave way to stuffing. All through my teens I
was forced to fake flu as I trailed a forest of tissues.

Stuffing gave way to padding – a bra to bring out your
nonexistent best points. Bosom-enlarging creams; 'I must,
I must, increase my bust' exercises; blusher between the
breasts to create the illusion of cleavage . . . To B cup or
not to B cup was the *constant* question.

What made it worse, my best friend Louise was fan-
*tas*tically well-endowed. Out on the town together, no
sooner would we latch onto a couple of hot-to-trot
spunk-rats than she'd feel compelled to announce what a
bore it was having such big tits. Conversation would skid
to a halt. Whole rooms would fall into a cacophonous
silence as every male eyeball within a ten-mile radius

swivelled in her direction. It wouldn't have mattered if I'd been a nuclear scientist with more brain cells than you could shake a Nobel Prize at or a mystic guru spilling the spiritual beans on the Meaning of Life . . . the only depth in demand was in décolletage.

'Yes,' Louise would go on, plaintively, 'I'm thinking of having a breast reduction.'

'Why?' I'd hiss, resentfully. 'Aren't two the normal amount?'

Oh, I did find appreciative lovers: men who assured me, mid-grope, that 'more than a mouthful was a waste'. And I'd almost believe them . . . until, that is, I'd find the ubiquitous box of *Penthouse* magazines beneath his bed, the centrefolds well-thumbed. The first few I forgave. They were obviously weaned too early . . . But as the years rolled by, so did the stapled-navel-orientated boyfriends. They couldn't *all* have been bottle-fed, could they?

Day after despondent day I spent poring over those magazines thinking, 'Why don't *I* look like that woman?' And then it struck me. The truth is, *that woman* doesn't even look like that woman. Her body has been painted to create hollows and shadows and curves. Her gravity-defying breasts: supported by transparent sticky tape. The photos: air-brushed to remove any wrinkle, dimple, pimple, crinkle.

It was then I got militant. I bought a 'How Dare You Presume I'd Rather Have Big Tits' T-shirt . . . I wore it at home all alone on Saturday nights, while Louise was out on the town having Wild Jungle Sex with harems of male lover-slaves.

There are *good* things about little breasts, I told myself over and over. For starters, everything stops when you do. 'Jogger's Nipple' is an unknown ordeal to women like me. Sleeping on your stomach (something Louise could only achieve by digging two holes side by side in the sand at Bondi). Limbo dancing. Never having to wonder why you got the job. But it was pointless. I knew very well that men, all men, no matter how Politically Correct, no matter how good at doing sensitive things with mange-tout, are closet Benny Hills, obsessed with the fatty tissue situated between a woman's neck and navel.

But then, overnight, my Barbie fantasy became a reality. My bosom developed with polaroid speed. Finally, I had the sort of breasts that needed their own postcode. My chest looked like two tethered zeppelins ready for take-off. The pregnancy took second place to my long-awaited Barbie transmogrification. My wildest dreams had come true . . . *Then why wasn't I enjoying it?*

The trouble was, MEN HAD STOPPED TALKING TO ME. Oh, their mouths opened and words came out, but it was all addressed to the third button on my blouse. This wasn't just men I knew well, but total strangers, in bank, bus and train queues. All of a sudden everyone was looking down on me. It was as though I'd been decapitated. An 'A' score in the *Reader's Digest* 'How Good Is Your Word Power?' quiz, an awareness that 'Filet Mignon' was not an opera – in short, I was a girl who plucked her highbrows. Yet I was suddenly nothing more than a life support system to a mammary gland.

Half an hour into this kind of conversation with my cleavage, I'd have to glance down and say, 'Hey, when the three of you are through, lemme know, okay?'

But there was another reason I wasn't enjoying my newfound Mae West Mode. As gravity took effect, my normal sprightly gait was transformed into an angled shuffle. The Marks and Sparks lingerie lady encased my breasts into a support bra that had the erotic appeal of an orthopaedic shoe. There were so many flaps, loops, elasticated panels and clips . . . you needed an engineering degree to operate it. By the time my husband got the damn thing off, it was *morning*. The wretched contraption also left strap indentations only surgery could remove.

But there was worse to come. After childbirth, my Barbie breasts grew to Dolly Parton proportions. Finally I understood the real reason for bras: they're to stop an unfortunate situation from spreading. Not only was

I now wheezing from the tightness of my corsetry, but there was also the constant leakage. Breastfeeding may make you *look* like a Sex Goddess, but you are nothing more than Meals on Heels; a kiddie café; the fountain for youths.

I had to face the pathetic facts. Now that I *had* Barbie's big breasts, I wanted to be *small* again. The bewildering truth is that women are conditioned never to be happy with our breasts. Females with small breasts are injecting silicone pillows that leak and cause cancer, and the women with big breasts are struggling into asthma-inducing 'minimiser' bras and going under the knife for nipple realignments.

And is it any wonder we're confused? In this century alone fashion has dictated that women ricochet from the ironing-board chests of the 1920s; to the over-the-shoulder-boulder-holder sweater girls of the 1940s; to the Twiggy human-toothpaste-tube look of the 1960s; to the Cindy Crawford aerodynamic twin engines of the 1980s; to the Kate Moss bee-stings of the 1990s.

Imagine if male anatomy was prone to such fashion whims? 'Well, boys, this season it's *small* penises. We want them lopped and chopped.' Then, 'Gee, boys, the new look is BIG. We want them long and strong. It's penis implants and the 'Wonder Y'. (The padded Wonder Pant for Men, can you imagine it? The slogan would read, '. . . No, I'm just Pleased to See You.')

But men are more or less liberated from this anatomy angst. Think about it. Have you ever met a man who thinks he's ugly? Physically inadequate? Or even just a little bit *plain*? The flabbiest, chunkiest, most chunderous, aesthetically challenged bloke in the world secretly thinks of himself as an Arnold Schwarzenegger look-alike . . . Perhaps men have magic fairground mirrors that transform them, in their mind's eye, into a Greek Adonis? . . . While a woman's mirror distorts her into a demon. Ask any woman, even a top model, and she'll tell you that she has the kind of figure that looks better in clothes. (A man actually once said this to me. Needless to say, I looked even better when I accessorised his testicles as ear ornaments.)

Two babies down the track, and my bosom has shrunk back to its usual undernourished state. I'm now using Crone Creams and *still* having trouble filling out that trainer-bra. My breasts seem to be in *remission*.

But if there's one thing I've learnt from all this, it's what *not* to give my little girl for her birthday. A Barbie.

Bra Gras

KATE McCARTNEY

I'm not great at knowing what do with weekends. When I took on a fleet of freelance jobs two years ago, I found out what new parents have always known: it is possible to subsist in a lower stratosphere of existence on four hours' sleep a night and no human contact. And absolutely no weekends. So, when an empty Saturday floats down from the isthmus, perfectly formed and full of promise, I have no idea what to do with it. It's like I've been handed a chinchilla with a problem incisor and a short volume on rodent dentistry and told just to roll with it.

On these rare occasions, I've tried my very darndest to be one of the leisured people. I've tried to sleep in, but I still wake at seven; I've tried to drop in spontaneously at friends' houses, but my unease makes me seem like I'm about to drug them and steal their identity.

When I bake, I start fires; when I walk dogs, they hump old peoples' legs. I'm just not good at free time, so I don't do it.

So, one quiet Saturday, out to breakfast with a group of lady friends, my bottom cheeks have barely come to rest on my seat before I start consulting my list of long-standing chores. I've been adding to this list since the late nineties. It now includes taking up a metric tonne of pant legs, doing my tax returns from the years 1999 to 2003, and taping the final episode of *Moesha*. Obviously some tasks are more achievable than others. However, this expansive Saturday is still a chance to work through a decent chunk of business. And number one on the list is getting a proper bra fitting.

I haven't been fitted for a bra since I first got one as a pre-teen in 1991. Not being particularly large of bust, I went for years without regularly wearing one. Then, after an appointment with a Bowen therapist went horribly afoul, I stopped wearing one altogether.

George was in his sixties, with a white beard and a fondness for loose natural fabrics that made me suspect he thought he was God. He kept me immobilised on a treatment table, poking my torso like it was a badly ventilated cat-box. After the assault he let my body 'settle', presumably to allow white blood cells to coagulate around my new wounds, and used this rest time to lecture me on subjects as diverse as boat maintenance, the Dutch milk products he could digest, and the perils of underwire bras. Using my boobs as a convenient reference, George pointed to sites of possible tissue damage, scarring and lymphatic seepage. The speech was finely tuned and was clearly designed to take the listener on the most harrowing narrative arc since *Sophie's Choice*. So after an hour of hearing about how I was holding my boobs against their will, I left the session with bruises, a sound comprehension of motorised catamaran hydraulics, and a deep suspicion of any undergarment that crept above the navel. And for better or worse, my boobs have roamed free ever since.

But now that I've entered the last years of my twenties, I've noticed that when I move, my boobs join my arse in following a demi-beat behind the rest of my body. At first this was only when I broke into a jog, but more recently it's extended to walking and even shifting about at my desk to find a pencil. This doesn't upset me, because it's the beginning of something momentous. My boobs are finally getting bigger. At last they have acquired the womanly gravitas I always knew was coming. Oh, yes. It's something I've been expecting since 1990, when a body double posing as Julia Roberts slipped out of her lycra at Richard Gere's feet and imprinted her cleavage on my psyche.

Now, I'm not entirely sure which member of my family thought it was appropriate to take their nine-year-old to the cinema to see the charming tale of a hooker and the man who paid for her services. Perhaps *The Rescuers: Downunder* was too rodent-focused. Perhaps *The Labyrinth* had too many shots of David Bowie's penis only nominally obscured by spandex. At any rate, as a young girl on the cusp of puberty searching for easily digested female role models, *Pretty Woman* certainly left an impression on me. I learned quite a few things from that film. For one thing, Richard Gere is, and will always be, a giant conker. Prostitution is a really good way to meet people. Julia Roberts has the mouth of a whale shark. More than that, however, I remember vividly the boobs of JR's body double. I understood that one day, when I assumed my rightful place as a Woman, I would look that good in a lilac satin matching set with black lace inlays. I would reach twenty years of age and not only would my legs sort of elongate like pulling taffy, but overnight I would grow a bountiful cleavage that just effortlessly spilled over the top of a French cup. It was going to be so great.

It has taken a little longer than promised by *Pretty Woman* all those years ago, but I finally have big boobs. In light of their new prominence, I've decided that I'm finally woman enough to graduate from a black crop-top to something more befitting my age and my new heaving bosom. My one white bra that I reserve for formal occasions was bought when I was still trying to get into nightclubs with my sister's ID and praying that I hadn't already missed a definitive Coolio remix. But that bra is now a permanent shade of dust, and has suffered significant structural damage that makes one boob fit snugly under my chin and the other loll about my knee. Worst of all, the lace insets that gave it its original jailbaitish charm in 1997 now make it look like it's been chewed by a large, powerful baby. It's time.

At breakfast, my girlfriend decides to join me on my bra-fitting expedition. She hopes to correct a recent fitting with a bra salesperson who assumed that, as a young woman, Alice wants her boobs to look as pendulous and bovine as possible. Since then Alice's boobs have been acting as percussive counterweights when she walks. Although this has made it easier for me to recognise her without my glasses, Alice is pretty over it.

Excited at the prospect of remedying her bra situation, she tries to recruit our other two friends at the table to the cause. As with many large-busted women, Selene and Marg have both spent much of their time since hitting puberty searching for bras that don't make their busts look like Scandinavian office shelving. Years of disappointment at the hands of bra manufacturers have left them broken and without hope.

'I got my first bra when I was ten,' Selene explains, 'and I've been uncomfortable ever since. That's twenty years. People thought I had a personality disorder. Turns out it was just my bra.'

'Exercise is the worst,' says Marg, shuddering. 'At school they made us jog. At the time I didn't know what would happen. I mean, how was I supposed to understand? I was so young. But then the bouncing began . . . and then the chafing . . .' She trails off, lost in the horror of her own memories.

Alice grabs my arm. 'Don't you see? This is bigger than the both of us.' I have to agree that it is.

So the four-woman Boob Squad is born. We high-five to make it official, leap into the car with delightful synchronicity and head towards our destination as fast as the Volvo can take us. As we reach speeds of 55 kilometres per hour, our excitement grows. At any other time we might have taken a moment to consider the meaning behind our eagerness to purchase such a humdrum essential item. Like the Friday night I spent gazing adoringly at a set of new bath towels, stroking their satin piping and vowing never to use them to clean up soup, this bra thing is just another nail in the coffin of our youth. But for the moment, we don't care a jot. Sure, we're getting older, but with that comes a new phase of womanhood and its major tool is the bra. And thanks to a new generation of lingerie manufacturers who, we're quite certain, lovingly fashion their creations from spiderweb fibres to our most idiosyncratic specifications, our womanly assets are going to look and feel totally awesome.

When we arrive at the department store, the lingerie section is at the end of its post-Christmas stocktake sale. It's like someone's dropped a large clump of women, excitable signage and lime striped G-strings into a snow dome and shaken it vigorously. In the expanse of floor between the dressing rooms and the counters, the racks of seamless underpants, halter bras and the women who fight over them twist and contort together in a giant amorphous mass. It's a Bruegel painting come to life: a sombre lesson on the perils of excess and vanity, wrought from above by fluorescent lighting. I now remember why I never go shopping.

Yet, so ensorcelled are we that we skip through the carnage like it is a colourful, perfumed Utopia and head straight to the fitting rooms. They're packed tightly with women and visibility is low. We wander around trying to find someone in charge of bra fittings and finally happen upon a young sales assistant cowering behind a mound of underpants. After a series of negotiations as delicate as the handover of Hong Kong, she emerges and shows us to a change room, telling us to wait, *very quietly*, for Angela, the senior bra-fitter. She draws the curtain closed just as customers pick up on her scent and descend upon her. We never see her again.

The dressing room allotted for bra fittings has all the charm and light-filled spaciousness of a motel air-duct. After a lot of elbows up each other's nostrils, we adopt a frieze-like composition against one wall and concentrate on not moving, lest we fuse together in a godless perversion of nature like one of those pre-packaged meals that feature both dinner and dessert.

After a short time the curtain is pulled aside and a small woman in black bustles into the cubicle, introducing herself as Angela. In heels, she only comes up to my shoulders. Being 5'5" myself, it occurs to me that this woman has spent her entire adult life at eye level with the average woman's boobs. She probably had little choice about becoming a bra-fitter. Boobs obscured her vision when she was walking down a busy street. They stamped her library books and gave her samples of gouda at the deli. Just like a fifteen-year-old boy, boobs are Angela's world. It was meant to be.

And, like so many people in history with the heavy yoke of destiny on their shoulders – and also maybe because it's a Saturday at the end of stocktake – Angela has no time for idle niceties. She's not icy or unfriendly, rather she's a seasoned retail professional who, like an ungulate on the African savannah, has learned to emit just enough energy to stay alive in her harsh, unforgiving environment. Angela surveys us behind her pleasant, economical smile.

'Good afternoon, ladies,' she says. 'Who's first?'

Alice puts up her hand. Angela steps towards her and inquires after Alice's bra size. Upon hearing that Alice passes herself off as a 10B, Angela raises a pencilled eyebrow and looks sceptically at Alice's chest. Alice gets nervous.

'At my last fitting,' she stammers, 'they told me to bend over and jiggle my boobs until they filled the cups like udders —'

Angela snaps her head up, aghast, and puts a hand on Alice's shoulder.

'Listen to me,' she says, staring into Alice's eyes. 'Your breasts are not udders!'

'Okay,' Alice says.

'You are not a cow. Say it!'

'I am not a cow,' repeats Alice.

Relieved, Angela releases her and smiles at the rest of us. Her retail mask has already slipped a little and behind it seems to be a woman genuinely concerned with the wellbeing of boobs and their owners. It is incredibly endearing. Smooshed up against plastic hangers and a G-string that none of us own, we all fall a bit in love with Angela.

'Okay then,' Angela smiles at Alice. 'Please take off your top and leave on your bra. I'll leave you to do that in private.'

Angela backs out of the change room and pulls the

curtain closed with a flourish. All is silent. Outside the change room, I can see her shadow hovering on the carpet. It doesn't move. We look around at each other. Alice takes off her top, uncertain. Then we wait, listening to Angela breathe outside the curtain. Eventually, after what she must have deemed to be an appropriate amount of time, Angela clears her throat.

'Is everyone decent?'

Alice looks down at her bra and then around at the team. We shrug.

'Yes,' Alice answers gingerly.

The curtains part and Angela glides back in, regarding Alice with a keen, critical eye. The bra-fitter looks calm, poised, focused, like an Olympic diver about to jump or a science teacher about to instruct a group of Year Nines in sex ed. It is exactly the way I always wanted to appear during my one semester of yoga classes. Except where Angela has affected the eyes-at-half-mast look of a Zen master, I always looked like I was trying to let out an extended fart without anyone hearing.

Angela slowly lifts up her hands. Her fingers, I notice, twitch slightly. She takes a breath.

'Right, let's get started,' she says.

Now, people talk about the experience of watching a master craftsman at work. Up until that point the closest I had come was a YouTube video of a Canadian woman making a poodle sculpture out of dried macaroni. But

Angela makes that woman seem like, well, someone who makes poodle sculptures out of macaroni.

She comes up behind Alice and rests her hands lightly on Alice's ribs, just below her boobs, as though she's about to lift her up. Angela's palms are flat against Alice's body but her taut fingers seem to search for something beyond the realm of our feeble mortal perception. Then a pause. I realise that no one is breathing. We lean in. Finally Angela takes her hands off and looks at Alice in the mirror.

'10C,' she announces.

Everyone exhales in unison. Everyone, that is, except Alice. She opens her mouth to protest but Angela merely lifts her hand to silence her.

'10C,' reiterates Angela. 'I'll go get you a selection of bras.' She leaves the cubicle.

Alice looks at us. '10C?' she snorts. 'There's no way. I mean, look at them.'

We all study her boobs. After a while, I'm siding with Alice's old bra. Angela was kind of baroque and fun, but she's patently gone mad from the amount of cleavage she's seen in her lifetime. A little like what's happened to Hugh Hefner. And Anne Heche.

In time, Angela returns with a selection of fluffy, silky bras that look like cast-offs from the Pussycat Dolls' wardrobe. Or the entirety of the Pussycat Dolls' wardrobe. She hands them to Alice.

'These are 10C. Try them.'

Alice looks at them, dubious, but tries one all the same. Angela performs a series of complex checks on the bra that are a cross between semaphore and a mattress-spring test. Eventually, she takes a step back.

'10C. Just like I said,' she says, triumphant.

Alice turns around. The bra fits perfectly, exquisitely even. And not only does it fit, but its aqua animal-print satin frames her boobs like eighteenth-century bonbon wrappers. Everyone murmurs appreciatively.

'You look like a really expensive prostitute,' sighs Marg.

'I had no idea,' says Alice, regarding her new cleavage in the mirror. She turns to Angela. 'Is there anything with less, um, tasselling? Because I work with kids.'

Angela gives her a little squeeze, beaming.

'No, no. The best thing about you is that all the designers make your size. So you get the pick of the best bras.'

'You don't think they're a bit cheap?' Alice says, concerned.

'Cheap!' Angela roars with laughter. 'These are ninety dollars each!'

She hands Alice something sheer with lace nipple covers, claps her hands and turns to the rest of us. 'Okay, ladies. Who's next?'

Marg puts up her hand. The wall frieze shifts into its next position and the ritual begins again.

Angela lays her hands upon Marg. We hold our breath

until she announces Marg's true bra size, like the sex of a newborn child.

'16E!' Angela cries to the heavens, perhaps expecting a thunderclap. It wasn't cued up.

'That's two sizes more than I'm wearing!' Marg says, horrified.

'That's right. And you two can share.' Angela points at Selene, sitting flat against the wall.

Selene looks confused. 'Me?'

Nodding like a sage, Angela glides out of the change room, quickly returning with a new selection of bras. These ones are entirely different from those that Alice had been given; featureless but for scars of hardy reinforced stitching. They're all 'skin'-coloured, if the definition of that word can be broadened to include an entire spectrum of hues in 'Old Band-Aid', 'Fatty Deposit' and 'The Undead'.

'These will minimise,' says Angela, handing equal piles to Selene and Marg. 'These will lift and separate. And these,' she says, hanging up some bras that look like cinder blocks, 'are for exercise.'

Sure enough the bras fit. And despite their colour and elasticity that could prevent a dam leak, both Marg and Selene have to admit this is the most comfortable they have ever felt. And once the actual structures are hidden under their T-shirts, their boobs look incredible. But despite the depth of this revelation, neither Marg nor

Selene are particularly happy. Marg gives a deep, disappointed sigh.

'It's just,' she says, 'I thought maybe this time I could get something with lace. I mean, lace that wasn't hiding a buckle . . .'

'I think my grandmother has this bra,' Selene says sadly.

'Yes, it's a good seller!' Angela beams.

Alice approaches the mirror and puts a hand on each of their shoulders.

'You know what this means, though?' she says kindly. 'You two have really huge bazoongas.'

'That's true,' Marg says. 'Two sizes bigger than we thought.'

'Yeah,' says Selene. 'We're completely stacked.'

'You could be in porn,' Alice adds helpfully.

'Yeah! Seedy jugs-specific porn!' Selene said, brightening. She has a thought. 'Hey, we could borrow your new bras, Alice!'

'That's true! Although they're going to be a bit small,' laughs Alice.

'Not that small – 10C!' Marg says, slapping her on the back. Alice smiles. Selene and Marg smile back at her.

I watch from the sidelines, a big, toothy grin plastered on my mug. I'm not just happy for them. I'm happy for myself, too. If these three ladies are anything to go by, women underestimate the size of their boobs *all the time*.

Clearly every woman in the world is at least a size bigger than she thinks she is. I wait, excited and ready to find out my true bra size.

Angela turns to me. 'Are you ready?'

I smile at myself in the mirror. 'Born ready,' I say, and take off my jumper.

Angela winces at my impropriety. With her fingertips, she lightly gauges the circumference of my frame then turns me around to scrutinise my cup size. She tut-tuts under her breath.

'What are you doing wearing a crop-top?' she asks.

'I know I shouldn't,' I say, a bit cocky. 'It's not doing my bust any favours, you know, *gravity-wise*.'

'Well, it's certainly not giving you a good shape.' Angela wrinkles her nose. She takes her hands off my ribs and looks at me in the mirror.

I smile at her. She smiles back knowingly. This is it. Take a seat, Shelley Michelle.

'12A,' she announces, and bends down to pick up a bra.

'There must be some mistake,' I whimper. 'I was an 8A . . . before . . . in 1991 . . . they're not any bigger?'

'We've got some good buys on the sale racks for you,' Angela says over her shoulder. 'Something to give you shape. I'll go and get you a selection.'

'Are you sure it's not the cup size that's gotten bigger?' I ask.

'No, no. Your cup size is the same. It's just your back.

Your back is wider – much, much wider – than you thought,' Angela says.

'But, but, but —' I protest.

Angela closes the curtain on my stuttering.

She comes back a few minutes later. 'Here you go,' she says, handing me my new tools of womanhood.

I stare at them. They're hideous, the same miserly pieces of cloth I remember receiving when I was eleven.

Sure, the turn of the millennium has heralded a new array of colours and materials and cup shapes, but nowadays the one defining feature of my bra size is the eighteen layers of humiliating compensation padding that every manufacturer assumes you want. And those that don't have the padding are affiliated with Bratz figurines and have 'My First' as part of the product name. The message is clear: I should feel embarrassed by what I've been born with and pretend that I'm something that I'm not. And soon, God willing, there will be no obviously small-chested women left, driven to extinction like the polar bear and the Monaco Bar.

But instead of dispiriting me into a state where I might purchase one of these items, the revelation makes me narky. Narkier than when I tried to give myself a bikini wax after a long, featureless winter. Narkier than when I realised Gwyneth Paltrow was about to win an Oscar. *Pretty Woman* had lied to me. My boobs have nothing to do with me becoming a woman.

They don't have superpowers. They don't make me funnier or better at ballsports or able to body pop in a nationally televised dance competition or anything else I hope to achieve as a woman. They're just boobs. They're a bit lumpy and sometimes have strange single hairs that grow towards the sun. They're subject to outbreaks of rack-ne that always manage to synchronise with the first hot day of the year. My nipples like to announce themselves at severely inappropriate moments, and despite their size, I still can't figure out how to keep it all inside even the most papal-grade swimwear. Most of all, my boobs are always going to be small. And I'm pretty fond of them for looking like that. Faced with a selection of bras that feature chicken fillets lurking inside each cup, or claim to stabilise our orbit, or imbue us with subsonic levels of sexual allure, I realise that ultimately neither Marg, nor Alice, nor Selene, nor I need these things to stake our claim to womanhood.

So I return everything to their hangers, and thank Angela for her time. With the rest of the Boob Squad in tow, I head home – braless, but slightly fatter. Next time I've got a day off I might just buy that DVD box set of *Moesha* I've had my eye on. 'Mo to the E to the Mo to the E. A new day is dawning. It's me, it's me.' Now that's what I call a woman.

Come to Mummy

SARAH MACDONALD

I've now been immersing myself in India's spiritual smorgasbord for eighteen months. At times I feel god-filled, at other moments slightly spiritualised, but mostly I feel like I'm failing. It's as if, after scrambling to the top of the wall that separates doubt and dharma, I fall dumpty-down into bad thoughts and bad living. Between faith and faithlessness is a sea full of sharks that pull me down into the depths of doubt, rip any emerging happiness from my heart and spit me back to the surface of cynicism.

The main predators are male.

India is a man's world. As a result of female infanticide, where girl babies are aborted, undernourished or murdered, there are fifty-two men for every forty-eight women. In northern India the ratio seems higher – in the streets of Delhi and Mumbai gangs of guys are out in force, strutting and swaggering hand-in-hand, smiling and sneering with bravado. It seems no one can adore these lads as much as they adore themselves; one of the most popular T-shirts stretched over scrawny chests and pot-bellies this summer declares 'GOD I'M GOOD'.

It's easy to laugh when Jonathan is around but he has flown to Calcutta for another urgent story and I'm stuck in Mumbai alone and extra-sensitive to being encircled by giggling idiots and silent stone-faced stares. I'm fed up with having entire busloads stare down at me, of truck-drivers motioning cabin mates to cop a look, and of being constantly followed. And I'm especially sick of the cocky display of the penis. It seems many Indian men have a chronic urinary tract infection – they piss proudly beside the road, up against buildings and in every park. Those with stronger bladders just seem to love the *lingam* – there are more hands on dicks here than at a hip-hop gig. What's worse are the occasional bastards in a crowd who grab at my crotch or pinch my breasts. It doesn't happen often, but it's infuriating, especially when it's dismissed as 'Eve-teasing' by lazy police. Even at home I'm not safe – once a week a mystery sicko calls to try to talk dirty, or just to say, 'Hello, howww are yooou, I loooove you.' The Indian overload of male attention is dehumanising and debilitating and makes forgiveness, love and understanding of fellow humans almost impossible.

Of course these men are a highly visible minority who

are uneducated and powerless in other parts of their life. I also blame the new cable TV channels. *Baywatch* is big here. Perhaps many of the millions of men who watch it believe all we foreign females want is to shove a piece of lycra up our butts, run towards them without moving our upright nipples and then seduce them on the spot.

I'm still wearing my baggy *salwar* suits, but then again, so do the prostitutes. Apparently the only way to spot a sex worker is to look in her eyes; like a western woman, she will stare back. I've learned to look down all the time but that only contributes to my dejection. I used to worry about losing my kudos and place in Australian society. Now I fear I'm losing my identity as a human being. When I'm with Jonathan it's common for men to say 'hello, sir' and engage him in conversation, while ignoring me completely. It's better than being hassled but at times I feel I don't exist.

I need a shot of female spiritual empowerment.

While I suffer a strong aversion to gurus, I hear of one who might be able to help me deal with India's men. Mata Amritanandamayi sounds like a saviour; 'The Mother of Immortal Bliss' claims to be the living manifestation of all the divine goddesses of the Hindu pantheon combined. Perhaps if I can get some *shakti* or goddess power I can find a way to stop my blood boiling or at least discover how to get blokes to leave me alone. If not, then at least I get to see an Indian woman who is respected, worshipped and adored by hundreds of thousands of men. There's a rumour that the Mother of Immortal Bliss transmits this power with a hug and a kiss – including to blokes! Barring dark corners of cinemas and under bushes, I've never seen such a thing in India; public displays of affection are confined to male mates. This taboo-breaking religious rebel lives in Kerala – the only state where women outnumber men and where matriarchal tribes once ruled. Kerala was my favourite state when I came to India all those years ago; I decide to return.

I fly from Mumbai and as we land in Kerala I feel I've left India far behind. In the north, Mother Earth chokes in clouds of dust; she's decrepit and worn down by centuries of invasion, plundering, squandering, depletion and desertification. Kerala, in comparison, is a young fecund mother of abundance. Big wide wet rivers snake through acres of fat coconut palms with electric green leaves. Pineapples, mangoes and coconuts sell under the shade of flame flowers and frangipanis. Above is the first big blue sky I've seen for months, and beside the road lurid billboards advertise computer jobs in Australia, gold, jewels and movies starring bosomy babes and men with lipstick. The Keralan people are beautiful, with big round bodies, wide smiles and dark skin. The women wear jasmine flowers in their hair, mu mu dresses and bright saris, and the men, all hail the men! The southern spunks are either ignoring me or smiling to my face. I smile back, safe that their looks aren't sleazy.

Kerala has been a communist state for much of the last half-century and since independence has had the highest rate of literacy and the best health care in India. Marketing itself as a retreat for stressed western capitalists, it's importing bodies and exporting a divine soul. The state's Holy Mother has just returned from Europe and Australia, and is about to set out for Japan and the United States. It's May and the southern summer is horribly hot and muggy. It's not the ideal time to visit her ashram, but it's the only chance I may have for a holy hug.

Sweltering in a tin can taxi that bumps along sandy roads, I finally come to the coastal backwater town of Vallikavu. I squat in a small canoe crossing the deep dark lagoon, gliding under fishing nets suspended from bamboo poles like giant spider webs waiting for prey. Flies feast on my sweat and mosquitoes spear my slippery skin. Drums begin to beat, becoming louder and faster as we approach the bank. My heart takes up the ominous rhythm. I shut my eyes, fearing I'm being sucked into the heart of darkness.

I open them to see Barbie's world.

Mata Amritanandamayi Math, the main ashram of the Divine Mother, is a candy-coloured kingdom. Nearly everything is pink – the phallic fifteen-storey high accommodation tower, the hospital, the Ayurvedic centre, the shops, the canteens and even the temple. Rising up in a series of storeys crowned with small domes, the Hindu temple, or *mandir*, looks like a pile of giant cupcakes topped with marshmallows. Spilling out the doors and teeming all around are thousands of devotees. I've arrived on a '*darshan* day'; inside the pink temple of love, Amma (as the Holy Mother is affectionately known) is hugging her disciples.

I leave my bags and let the swarm carry me into the temple's holy hive. Balconies drip with devotees, the floor softly heaves with the brightly coloured bodies of hundreds of men, women and children. Up front, Indian white-robed *brahmacharis* (monks and nuns) are chanting holy *bhajan* hymns, and the room vibrates with a drone of harmonium, tabla, clapping, chatting, snoring and singing. It's stinking hot and a sticky cocktail of body odour rises. Amma's face is everywhere, on the clocks, on the walls, and on the faces of the goddess statues. But I can't see her. On the stage, two chaotic conga lines of men from the right and women from the left, meet in a bulging knot of pushing, pleading pilgrims. Every couple of seconds the bulge engorges, pulsates and then pops out an ecstatic or weeping being. Within the bulge is the Holy Mother.

'You're here for *darshan*? Mother wants westerners, come,' whispers a western woman at my side.

Suddenly I've joined a queue of five foreigners push-ing in, ahead of the Indian queue of thousands. Within moments I'm halfway up to the sacred stage. I don't feel like a hug. The humidity is horrific, my thighs are stuck together like two wet slimy flounder fish, my hair is plas-tered to my skull, my face is red, blotchy and sticky, and my body is bumpy with an angry heat rash and infected mosquito bites. I also have onion breath from lunch.

'Don't worry,' comforts an American grey-eyed, ghostly pale girl in front of me. 'Mother loves all without conditions and without limits; she is pure, unconditional, beautiful love.'

Western helpers in white saris are on all sides of me. One gently wipes the sweat from my face and then roughly pushes me into the backside of the devotee in front. She rams the woman behind me into my spine. The next helper shoves me forward towards the churn-ing Mother mass. Before I have time to compose myself I'm in the centre of the heaving hive. A disciple squatting on the floor yanks me to my knees, grabs my bottom in both hands and pushes it forward. Unseen arms take my hands and put them on either side of Amma's feet and clawed fingers roughly tilt my head to one side. I'm in the lap of the Holy Mother! Before I'm tucked into her sweaty armpit I catch a quick glimpse of a short, plump body wrapped in white cotton, a sweet round face with slightly bucked teeth and the glint of a nose ring against dark skin. She looks like my cook Rachel. Amma puts one hand on my shoulder, another behind my neck and babbles in my ear: 'mooneemooneemooneemooneemoo-neeeemoooooneeemooooneemoooonee.'

I feel a kiss on my cheek, a sweet pressed into my hand and I'm yanked up, pulled away and pushed off the stage. The entire encounter has taken about five seconds.

'Isn't she wonderful?' the woman behind me raves with a rabid look in her eye. I nearly burst into tears of disappointment.

I felt nothing.

Mother, as I'm told to call her, is not the first manifestation of the Divine Goddess in India, but she's definitely the most popular at present. I buy her official biography from the shop and read the story of a spiritual Cinderella. The fourth of thirteen children born into a poor fishing family in 1953, Sudhamani, as she was known then, grew up right here. She was dark blue at birth (like Lord Krishna), laughed as she took her first breath and then promptly sat in the lotus position. When she was six months old she walked and talked and went dark brown. At two she said prayers, at five she composed her own devotional ditties, and at seven she began meditating. For some reason, Sudhamani's family didn't see this brilliant development or even the blue skin as anything significant – they thought the girl was ugly, so they pulled her out of school when she was ten and made her the family servant. She worked happily and endured bloody beatings before becoming a teenager obsessed with merging with God. According to the book, 'The sounds of Krishna's flute played within her, she danced until God intoxicated and fell on the beach losing consciousness.'

At twenty-one Sudhamani manifested the divine moods of Krishna, turned milk into pudding, ate burning camphor and tongue-pashed a cobra. She foiled murder attempts by her detractors and marriage plans by her parents. Sudhamani died. She resurrected. At twenty-two she 'merged with the Omnipresent, the Omniscient and the Omnipotent Being; the Divine Mother.'

The foreigners' information centre at the ashram gives me a key to a tiny room high in the pink tower and a list of rules. The German boy on duty also recommends I meet Amma's right-hand man, translator and spokesman Swami Amritaswarupananda Puri. I take a cold shower, then travel to the back of the temple where the swami has an office. A rotund, long-haired, bearded dude in an orange caftan opens the door and motions me to sit opposite him. I ask him about when he met his guru. In eloquent English, the swami softly tells me he was a student called Balu when he first came here, and his first hug sounds much more auspicious than mine was.

'She told me she was my mother and I was her child. These words entered deep into my heart. I burst into tears and became enraptured with inexplicable joy. This is what I had been searching for, love in all its purity. Motherhood in its universal essence had assumed a form. I saw the universe of love overflowing with divineness, an experience of complete peace of mind beyond space and time.'

'You saw all that in a hug?'

'Yes, I did,' he smiles serenely.

Balu had found his guru and his God. Soon he was so in love with Mother's love he became oblivious to the world. He couldn't sleep and had to be near her. Amma initiated him with a meditation mantra, and sent him out of the ashram to earn a Masters degree in philosophy that he believes he only passed with her divine intervention. Together they began to initiate other devotees and the ashram grew.

The first westerners started coming in the early eighties. Swami tells me that one is still here. In a tiny, homely, yet starkly simple flat high up in the pink tower, Sharadumba greets me at the door with a gentle but sickly smile. She doesn't go out much, as her liver almost stopped functioning on a tough tour with Amma last year. Twenty years ago Sharadumba was a Buddhist who meditated on the female manifestation of Buddha energy, Green Tara. When she arrived at the ashram, Amma greeted her on the dock with the words 'Green Devi' (Devi is a Hindu goddess). The American saw Tara in human form.

'I left many lifetimes of Buddhism to belong to Amma who is all pervasive consciousness, like the Buddha.'

Sharadumba swears she saw miracles here and tells me the story of a leper called Dattan.

'He was reptilian, his skin was hanging off, he had missing eyelids and massive lesions on his skin, yet a certain dignity about him. He would get *darshan* last. Amma would hug and kiss him – she'd stick her tongue in his puss-filled lesions, put sandalwood on him and dress his wounds. I almost threw up the first time I saw it. Apparently he's cured now.'

Sharadumba is a darling and radiates goodness, but I go to my dorm room feeling repulsed and revolted by this story. What kind of a being would lick a leper? Yet as I fall towards sleep, my disgust turns to shame. Even if I don't believe in miracle healing, if this licking story is true, the Mother has performed a miracle of some sort. She must be capable of absolute, indisciminate love and affection. I resolve to try to open up to the Mother's love.

First, I embrace her ashram's routine. It starts at a quarter to five. In the temple, the first ripples of heat rise with waves of rapid, tongue-twisting Sanskrit. A swami leads the recitation of the one hundred and eight names of Amma – the qualities of the guru. They hail her as the 'manifestation of the absolute truth', as a being 'whose greatness is unsurpassable' and as 'the life and saviour of the state of Kerala'. Next are the one thousand names of the Supreme Mother (or Devi), each carrying a different shade of philosophical meaning. Such chanting is believed to guarantee the protection of God and ensure our physical and spiritual growth. It puts me to sleep; the rhythms of adoration caress me like a motherly hand stroking my brow.

While Amma might love us without distinction, her ashram is strictly divided to ensure there's not too much of the wrong kind of loving between the sexes. Men and women have separate rooms, yoga times, temple queues, mother hugging sides and swimming times. Later in the day I head to the pool, which is like a warm bath and has a cling-guard rather than a lifeguard – a pale, skinny French devotee who checks we are all wearing full leg-covering caftans in the water. The fabric billows out and swirls around like seaweed. We then have to pass an inspection to leave. The cling-guard warns, 'Suits stick when wet, do not go sexy.'

I laugh and she stares at me, shocked and stern. I wait until my *salwar* is dry enough for a twirl inspection; she grunts and lets me go.

Far more noticeable than the women–men divide is the western–Indian divide. I am given strict instructions by the 'foreigners' registration office' that I must eat at the 'foreigner canteen', shop at the 'foreigner shop', and I am encouraged to buy the all-white 'foreigner uniform'. I pay the 'foreigner rate' of one hundred and twenty-five rupees a day (five dollars), while the locals pay thirty (one dollar). The Indian monks and nuns work hard printing and binding Amma pamphlets but otherwise they live rent-free, while the western devotees pay eight thousand American dollars for a flat or a VIP travel position with Amma. This doesn't really bother me; westerners generally can afford more and I'm thankful our cash pays for a smaller *darshan* queue. When I find out the extra rent also earns me the privilege of doing *seva*, or divine selfless service, I'm also happy to participate.

I feel the joy of giving as I build up blisters washing the floor of the massive auditorium. But as I start sweating onto the endless piles of *chapatti* dough my righteousness wears off, for a huge group of Indian visitors has gathered to laugh at how bad our round bread looks. I suggest to the Italian devotee with blonde curls beside me that perhaps the Indians could also do some divine service.

'Don't,' she says sharply. 'Remember, we westerners have more ego. We need to do this work to get rid of bad karma and to make Amma happy. Obedience to a guru destroys the ego that separates us from God.'

The reason the devotees meekly obey the Mother in a way they've probably never followed their parents is that they truly believe she orchestrates the minutiae of their lives. An emaciated, balding, middle-aged Mike from Manchester tells me she got him a job and then took it away so he'd come here. Lanky, lithe Bob from Iowa (whom Amma has renamed Hari) saw his saviour in a vision where she danced suggestively as Krishna. He then let her decide his fate and at every hug he asks her questions through the translating swami and always obeys her answers.

'I will leave when she wants me to, until then, I'm hers,' he blissfully babbles.

Hari's pale freckled wife Sharona saw Amma in a dream dressed as Kali – the fearsome goddess that wears human skulls as a necklace. Sharona says she succumbed to the divine agent that killed her ego and since then life has become easy. Amma does ninety per cent of the internal work on her, bringing about the situations and challenges that will lead to transformation.

'We are completely connected to her, she knows everything about me. I project everything onto her, my love and my dislike, I pray to her, I talk to her, I write to her. I observe her and I know how to be.'

This primes me for a second *darshan*. Sharona promises me Amma will give me what I need, and suggests I ask a question in my mind that Amma will hear, understand and answer. I have my fourth shower for the day, wash my hair and brush my teeth but after ten minutes in the hall I'm sweaty, red-faced and blotchy again. Amid the push, shove, knee-crunch and head-yank I concentrate on my question.

'What is my purpose, what does God want from me?'

Again, the flash of the nose ring, the gentle hold of the neck and the whisper in the ear. The answer, my purpose in life is: 'rootoongarootoongarootoongarootoongaroo-toongarootoonga.'

My shoulder nearly dislocated by the yank out of the Mother's midst, I wait for a vision. Is the purpose of my life to root?

A five-second flash of nonsensical babble is hardly inspiring faith. I go for a cup of tea and watch Amma's children. The Indian devotees are enjoying the ashram like it's a holiday camp with a divine counsellor. The kids spend the day riding the elevators; the women chat and do each other's hair and the men sleep, drink chai or play badminton. The westerners, in contrast, seem pious and precious. Many are sullenly silent, a number are frequently crying and some are very snappy. One yells at me for serving her a small dinner portion and another refuses to let me owe one rupee (four cents) when I'm a bit short of change. I'm lectured for eating eggs and my jokes are received with stone-faced stares. I see one girl lie to get given an extra *darshan* hug and I observe a lot of pettiness, pushiness, jealousy and competitiveness for Mother's closeness and attention. This family seems dysfunctional.

The saintly Sharadumba is one of the few not infuriating me. She agrees that the devotional path is not a pretty process, but says it's essential.

'The jealousies, pettiness and pushiness are the devotees' *vasanas*, their latent tendencies caused by bad karma. Amma encourages the jealousies to purify them all.'

Perhaps the impatience and annoyance are caused by my own bad karma and Amma is purifying it while giving me a good laugh at the same time. But could the Mother get annoyed as well? In a little afternoon lecture to the devotees she seems frustrated and talks about small-mindedness. The swami translates.

'I'm trying to give my children time but the situation is changing. As ashramites, we are all in heaven, be brave and not afraid and don't be so glum, you'll give yourselves heart attacks.'

I nearly applaud.

Perhaps the saner devotees have all gone. When the inner work is over, Amma's children are sent out to work for certain charities. The Mother still lives in two tiny rooms here and money collected goes to an orphanage, secondary school, a widows' pension and housing projects for the poor. Her trust also pays for medical dispensaries, a world-class hospital in nearby Cochin, an aged-care home, a tribal school, a college for the speech impaired, industrial training courses, colleges and a computer institute across the river.

What with all their good work and their willingness to help me, I'm feeling guilty for judging the western devotees. And it seems they show more compassion than their Indian counterparts. At dinner I sit with an Indian girl, Uma, who prefers to hang out in the foreigners' section than with the locals. She came here to study computers when her daddy died but the *brahmacharis* didn't accept her and burnt her hand on the cooking pot; she solemnly shows me the scar. Uma says many of the Indian monks and nuns also don't like the paying pilgrims.

'They are believing that you are from a culture that does bad things. They think you are all on drugs.'

'Uma, sometimes I think India is just one big drug trip,' I answer solemnly.

Before bed are *bhajans*. I join thousands gathered under a massive chandelier in the new auditorium to sing with their saint. Amma only finished hugging five thousand devotees two hours ago, yet she comes out looking fresh in a clean white cotton sari. Backed by a huge rainbow and some dinky Casio keyboard playing with tapping tabla she transforms into a Diva, singing and directing the clapping faster and faster. At a song's peak she leans back and throws both arms up motioning like she's juggling a giant ball or a small world.

'She's calling down the Divine Goddess,' the girl beside me gushes.

The Divine Goddess must make Amma happy. She lets

loose a guttural sound and a cackling laugh that's ampli-
fied by some reverb. We chant the sacred syllable 'OM'
and then some Sanskrit verses. Amma strides off smiling.
A small group of pilgrims push and trip over each other
to be the closest trailing her every move.

Sunday morning, five o'clock and I look down from the
tower roof to see the hive has swelled overnight. A python
of pilgrims snakes around the temple, out the gate and
down the path. On Sundays Amma does two *darshans* – one
as Amma and one as a manifestation of the Divine Devi.
People are pacing themselves for a long day. They're
sound asleep in the corridors, doorways, gravel heaps and
stairways or standing stoically in huge queues for the shop,
chai, toilet, lifts and, most of all, *darshan* tokens.

Through the heat of the day Amma hugs eight thousand pilgrims at a rate of twenty a minute and twelve
hundred an hour. She finishes at three-thirty, and at five
is back in the auditorium to sing. The crowd has swelled
again. More than fifteen thousand people are here for a
hug. Entire families sit clinging to their luggage – women
dressed in their best silk saris with fresh flowers in their
hair clutch children dressed as Krishna. Old grandmas
and cripples stand on the edge of the crowd. The heat
and humidity are so incredible that the heat rash has
spread all over my body – I haven't been dry for days.

Above us, somehow Amma seems younger, refreshed and blissed out. She gives a lecture in the local language and then leads some songs. As the final 'OM' rings out, the doors jerk shut on the stage. The crowd is at critical mass. It chants for the costume change that signals the beginning of Devi *darshan*. This is the external manifestation of Amma's oneness with the Supreme where she'll take off two of the veils that separate we mortals from the divine, enabling us to glimpse the ultimate truth of existence. It's like waiting for the opening show at Mardi Gras. The heat rises to hell-like levels; it sits on us like a low cloud and rains sweat smelling of onion and hair oil. The crowd is pushing forward, a sea of ecstatic people drowning in their desire for love.

The doors jerk open. Amma sits under an orange felt umbrella, looking like a small teenage girl playing dress-ups. She's in a red and gold sari with a huge silver belt, glittery earrings and a touch of make-up, and sports a tin foil crown on her head. Her swamis prostrate before her. The crowd surges and bows. Then it begins again. The Holy Mother is surrounded and swamped. The sick, the crippled and the love-hungry descend, desperate for a divine hug, a smile, and a few words. It's seven-thirty and the queue goes for miles.

I go up onto the stage to give *prasad*. This is an honour reserved for foreigners and strictly timed with a stopwatch to two minutes. I hand Amma little packets containing a bag of sacred ash and a single boiled sweet that she gives to each devotee. Up until this moment I've thought perhaps the Mother was divinely mad, but as I struggle to keep up with her pace, I realise she's too cool to be crazy. Surrounded by shouting, screaming, pushing and pandemonium, she is systematic, disciplined and patient. Each devotee is given the routine hug, kiss and *prasad*. Those who are crying get an extra pat or are invited to sit close by. Amma occasionally looks cranky but is usually smiling. She's highly disciplined love in motion. Apparently she never has a day off and hasn't cancelled *darshan* in thirty years.

I find the intensity exhausting and have to go and lie down for a couple of hours. When I come back at four a.m. the music is still going strong, the queue still growing, and the hugs still happening. It occurs to me that the only time I've ever felt absolute and unconditional love for everyone and everything was when I was possessed by a chemical goddess. Perhaps Amma's Devi *darshan* will awaken the natural ecstasy within me or at least crack my ego, doubt and bad karma. At five I'm up on stage. The helpers are even pushier than before. I tell one that Amma hasn't told me yet what God wants.

'Ask her for something more superficial then, hurry up, quickly.'

I'm knocked to my knees and my head is again in the vice. I don't have time to think. But I'm feeling cheeky.

'*Amma*,' I say in my head, '*give me bigger boobs.*'

I'm pulled out before I even register the hug, the kiss and the divine ditty.

I push to the middle of the melee, limp with dehydration and disappointment. That's three strikes of the divine and I'm out. Beside me, a shrunken old woman sits whispering to a plastic Amma ring on her finger. Beside her, a young French girl sits rocking, her arms wrapped around an Amma doll – a gollywog in a sari that costs one hundred and eighty American dollars. The girl's head lolls back, then jerks forward, her eyes roll and spin, her mouth flops open and she drools. She's hysterically high on Amma love, drunk on desperation for divinity. An elderly English woman collapses weeping and is virtually carried off the stage.

Can you feel pity for the divine? I'm overcome with sorrow for the Holy Mother surrounded by such grasping, pulling, demanding, desperate people. I need to get out. I walk away to watch the nuclear red sun come up over the canal. Ignoring the music and the mayhem, it kisses the earth from below and blows away the mist snaking through the trees. Fishing boats chug in from the sea. I gain strength for the finale.

At eight in the morning the queue is like the magic pudding, still getting longer and longer. The flopping doll-hugger is still rocking and salivating, oblivious to the surrounding mosh pit. I try to enter the trance of the true devotee and fall asleep. At nine-thirty I wake up to realise Amma has been going for fourteen hours without a break for water, a wee, or a stretch. The *bhajans* are picking up in speed again and at ten the line suddenly stops growing. She gives her last hug, stands up and staggers to the front of the stage. A devotee beside me grabs my arm.

'Trust your heart and not your head, what's your heart saying?'

I tune in. It's beating 'bullshit, bullshit, bullshit' in time with the tabla.

Amma throws flower petals. The mass of arms and legs push against the stage. Thousands raise their hands and beg for love. The Mother falters and almost falls. She slowly scans the crowd, her exhausted eyes full of absolute patience and love. When she sweeps my face the bullshit-beat stops. I feel my heart melt, contract, and then explode. A supernova of love sends sparks of pity, compassion, admiration and amazement through my being. If God is the source of pure love then Amma's an avenue. I feel the touch of a pure soul, of a saintly grace.

My suspension of cynicism could be hype or hysteria, momentary madness, the drug of exhaustion or the power of group suggestion. Whatever it is, it fades by lunchtime. I just don't have the good karma, innocence or absence of ego that will allow for the surrender and deep devotion to a guru. Yet I bow before Amma's patience, compassion, strength and the power of her ability to love such annoying groupies. And I hail a saint who tears at taboos, especially ones that restrict physical intimacy. If everything happens according to her grace, she must want the story to end like this: without resolve.

And yet, there is some. By the female *shakti* power invested in me by the Hugging Mother I resolve to give the men of India a better go, for I realise I have been judging them too harshly; they are creatures of habit and conditioning, and if I can treat them with something closer to love than hate, perhaps they will respond and respect me. I buy a kitsch little plastic red ring with Amma's face on it to remind me that love is a powerful tool. I walk out of the ashram faithfully feminine, with my head down but my heart open.

The Mother Hugging Divine Manifestation of the Supreme Goddess has done it. My breasts are getting bigger!

It's a month since I made the wish in her lap and my boobs are blowing up like balloons. Even Rachel notices.

'Sarah, what have you done? Your women things are growing? Isn't it?'

Jonathan, who has now been home for a whole week,

is rather impressed with my new assets. I know he's planning a surprise party for my birthday so I go shopping for an outfit to show them off. In the wee hours of the morning of the day of my party the phone rings. There's been another South Asian tragedy – the Crown Prince of Nepal has shot his entire family – and Jonathan has to fly to Katmandu immediately. The party is cancelled. We've now been married for six months and have only been together for about six weeks.

I spend my birthday alone, sulking and, as Indians say, 'paining'. And I'm literally paining, too, for my breasts are not just growing they are hurting. The pain builds so much I can't sleep on my side; at times it feels like a hot skewer is piercing through my nipples and I think I can feel major lumps of hardness.

Nearly everyone I know has abandoned the Delhi summer and Jonathan is too busy in Nepal to be of any comfort or help. Mindful of the Indian modesty, the ABC's insurance company takes a day or two to find me a female doctor who will touch my breasts. But they can't find one with a bedside manner. She has a quick grope behind a curtain.

'Listen, I don't think it's cancer, but you are old, you have no children and you are western, that's all very bad. Veeeeerrrrrry bad. You have to have mammograms and the like.'

The insurance company flies me home to Australia for

tests. I spend the trip with my face at the plane window worrying. Again, the reality of mortality is harder to face than the meditation on its inevitability. My parents are grim-faced at the airport. It hurts to hug them. We head straight to a specialist who orders a mammogram and ultrasound. Three horrible hours later I'm called into his office. The doctor gravely explains he cannot find any cancerous lumps but it appears I've suffered a massive hormone explosion.

'What on earth were you doing a month ago that could have triggered an extreme oestrogen flow?'

I can't tell an Australian doctor about Amma and my wish within her holy hug. He may commit me. But what do I tell myself? Did the Divine Mother's powerful presence activate my female hormones? Is she sending me a message to come back to her? Or is she cursing me for my cynicism? I take off my plastic Amma ring; freaked out and frightened, I decide to forget faith in her for a while. The doctor prescribes vitamin B and rest, and when my period begins my breasts stop hurting and begin to deflate.

The Role Model

MONICA McINERNEY

When I look back at those strange, sad months of last year, it's as if we had joined a cult. Four sensible women in our late thirties, friends since school, but somehow, without noticing, we lost our reason and perspective, and so much else as well.

It began with the arrival in our town of the new doctor and his wife. He was comfortingly like the old doctor: in his early fifties, short dark hair, kind face. The sort of man you wouldn't look twice at in the street, which was a relief when you had to undress in front of him in the surgery. His wife, however, was something else. Tall, fine-featured, slender as a model, beautifully groomed, and at least twenty years younger than him, which made her just a few years younger than the four of us.

Our town was a small one, with the usual amenities:

one main street of shops, two pubs, three schools, a small hospital and a good medical centre that served the communities for one hundred kilometres around. There was little to distinguish it from dozens of other Australian country towns apart from its proximity to a large lake, which meant for several months of the year it became a holiday haven. We were used to our country lives being invaded by the city-ites, as we called them, but they never raised any envy among us. It was like watching migratory birds fly in, make a lot of noise and leave. When my three friends and I met for our usual Saturday-morning coffee at one of the lakeside cafés, we liked to guess at the amount of money these holidaying women had spent on their clothes or shoes or swimsuits, but they didn't bother us. We knew they'd be gone soon and we could go back to our own lives.

Caitlyn, the doctor's wife, was different. She was here to stay. Caitlyn, with her designer wardrobe, sleek hair, close-fitting clothes and the something else that we couldn't quite put our fingers on. Aloofness, my friend Jenny called it. Stuck-up-ness, Susan called it. Snobbery, Alice said. I was undecided at first. Maybe she was just shy, I suggested.

'Shy? She's got more confidence in her little finger than I have in my whole body. And as you can all see, I have a lot of body.' Susan was an ample size 18, curvaceous and brown-skinned. 'I've asked her over for coffee three times, and she's cancelled each time, said she wasn't feeling well. The last time she cancelled I saw her an hour later, picking up her husband in their car – a new-model Mercedes, of course – and she looked fine. She saw me, I know she did, and she looked away. Guilt written all over her face.'

'You're just jealous of her.' We'd been friends long enough to speak the truth like that. But Susan still took offence.

'Jealous of what?'

'Her figure. Her looks. Her relationship with her husband.'

Susan poked out her tongue. She used to do that to me at school too. It meant my words had hit home, even if she wouldn't admit it.

The truth was we were all a bit jealous of Caitlyn's relationship with her husband. We'd all seen them talking over dinner in the town's one high-class restaurant, her leaning her head on his shoulder, him stroking the hair from her face, holding her hand, as though she was some precious object. When we went out with our husbands, we went as a group. They talked to each other about sport and business while the four of us talked about every other single thing. As for public displays of affection, forget it. The idea of going out with our husbands, in pairs, was out of the question too. People in the town would think the 'Gang of Four', as we were known, had had a falling-out.

'They must be newlyweds,' Jenny suggested.

'They're not,' Susan said. 'They've been married for ten years. Her husband told the receptionist at the medical centre who told her sister who told me. They had their anniversary just last week.'

'Where did he find her? The local primary school?'

'She's older than she looks. Thirty-four, I was told.' Susan was very good at finding out people's personal details. She worked part-time in the council office and had access to a large database. She swore she never looked up information on any of us, but I wondered sometimes.

Alice sniffed. 'She'd better get a move on with the kids, then.'

The fact Caitlyn didn't have children created another barrier, in a way. The four of us had seven kids between us, ranging in age from ten to fifteen. We'd had to put a ban on talking about them at our coffee mornings, otherwise the time would have gone before we'd even started on our husbands.

By unspoken agreement, we switched the subject from Caitlyn to a different, favourite subject.

'I've been thinking about dieting again,' Alice said.

Jenny put down the last few centimetres of her croissant. 'Me too.'

'Me too.' I didn't have any of my croissant left to put down.

Susan pulled a face. 'That's all I think about. Diets and food. Food and diets. Food always wins.'

'It's the thought that counts,' I said. 'Anyway, you're beautiful just the way you are.'

I know a lot of women say that to their friends and mean it, but in our case, it was a lie. The truth was that each of us was overweight, by at least ten kilos. We had been for years, since we started having children, not finding time to exercise, excusing ourselves our morning biscuits and afternoon snacks, eating the kids' leftovers . . . The weight had just crept on, but because it had happened to all four of us, it kept us on an even keel, so to speak. Several years earlier, Jenny had got a bad stomach bug and lost nearly five kilos in two weeks. It upset the equilibrium. She'd been as anxious to put the weight back on as we were anxious for her to do it.

'I got this flyer in the post last week.' Alice held up a piece of yellow paper. She worked in the pharmacy and was a fount of knowledge on all matters medical and cultural. The pharmacy window was the display area of choice in our town, for everything from lost-dog notices to Cars 4 Sale to advertisements like this one.

The writing was black and bold:

Overweight? Over it?
CHANGE IT.

The flyer went on to explain this wasn't the usual calorie-counting deprivation regime. The instructor would go to the core of her clients' weight problems, using a new approach. Our town had been chosen for a pilot program. If anyone signed up for ten weeks, they'd get the last two weeks for free. That appealed to all of us. We'd been to enough weight-loss sessions over the years as it was, eventually tiring of handing over the price of a nice lunch to be told how much we weighed. We could do that at home for free.

We were all on time the next week for the first meeting. It took place in the small room at the back of the medical centre. To our relief, there were only the four of us. Possibly because Alice hadn't put the flyer back up in the pharmacy window.

The instructor came in a few minutes after us. She was a petite, sharp-eyed, well-groomed woman in her sixties. She nodded a welcome.

We settled into our chairs, waiting for the pep talk, the jokes, the charts, the discussion about portion size, the shock news that there were as many calories in one glass of wine as there were in fifteen cream buns.

But there was no welcoming smile. No motivational 'I used to be overweight and now I am thin' photos. Instead, the woman briskly introduced herself as Margot – she didn't give a surname – and then left the room, returning wheeling a full-length mirror. Still unsmiling, she asked each of us to go and look at ourselves for a minute, in turn, and then sit down again.

We did, fighting back nervous giggles, not daring to look at each other, unsettled by the silence in the room.

'Have you all had a good look at yourselves?' she said after we'd sat down again. She still wasn't smiling.

We nodded.

She was silent for a few minutes, staring at each of us in turn. All our smiles had gone by now too.

When she spoke again, her voice was low, firm and cold. 'Aren't you ashamed? Embarrassed? Disgusted?'

Susan gasped.

Margot continued. 'You should be. How could you have let yourselves go so badly?' She looked directly at me. 'Have you seen your back view? You're twice the size you should be. As for you —' she looked at Jenny, 'where is your self-respect, coming out in public wearing clothes as baggy and shapeless as that?' Another laser glare, this time at Susan. 'You must have been pretty once – what happened?' Alice wasn't excluded from the insults either. 'You're not pregnant, are you?' Alice shook her head. Another long pause. 'Well, you look it.'

This time there were four gasps, one from each of us. Susan rallied first. 'How dare you? We've come here to lose weight, not be insulted.'

'You deserve to be insulted,' Margot said in that same steely tone. 'And I'll tell you something else. You *will* lose weight with me. Because I'll say it like it is, every week, until you've lost all this lard and turned back into attractive women. Because you're not attractive at the moment, are you? You don't look it and you don't feel it, no matter how much you might pretend otherwise.'

More gasps, but somehow, just then, there was a subtle change of mood in the room. She was right.

On and on she went, in the same cold voice. She wouldn't be soft-soaping us, excusing us, making allowances. It was obvious we'd been doing that to ourselves for too long already. The same words kept coming up in her speech – weren't we ashamed, disgusted, appalled? Didn't we hate our ugly bodies, wobbly thighs, bulging stomachs? A childhood saying came back to me: *Sticks and stones may break my bones but words can never hurt me.* The saying was wrong. Words could hurt and Margot was choosing the most hurtful of them with perfect aim and precision.

She asked questions but didn't wait for our answers. She talked about our poor husbands, having to get in bed with these revolting bodies. Had we all been thin on our wedding days? Yes, we had, but she didn't wait for that answer either. On she went about our husbands, how they had every right to leave us; we weren't the women they'd married; we'd become lazy and uncaring; showing them as much disrespect as we showed our own bodies.

Mid-diatribe, something outside the window caught

her attention. Not something but someone, in the car park of the medical centre. It was Caitlyn, getting into her husband's Mercedes.

'Look at her,' Margot said.

We looked.

'What has she got that you four haven't? I'll tell you. Self-respect. Self-love. That's a woman who takes care of herself, who respects herself. You can see it in her figure, in her clothes, in her make-up. But you four?'

Jenny started to cry. I was too shocked. I wanted to leave. I wanted to throw insults back at Margot, but there was something frightening and compelling about her approach.

She was telling the truth.

She glanced at Jenny, then calmly reached for her bag. 'That's all for today.'

Our shock must have shown. Susan, always the bravest, spoke up. 'How can that be all? We should sue you for false advertising. Where are the tips and the diet sheets?'

Margot fixed her with a stare. I was uncomfortably reminded of a snake staring down its prey. 'You don't need diet sheets. You're grown women. You already know why you're fat.'

That word. Fat. Not overweight, not curvy.

'You eat too much. You don't exercise. So change it. I'll see you next week.'

The door closed behind her, not with a bang or a slam, but with a firm, sharp click. We were silent for a moment and then the room exploded into noise. Anger, astonishment, and even – eventually – some laughter.

'She's a witch,' Jenny said, shuddering. 'She's flown up from the underworld.'

'More of a bitch than a witch,' Susan said. 'I've never heard anything like it in my life. She can't get away with that, can she?'

'We're the ones who paid to meet her,' I said. 'She didn't force us.'

'Well, she'll be talking to an empty room next week, I'll tell you that.' Susan's expression changed as she looked at the rest of us, from outrage to surprise. 'You're not going to come back, are you?'

Another brief silence.

'It's a different approach,' I said. 'Maybe there's something in it.'

'A different approach? Insulting and offensive and belittling . . .'

'I wish she could belittle me,' Jenny said gloomily, rubbing her belly.

We laughed and a little more tension lifted. A knock at the door got us moving. Someone else needed the room. We all had to go and do shopping, pick up the kids, go back to work.

'Let's keep all of this to ourselves,' Alice said in an

oddly urgent voice as we walked out together. 'We'll give her a second chance, but no one needs to know how awful she is, do they?'

That was the first mistake we made. We agreed to keep quiet.

The second week was worse, if possible. More insults. No weighing – 'You've all got scales at home, haven't you? Use them. You don't need me to tell you you're carrying too much fat.' For an hour she hit us with a barrage of insults and each one of them stayed with us.

It wasn't Caitlyn's fault that she happened to be walking down the main street as the four of us came out of the second meeting. Or her fault that, yet again, she was beautifully dressed, her clothes skimming her model figure, her posture perfect, her whole image so feminine and graceful. We felt like four elephants coming across a deer in a forest clearing. But – and I know I wasn't the only one to think it – seeing her again was like a sign. She was the finished product. We were the raw, unshapely materials. Margot was right. We *were* disgusting. We *were* fat. We felt like our bodies *were* revolting. But we didn't have to be like that. We could change.

Looking back, our obsession started that day. We didn't go so far as taking clandestine photos of Caitlyn and sticking them on our fridges, but we came close. If we felt ourselves slipping, reaching for the chocolate or the biscuits, we'd ring each other and talk about Caitlyn.

We even developed our own dieting catchphrase around her. I was the one who coined it. At a party once, I'd met a woman wearing a necklace with the letters WWJD. I asked her what the letters stood for.

She smiled, put her hand on mine and said, 'I'm so glad you asked. It stands for What Would Jesus Do? It's how I live my life, every day, from moment to moment.'

Alice, Susan and Jenny had laughed about it when I told them afterwards. I remembered the phrase that day as we spoke enviously about Caitlyn.

'I need to spy on her,' I said. 'Live my life the Caitlyn way. Ask myself every day, moment by moment, WWCD? What Would Caitlyn Do?'

It was a joke that quickly became serious. We started living our lives by what we termed the Caitlyn creed. Would Caitlyn eat that biscuit? Of course she wouldn't. Would Caitlyn put butter on her toast? No, she would not. Would Caitlyn serve chips instead of salad? Would Caitlyn decide she was too tired to exercise? Would Caitlyn sleep in or go for an hour's walk every morning? We knew the answers. And if we kept doing what Caitlyn would do, then we would soon be as thin as her, wouldn't we?

We didn't tell Margot about Caitlyn. There was never much conversation with Margot anyway, and we certainly didn't want to draw any more attention to the perfect Caitlyn, in case Margot got it into her head to invite her to one of the meetings and parade her naked in front of us. Margot was busy enough with our four bodies. Week after week, she would pick on a particular area, force us to stand in front of the mirror and look at it, insult us, harangue us. Hips one meeting. Waists the next. Breasts after that.

We'd undressed in front of each other since we were at school together, but even so, it was slightly embarrassing to do it. The light wasn't flattering in that meeting room, even after Margot had, thankfully, drawn the curtains.

Silent and stony-faced as always, Margot would inspect each of us in turn like an army major on parade duty. We could feel her glances at our tired old bras, our stretch-marks, our bulges.

'Didn't you ever *look* at yourselves before? Realise how ugly your bodies are?'

She never encouraged us, never praised us. And yet we kept going back to her. We even upped the meetings to twice a week. Our suggestion, not hers. Why?

Because it was working.

Because all four of us were losing weight. And not just a little bit. A lot of weight. It was like some kind of miracle.

Whenever any of us reached for something sweet or fatty, or for a second helping, or for something fried, we'd hear Margot's haranguing voice, heaping scorn on our bodies, insulting us. That voice, combined with a mental picture of who we wanted to be – Caitlyn – was more powerful to us than diet pills, gym memberships and weekly weigh-ins put together.

Our husbands started to notice a change. Our kids noticed, first that the cakes, biscuits and chips had disappeared from our houses, second that we had stopped driving them everywhere and were making them walk instead. Shop assistants, other friends and our relatives noticed. The more comments we got, the more driven we became, the more obsessed we grew – with our bodies and, increasingly, with Caitlyn.

We'd call each other if there was a Caitlyn sighting, discussing in forensic detail her figure, her hair, her shoes, her accessories. We'd also ring if we'd managed to dress in a pair of jeans or a skirt long consigned to the back of the wardrobe. We still met every Saturday morning, but only for a quick black coffee before we did an hour's walk together around the lake. We did that walk every day, sometimes even twice a day.

As the weight kept disappearing, some of the compliments from our families and friends turned to concern. Questions were asked. Were we on diet pills? Had we had liposuction? What was going on? Was it healthy to lose so much, so quickly? We became very skilled at deflecting their questions. We kept quiet about Margot's methods, just murmured about feeling extra-motivated with summer coming, tired of having trouble finding clothes to wear, the usual reasons. We didn't want anyone else coming to Margot's meetings.

I often wonder if Caitlyn had any idea how obsessed we all were with her. I'd see her in the supermarket, or walking down the main street, or out with her husband. She smiled at me once or twice, a nice, shy, inviting smile. I could have started a conversation with her. Invited her and her husband out for a drink. But I didn't. How could I talk to her about ordinary things like the weather, or something in the news? She wasn't an ordinary woman any more. To Alice, Susan, Jenny and I, she'd become the equivalent of Cindy Crawford or Elle Macpherson living in our town. We could look at her, yes, but talk to her? No way. What could we possibly say? Why would she be interested in us? She was the perfect one; we were the imperfect ones. But we were working hard to close the gap.

The weeks went by. Two months after that first meeting with Margot, we had each dropped nearly three dress sizes.

We were seriously the talk of the town. 'What's your secret?' 'You all look so great.' People who had never dared suggest we had weight to lose were boldly telling us how much better we looked now we were thinner. Each word of praise was more motivation.

Then Caitlyn went away. It took us four days to notice and another day to find out for sure. Yes, she and the doctor had gone on holiday. Margot's meetings went on, the insults as bad, the competition between us as fierce, the weight loss as sought after, but something was missing. Someone. Our motivation. Her.

To our amazement, Margot noticed we were distracted. 'What's wrong with you four?'

Out it poured. We told her all about Caitlyn being our talisman – or taliswoman. Our idol. We were sheepish about it, expecting to be admonished. We were admonished about everything else, after all. But Margot approved. She asked us to describe her, and nodded thoughtfully, saying she recalled seeing her that day in the car park.

'You've made a good choice. I remember her. Elegant, thin, well groomed. And so can all of you be. If you keep that greed of yours at bay and keep taking good hard looks at yourselves, that is. You're only halfway there, you know. You think you're thinner, but each of you still has a serious weight problem. When will this Caitlyn be back?'

We didn't know but we wanted – needed – to find out. Jenny made an appointment with one of the other doctors on false pretences, finishing the consultation with an apparently cheery, innocent inquiry about the new doctor and his wife and when they might be due back from holiday.

'We're not sure,' he said.

We were outraged. How could they not be sure? Typical doctors, taking holidays when it suited them. Didn't they realise we *needed* Caitlyn?

Nearly two weeks later, we saw her again. At least I saw her, and rang the others. We all made excuses to get down to the main street as soon as we could, before she finished her shopping.

The first thing we noticed was that she looked different. She had a new, shorter hairstyle for starters. But even the shape of her face had changed. Her cheekbones were more pronounced, her skin even paler, her lipstick a bold red. She looked like Audrey Hepburn or a Parisian model. And not only that. We didn't know how she had managed it, but there was no escaping it. She was even thinner than before.

Susan asked around and got all the answers. Caitlyn and her husband had been to a spa in Indonesia, she reported back to us. One of those five-star luxury places. She'd obviously had the works. Colonic irrigation. Botox. Fasting. Mudwraps and facepacks and seaweed baths. Some sort of collagen implants too, judging by those new cheekbones.

We weren't just envious now, we were angry. That was unfair. That was shifting the goalposts. We could afford to eat less and do more exercise – doing that saved us money, in fact – but we couldn't head away to some glamorous resort to be pampered and fussed over and operated on.

Something changed in all of us then. We turned on Caitlyn. All four of us. Alice had always liked to gossip, but she wasn't usually vicious about it. Yet she started being spiteful about Caitlyn, suggesting she was a gold-digger, had a father-figure complex, that there was something, well, a little bit *creepy*, didn't we think, about her husband being so much older than her? Once it was said, it changed the way we viewed her and the doctor when we saw them out together. What had been a source of envy to us – their whispered conversations, his attentiveness, the public displays of affection – now looked sordid.

Word went around, fuelled by gossip – from us – that Caitlyn was even younger than we thought. A rumour started that she had actually once been engaged to the doctor's son, and had then set her sights on the doctor himself. It wasn't true, of course. I don't even know where that story came from. Not from us, I know that. But once it aired, it was out there and there was no way of getting it back. It grew into other stories, travelling around the town, increasing in size and detail each time we heard it. She'd actually gone away to Sydney, not Bali, and not on holiday but to have an abortion. She'd told her husband she never wanted to have kids and she meant it. No, another rumour announced, it *was* a holiday, but it was because their marriage was in trouble and it was a last effort to stay together. Then someone else said they'd seen the doctor's son in town, all three of them out dining together. Was it a *ménage à trois*?

As the gossip swirled around the town, we saw Caitlyn less and less. I spotted her in the main street one afternoon and actually crossed the road to avoid passing her. I told myself that I needed to keep a distance, to keep her on that pedestal, to keep my goals intact.

A month later the doctor and Caitlyn went away again. Another holiday, Alice heard. Well, so what? we told ourselves. We didn't need her any more. We kept paying Margot to insult us twice a week. She had put up her prices but we'd have paid whatever she wanted by this stage. I was now a size 12 for the first time in my life. Jenny and Susan had lost fifteen kilos each. Alice was winning, down sixteen kilos, but then she had had the most to lose. We bought new clothes. We flaunted our new bodies. We barely ate anything any more. We were too busy exercising. We told each other we had never been so happy.

I was at home when I heard the news. Jenny rang me. I had to ask her to tell me three times before I believed it.

'Dead? Caitlyn's *dead*?'

I asked Jenny all the questions she had been asking people too. How? An accident? When? Where? There's no mistake? Caitlyn's *dead*?

Jenny didn't know any more details. She'd heard it from her cousin who had heard it from the medical centre receptionist who'd taken the call from the doctor's son. No details, just the basic facts.

If there had been a swirl of gossip about Caitlyn before this, there was now a hurricane. It was a car accident; the doctor had been drink-driving. No, she was a drug addict and she'd overdosed. No, it was suicide. No, the doctor had killed her and was now covering it up.

I didn't go to Margot's meeting the morning after I heard the news. The others did. They were as shocked by the news about Caitlyn as I was, but they still went. Jenny rang me straight afterwards. I listened, but only barely. They'd told Margot about Caitlyn. That the perfect specimen, the role model she'd held up to us, was dead.

'Do you know what she said then?' Jenny was crying.

I didn't answer. I didn't want to hear what Margot might have said.

'She said, "Sad, yes, but it doesn't change the way she looked when she was alive. Keep that image in your minds. That's your goal."'

None of us went to the funeral. It was held in a town a hundred kilometres away, where Caitlyn had grown up and where she would be buried. I didn't hear any details about it until the following week.

I had decided to go back to Margot's meetings. I thought it would focus me again. I was finding it hard to care about dieting and exercise any more. I needed that hectoring voice in my ear: 'Hate the body you're in. Love the body you'll get.'

I was early, for once. The others weren't there yet. As I waited, the receptionist came into the room with some files. We got talking. About Caitlyn, unsurprisingly. The receptionist had been to the funeral, she told me. It was beautiful. A celebration of her life, the way a good funeral should be. Her husband had given the eulogy.

'Everyone was crying by the end. He loved her so much.'

'How did it happen?' I asked, choosing my words carefully in case it had been an overdose, or suicide. I had to know. The rumours were still flying and the truth hadn't reached our ears yet.

She looked at me as if I was a bit stupid. 'Her cancer came back.'

'Caitlyn had cancer?'

'That's how they met. He was doing a research paper about her. That's why they moved here.'

I don't remember the questions I must have asked, but I soon knew the story of Caitlyn's life. She was diagnosed with breast cancer in her early twenties. She had fought it with chemotherapy, lifestyle changes, determination, and won. It was how she and her husband had met, the year she turned twenty-three. Already divorced from his first wife, single and a workaholic, he'd been undertaking research into alternative cancer treatments. They had fallen in love. Yes, they had both always known there was the possibility the disease could return, but they lived life well and joyously. Eighteen months previously, there was a bad test result. They decided to change their lives. They moved to a country town. Our town. Hoping the slower pace of life, the fresh air, living in a close-knit, friendly community could help Caitlyn. Close-knit community? We had barely spoken to Caitlyn. As for help her . . .

The receptionist told me there were attempts to fight the cancer with trials of new drugs. Visits to alternative-therapy centres in Bali. Attempts to live a normal life. That's why people hadn't been told. Caitlyn had wanted friendship, not sympathy.

The doctor's eulogy had been so honest and so sad, the woman said. He'd spoken of the two of them real-ising that this time her body wasn't strong enough to fight it again. He talked about his love for her spirit, her humour, her zest for living, her kindness, her gentleness. Of how much he would miss her. Of how much she had meant to him. Of the plans they had made together, the children they had longed to have together, the memories they had still managed to make.

Even as I listened, my own thoughts were crash-ing into my head, the pieces falling into place, the real story of Caitlyn pushing out the fantasy we had created around her.

Caitlyn wasn't thin because she dieted. She was thin

because she was so ill. She hadn't changed her hair for fashion reasons. She'd bought a wig to cover her baldness, a side effect of her treatment. Her husband hadn't cared for her so tenderly because it was a winter–spring romance. It was because he knew better than anyone that she was not going to be with him for very long. Each of those loving glances, those romantic dinners, had been precious moments in a long, sad, drawn-out farewell to the woman he loved. Those shy, inviting smiles she had given me had indeed been that – invitations to be her friend. And I had ignored them.

I left the medical centre then, before the others arrived.

I never went back to Margot's meetings again. Jenny went for one more week, before leaving midway through, calling me, barely able to speak for her tears. She came to my house to talk, rather than to the café. We didn't want any comments about our weight, our new bodies, our new looks.

She said that afternoon all that I had already decided. That it felt wrong to sit in a room, to be healthy and alive and yet be told to hate our bodies, our strong, healthy bodies. To hate our legs that had carried us throughout our lives, to hate our bellies and our breasts that had grown and nurtured our children. To think of food as the enemy and our bodies as battlegrounds when we should be celebrating our bodies and our lives every day.

Jenny and I decided I'd be the one to tell Alice, Susan and Margot that we didn't want to go to the meetings any more. Three times I tried to call them. Each time I put down the phone. In the end I wrote notes. Cowardly to the last, I didn't tell the truth. I said Jenny and I were too busy. Perhaps that wasn't a lie. We had decided to get busy. Busy being glad we were alive and enjoying all the good things that we could, while we could.

That was six months ago. Alice and Susan still go to Margot's meetings. Jenny and I heard that we'd been replaced by two other women within a week. Word spread. There are now twenty women attending the two meetings each week. I heard that Alice is planning on setting up her own group. I don't know for sure. Alice and Susan don't really talk to Jenny and me any more.

We see them quite often, though. It's a small town; it's hard to avoid each other. The most recent encounter was yesterday. Jenny and I had organised a picnic beside the lake, with our husbands, our kids and several other friends, including a new couple who recently moved to town. I met the woman in a queue at the post office. Where once I would have left it at that – a conversation about the weather – that day I took the extra step of inviting her for a coffee. She'd accepted even before I'd finished delivering the invitation. Since then we've socialised together at least once or twice a week.

I'd done the baking for the picnic – oatmeal biscuits

and the sultana cupcakes my kids love. I used less butter than I might have in the old days, but they still tasted delicious.

We'd just set out all the food and drink on the picnic rugs by the lake when Alice, Susan and five other women went jogging past. They looked great. Thinner than slim, tanned and toned muscles, fashionably dressed in designer exercise wear. They waved at us and Jenny and I waved back, sitting there surrounded by food. I knew what they were thinking and they knew what we were thinking. Jenny and I didn't need to say anything about them after they'd gone, though. We'd done that enough, for hours, talking about how guilty we felt, and how we hoped we would never let something like that take us over again.

I reached into the picnic basket behind me, took out the thermoses for the adults and the bottles of juice for the kids and passed around the sandwiches, cakes and biscuits. After lunch, we got up and played a game of cricket together, enjoying a beautiful day with family and friends.

I hope that's what Caitlyn would have done.

Elixir

FIONA McINTOSH

Nazira sighed. Her fingers ached from bathing two large and demanding women already this morning, and the worst was yet to come – a bridal bath. For Mistress Alhena, no less. She was easily the most difficult of customers to please and seemed to take almost as much pleasure in demeaning Nazira as she took from the scrub and massage that the bathhouse girl's dexterous hands were famed for.

Nazira was just twenty summers but her legend had been spreading for three years. She had shown a natural flare for the trade, causing Mistress Farak to cut Nazira's apprenticeship from four to two years. The hamamci had sensed that good money could be made from this intelligent and pretty girl who she and her husband had originally hired for their domestic household.

Mistress Farak and her husband Master Arif ran the most famous bathhouse in all of Percheron. Originally designed and commissioned by Zar Joreb, the present Zar's great-great-grandfather, its architecture was a work of art. The main dome's marble looked translucent from inside, and at night the building seemed to glow from the lantern light within. It was called Baja – in Percherese this meant double.

The Baja was the only bathing house in all of the city that serviced men and women at the same time, in separate halves of the magnificent pearl-coloured stone building. Each side had four chambers. In the middle of the house was the grand entrance hall with its massive marble columns, and arched windows that let in the cooling breezes off the Faranel Sea. This area was where men could meet, share a quishtar, relax with friends and acquaintances. Women had their own meeting chamber and here news and gossip were exchanged at a furious pace.

Its royal lineage gave the Baja lofty status and so it only attracted people of means, along with dignatories, theologians, philosophers, nobles, esteemed visitors from other realms – and, of course, their wives.

Alhena came from a wealthy family – her father an adviser to the palace – and her long engagement was finally to come to fruition. She would be married later today to the Head of the Janisseries. This most senior of soldiers was known simply as Qadiz and answered only to the Zar himself. Because of his status, Qadiz was the single biggest catch in the whole of Percheron.

Nazira had heard stories that he abused his power and was hated by the people. If these tales were true, she decided, Qadiz and Alhena would make a fine marriage and Nazira could only pity their children.

She stood, took off her robe, so she was naked, save the small loincloth around her hips, and began some stretching routines in the airy rest room that would help prepare her already aching muscles, especially her hands, for the important session ahead. She liked this chamber for its glass roof that afforded her a view of the sky – especially during a busy day when she moved from client to client, unable to step outside. A black slave entered the doorway.

'Is she here already?' Nazira asked, her tone almost a groan, as she reached for her robe.

Khaliya nodded. 'On her way. I just ran an errand for Mistress Farak and saw the entourage moving through the main bazaar.'

'Big?'

'Huge,' Khaliya replied.

'A reflection of her, then,' Nazira added drolly.

Khaliya gave her friend a glance of soft admonishment, looking around to check they were not being eavesdropped upon. 'I've set up chilled juices and a fruit platter in case she just wants to graze today. What do you think? I imagine she's nervous.'

Nazira's lip curled. 'Nervous? I doubt it. And she never grazes – she always eats with enthusiasm in between the bathing routine.'

'Well, Mistress Farak did warn me she's eager on the tooth, so I've put out some dishes of food – breads, salads, a spicy pea paste, some skewers of roasted meat. Surely she couldn't eat much more during bathing?'

Nazira gave a look of disdain. 'Last visit she told me that men preferred a fleshy woman . . . voluptuous, she said, like her. She said no man would ever want me and pinched what little flesh she could find to prove her point. But I know she did that just to hurt me.' Nazira shook her head. 'I really don't know why she asks for me. It's obvious how much she hates me.'

'She chooses you, Nazira, because you are the best natir I have ever trained,' said Mistress Farak, choosing that exact moment to enter. 'In fact, here's something to comfort yourself with, young lady. You would be better than any tellak in the men's quarters.'

Nazira smiled. 'Thank you, Mistress Farak. We shall never know, of course.'

The woman gave her a look of sympathetic agreement. 'And secondly,' she said, holding up a fat finger, 'she punishes you because you are too pretty and lithe for your own good and she, of course, is neither. The goddess Lyana granted that woman wealth, but not beauty, outside . . . or inside.' Nazira smiled self-consciously. Khaliya pulled a face at her.

'In fact,' their mistress continued, 'you're beyond pretty, Nazira, and I'm sure you know it. I'm surprised you never use it.'

Nazira adopted a wistful tone. 'What use is beauty?'

Both Farak and Khaliya raised their eyes to the ceiling. 'Here we go,' Farak said. 'I suppose astronomy or shirgak is preferable.'

'Beauty fades,' Nazira replied loftily, 'but the beauty of shirgak, for instance, only intensifies the more you play and understand it.'

'It's only a game,' Khaliya said, sounding bored, and threw a glance at their mistress, who winked back at her.

'Not to Nazira, I suspect. To her it is mathematical supremacy,' the older woman commented.

'Exactly,' Nazira said, eyes shining. 'A shirgak board is beauty itself.'

Both her companions gave her dismissive looks.

'Have you made up her potions?' Mistress Farak asked, glancing around with concern.

'Yes,' Nazira answered, sounding slightly vexed. 'I've already laid them out in the Shell Chamber; I have everything she needs to look her best for her nuptials . . . and

I've devised a unique perfume for her wedding night. I think it's why I'm so tired. I stayed up most of the night preparing.'

Mistress Farak tut-tutted. 'Is there any end to your talent, my girl?' Her tone was dry, but Nazira knew it was said affectionately.

'Even though it was for the sour Mistress Alhena, I didn't mind working hard. I think I enjoy my herbs and potions more than anything. They make me feel in control. I made a cream up last night that I think will help clear that complexion of hers.'

Her mistress shook her head. 'I sometimes wonder what you're doing here, Nazira.'

'You gave me a chance to earn my freedom from slavery, Mistress Farak. And then you granted me that freedom. I would never leave your employ unless I was to be married. I love my potions but they're a passion, like playing shirgak. I indulge when I can. Besides, I like it here.'

'Well, we don't want to lose you either. And I love your lotions and potions too. Perhaps we should make them more openly available to our customers, and not just our special clients who request them?'

Demand them, more like it, thought Nazira, keeping her face expressionless. But the notion of reaching the wider audience of the Baja was exciting. 'We can make any of them up within a day or so for clients if we have an order,' she replied eagerly.

Mistress Farak bustled her out of the rest room. 'Well, that may be, and we shall discuss it, but your next appointment is a vitally important one. Although I will admit she is one of the most difficult of customers that you must suffer, she is also extremely generous —'

'Not to me,' Nazira scowled.

Farak put her finger to her lips. 'Hush, child. She is extremely generous to the Baja that looks after all of us, and her new royal connections could be a boon for us. I would love for the Janisseries to start using the Baja. I think my good husband would even build a new set of chambers, simply for the soldiers – even a special wing for the officers.'

'Ooh,' said Khaliya, making a lascivious gesture over her bare breasts. 'The soldiers,' she drawled.

Nazira began to giggle.

Mistress Farak rolled her eyes in feigned horror. 'You girls! What is Percheron coming to when you young women are so salacious? I should ask Master Arif to spank you both but I fear he may enjoy it too much!'

The three women laughed. 'I'm afraid you lovely young things will never get the opportunity to lay hands on those fine young stallions – not unless they marry you,' said Farak. 'Beware!' she added, a stern glint in her eye now. 'Soldiers will make use of you and leave you. Don't fall for them.'

'We're never allowed to mix freely with men anyway, Mistress Farak. You have no reason to fret,' Nazira said, sounding weary.

'Where there's a will there's a way for lovers,' Farak said. 'I could fill a book of stories with the affairs of Percheron's bathhouses alone,' she said archly, holding up a finger to stop the girls asking any more questions. 'But I won't.' She shooed Nazira out. 'Go. You have but moments now. Make it a good session, my girl . . . One she can never forget.'

Nazira pulled a face but obediently went on her way, flexing and closing her fingers deliberately as she did so. She would need her fingers to be loose and warm for horrible Mistress Alhena.

Mistress Alhena swept into the main bathing hall, balancing on top of her tall wooden pattens. The mistress preferred to bring her own shoes rather than use a pair from the bathhouse.

A troupe of people marched behind her, carrying items wrapped in beautiful bundles: a silk embroidered peshtemal that Alhena would use to cover her modesty, and the special soaps she insisted on bringing in special tiny gold chests with holes at their bottom.

Mistress Farak made a big show of welcoming the important guest before handing her over to Nazira.

'Ah, there you are, plain little thing,' Alhena conde-
scended, staring down at Nazira from a great height.
'I'm always amused by how little there is of you,' she
said, shooing away the servant who offered to take the
small bundle she carried. 'But you have a strong pair of
hands and I shall need them today.' She looked again at
the hamamci. 'Mistress Farak, could you show my retinue where they can leave all of my belongings? And feed
them too perhaps,' she said absently. 'I haven't had a
chance to order them any food this morning.'

Nazira felt a flare of anger. Many in the retinue were
children, who already looked too thin to be missing a
morning meal.

'Come, girl, whatever your name is – lead the way,'
Alhena said over her shoulder. 'I have a very big night
ahead.'

And a very big backside, Nazira thought sourly, as she
fell in step. 'Er, this way, Mistress Alhena. We've reserved
the Shell suite for you.'

'I should think so,' the woman replied indignantly.
'What about my creams?' she demanded, tottering into
the private chamber, the pattens clicking on the tiles, her
large, magnificently firm breasts arrogantly prominent
beneath her all-too-thin robe. 'I trust they're all ready as
I ordered?'

What had so entranced Qadiz that he would choose
plain, plump Alhena over the well-bred daughters of

good families in Percheron, Nazira wondered? It had to be those ample bosoms; they were certainly impressive.

'They are,' Nazira said, realising too late that she was staring at Alhena's chest.

Alhena smiled, a lasciviousness underlying the gesture. 'I will need some special attention to these beauties today, girl. I see you looking at them and I'm not surprised – you have so little of your own,' she laughed.

Nazira swallowed her embarrassment, hoping she wasn't blushing too furiously. 'Here, let me help you undress.' She could barely reach the woman's shoulders because of Alhena's heels, lifting the woman's feet away from the endless swirl of waters over the marble.

Alhena groaned as her heavy day-garments were peeled away. 'Lyana save me, I'm so tired. How will I perform tonight for my beloved?'

Nazira did not respond. Instead she pointed to the milder of the two springs. 'Over here, if you please,' she said, careful to keep her gaze lowered.

'I want the hot bath, girl!' Alhena snapped.

Nazira curtseyed. 'Mistress Alhena, if you'll forgive me. You will find it a far more enjoyable experience if you use the tepid water first. To go straight into the hot springs – as I've mentioned before – is to risk scorching yourself. If you follow my suggestion your body will accept the heat and relax into the hot springs more easily.' Seeing the expression of thunder on her customer, she hurriedly added, 'I want your body to be perfect for tonight, rather than you feeling red or overheated . . . or swollen.' Nazira could not resist it. Impulsiveness was her flaw. Although the last word was loaded with sarcasm, it mercifully flew over the vacant head of Alhena, who was already clambering into the milder pool with the aid of a silent Khaliya, whose eyes bulged with caution at the natir.

Once she was seated in the pool, Alhena continued barking orders. 'I want my hair washed and brushed until it gleams. I want every inch of my body waxed, especially between my buttocks because I have heard Qadiz likes to —'

'Of course, Mistress Alhena,' said Nazira hastily, her embarrassment acute. 'I will ensure that you are smooth and polished and beautiful for your new husband. Above all I want you to be relaxed and calm. So please be still and quiet now.' Nazira pulled off her own robe, leaving her naked save a tiny strip of fabric that hung from her pelvis, and waded into the pool. 'Let's begin with your hair.'

Alhena retired to a small, private area reserved for high-ranking women, known as the Shell Chamber. It boasted beautiful designs of Goddess Lyana's symbol, the conch, used in various ways – from the shape of the room, to the etchings sculpted out of the marble friezes. Chilled pomegranate juice was served as Alhena lounged on a special divan, enrobed in warmed towels, her wet hair draped over the side. Khaliya knelt as she finger-dried the woman's black tresses, oiling them carefully with sandalwood, whose exquisite earthy notes Nazira had heightened with citrus and the famed crushed fromella seed of Galinsea.

'I hope you're using only Shahif's sandalwood oil. You know his —'

'His alone for you, Mistress Alhena. He provides for the Zar's wives after all,' Nazira cut across the woman's terse words as she too knelt and buffed Alhena's nails with a soft polishing stick. Again the insult was couched. Alhena, she was sure, wouldn't register that most of the royal wives began their lives as slaves, and were considered whores of the royal when they were sold into slavery as mere odalisques to the palace.

Alhena inhaled. 'It's very beautiful, but what have you added to give it that extra fragrance?'

Nazira demurred. 'It is a special recipe I have designed just for you, Mistress Alhena. It is the most beautiful fragrance I have ever created.' As she stood, Nazira regretted giving this perfume to Alhena; she wished now that she had kept it to share with her soldier lover. She glided sadly over to a cabinet from which she retrieved a tiny glass vial with an elegant stopper that Master Arif

had paid for Nazira to commission from the glass blower.
'This is for you, Mistress. It is your own perfume. A wedding gift from the Baja, with our sincerest wishes that
your marriage is blessed and ever happy.'

Alhena opened her eyes to slits, lazy and uninterested.
'Very nice. I just hope it doesn't make me think of you
whenever I wear it. Your voice wears on me, girl. Stop
talking!'

Nazira bit her lip. A look of warning from Khaliya
prevented her from smashing the little bottle at the
plump woman's feet. She hated Alhena for dismissing
her efforts with such carelessness. Master Arif had paid
handsomely for the beautiful vial, and Nazira was shaking with fatigue from her efforts to produce the finest set
of potions for this ungrateful woman.

Nevertheless, Nazira had promised her employer she
would reign in her vexation. She returned to her knees
and continued her work silently. In order to reach all
parts of her client's body, Nazira spun the woman around
on the raised platform. Here the hottest of all the waters
fizzed through holes in the marble and allowed the bath
girl to haul Alhena's large form across the massage dais
with relative ease. She was careful not to wet the woman's hair.

Finally, Alhena groaned. 'I ache. Did you deliberately
hurt me?'

Nazira smiled demurely as she once again wrapped

her customer in warmed towels. 'No, Mistress Alhena. Khaliya will brush your hair now. And you will feel the benefits of that massage later this evening.'

'When I'm pleasuring my new husband, you mean?'

Nazira's smile faltered.

'You're so shy, girl. I suppose you've never been touched by a man. Not so much as looked at.'

Nazira looked down. Neither was true but she certainly wasn't going to admit as much to this hideous person. In fact she was very much in love with a man, one of the very soldiers that Mistress Farak had warned her against. He was handsome and generous; from a good family of vineyard owners from the west. He was the second son of two. The first was ailing, might not see his third decade; Hazim stood to inherit all. He'd asked her to be his wife. His first . . . and only, as he had promised. Whether she could trust him, that was left to be seen, but it meant a life of serenity in a beautiful country house overlooking the vineyards. Hazim was young, romantic of heart. When Nazira gave him strong sons to work his fields, he would need no other women in his life. She smiled to herself. She was the romantic!

'Pah! She ignores me,' Alhena spat. 'Bring me quishtar!' she ordered.

'Sorry, Mistress. I didn't mean to.' Nazira nodded at Khaliya to fetch a brew of quishtar. 'May I take over the brushing of your hair?'

'As you please,' Alhena scowled. 'But you'll have to start the one hundred strokes again. Lyana knows the black slave couldn't possibly count.'

Nazira closed her eyes and drew a steadying breath. 'One,' she said loud enough for the woman to hear as she drew the ornate brush through Alhena's hair, beginning to gleam from all the attention. She continued counting softly, watching as Khaliya returned with a steaming pot of quishtar.

Nazira stopped at twenty strokes. 'Would you like it poured the traditional way, Mistress?'

'Yes, and cool it. I hate it when it burns my mouth.'

Nazira nodded at Khaliya, who set about the Percherese ritual of pouring quishtar from jug to jug, to release its flavours, cool it, and so that the maker could silently sing to it, imbuing it with her own mark of hospitality.

It smelled beautiful to Nazira. Only the best for Alhena, her senses told her. Mistress Farak must have insisted that Khaliya use only the finest quishtar of the rare northern berry. She paused again, this time at fifty strokes.

'Mistress Alhena, would you care to take a sip of your quishtar?'

Alhena did not bother to reply but sat forward to take the handle of the cranberry-coloured tea glass it was served in. Nor did she bother to thank Khaliya.

She took a sip of the quishtar, screeching in anger.

Before anyone could react, Alhena threw the glass and its steaming contents at the black girl. Khaliya screamed as the scorching liquid burned her bare skin. Thinking fast, despite her shock, Nazira grabbed a jug of icy water meant for cooling Mistress Alhena's brow and poured it over the weeping girl, lying prone on the floor.

'Stay there,' she whispered to Khaliya, glancing at a frightened Mistress Farak, who had run in after hearing the screams. 'I have something that could help,' she beseeched the hamamci, who nodded and took over.

Nazira fled the chamber but not before she caught Alhena's lazy drawl. 'The glass slipped from my hand when the quishtar burned my mouth,' she said to Farak. 'I'll send one of my slaves to take her place if she can't work any more.'

Nazira wiped a tear from her cheek as Mistress Farak explained Khaliya's fate.

'The physic's given her a soporific to help,' said Farak, resigned to allowing Alhena to get away with the cruel act.

Nazira sighed. 'I can stop the scarring, perhaps, but I need to make up a fresh lotion. It must go on her immediately.'

Her superior held a hand up. 'What you must do immediately is attend to your customer. Mistress Alhena has already waited for long enough. It is important we do not test her patience any further.' Nazira opened her mouth to protest her despair but Mistress Farak stopped her again. 'I know you understand why and that I can count on you. Now worry not about Khaliya. I will take care of her and you may see her when you have finished with the Faja's client.'

Nazira's lips thinned. It was the only way she could stop herself saying something she would dearly regret. 'I hope, Mistress Farak, that she pays you very handsomely because I cannot imagine that any amount of money is worth this much pain or torment.'

The older woman smirked. 'Nazira, she is not paying us anything at all. She expects this service free of charge. She believes her presence as the soon-to-be wife of the Janisseries is more than enough payment, because of the lustre she adds to our clientele. She also knows – as well as we do – that her husband's soldiers could make us a fortune if they chose to give us their patronage.'

'Free?' Nazira repeated dumbly.

Mistress Farak nodded. 'There is more, I'm afraid. I might as well tell you now. She has asked that you join her household retinue as her personal bather.'

Fury erupted. Nazira felt every part of her body swell with anger at these words. 'But, Mistress Farak, I am no longer a slave to be sold.'

Farak placed a gentle hand on Nazira's shoulder. 'Nor

will you be sold, my girl. You will go freely but you will do this for me because of what it could mean for the Baja. She will pay us for your services. You will be on permanent loan, shall we say.' Mistress Farak leaned closer. 'Although she refuses to allow you to tend to her husband. I don't think it's hard to guess why,' she added with a sly smile. 'Now, go, my girl. She wishes you to perform the full bridal cosmetology on her. Do not fight me on this other business. It is your fate.'

Fate? No! Nazira had worked hard and with diligence so that she could control her own destiny. She'd rather die by her own hand than be attached to Mistress Alhena.

In a daze Nazira returned to the Shell Chamber. Alhena was sprawled on the divan again, her hair being swept up into an elegant, high style and dressed with fresh linnaka buds by a different black slave, who looked understandably nervous. Nazira could see the girl's fingers trembling.

'I'll take over, Shandri,' she said softly.

'Ah, you're back,' Alhena snarled. 'In future, ask my permission to leave the room. And take that robe off. No one is to be dressed when they're attending me at my ablutions.'

Nazira was now convinced that Alhena enjoyed women's bodies as much as men's. It explained why she stared at Nazira's body so much and talked about it so often. Did it also explain why she was prepared to pay for her to join the marriage household? Nazira felt dizzy with illness at the thought of being answerable to Alhena's every whim. Who knew what humiliations this evil woman had in mind for her?

That morning, Nazira had woken to pleasant thoughts of a bright, free future. Yet Alhena's arrival at Baja threatened everything: Nazira's marriage, her love for Hazim, even the joy of making herbal potions was instantly tarnished by the notion that her life would be run by Mistress Alhena.

She could not bear it.

'I said take it off!' Alhena demanded. 'Lyana's Wrath! I'm going to teach you some new manners when you're working for me, my girl. I'll begin by granting you no clothes at all. You will walk around my suite naked at all times. You will be forbidden to leave the confines of that suite and its gardens.'

Alhena drew another breath for a fresh tirade. But now that she'd decided she could never permit herself to be 'owned' by this wretch, Nazira found her voice, and a new calm. She took advantage of the momentary pause by saying, 'Forgive me, Mistress Alhena. My hamamci explained that you wish to have some cosmetology. What is it that you would like?'

Alhena's eyes narrowed. 'That's a better attitude,' she snapped. 'I want my face to be made beautiful,' she began. *Impossible*, Nazira said to herself, but her expression betrayed nothing. 'My nails to be stained a deep red, I think . . . like the royals.' *Like your shame should be*, Nazira thought, politely nodding at the same time. 'I would have my body powdered and coated with the dust of gems.'

'Of course,' Nazira murmured, hoping privately that the crushed gems would get inside Alhena's body and scratch her mercilessly.

'And, as I plan to be wearing nothing for my husband tonight, I think I should have my nipples painted like the Zar's odalisques are reputed to do when he chooses them.'

Nazira gagged inwardly. It was the mark of a slave, and these days, a whore. She tried to find a polite way to say this. 'Are you sure, Mistress Alhena? It is —'

Alhena slapped her. The sting of it caught Nazira's breath.

'How dare you question me? You are a natir, that's all. Barely more than a slave and you have the gall to interrogate me.'

Nazira refused to raise her hand to her cheek. But it was the first and last time, she decided, that Alhena would touch her.

'Forgive me,' she whispered. 'I was going to say it might taste strange.' She knew this would appeal to the woman's vanity.

Alhena laughed. 'My husband will love the way I taste. Get on with it.'

'I will prepare the painting paste, Mistress. Shandri?' The slave looked questioningly at Nazira. 'We will need the staining ink – vermilion – for Mistress Alhena's nails, and some of the gem dust from the cabinets. Mistress Farak has the key.' She nodded to send the girl on her way. 'I won't be long,' she said to Alhena.

'Stop chittering and get on with it, girl.'

Nazira moved over to her trunk of ingredients, in which she kept the tiny chest containing the special salves, potions, unguents and creams that she had laboured over for Mistress Alhena. And now her hands moved rapidly, tipping various ingredients into her pestle and mortar. She crushed them, working adeptly to turn the small puddle of leaves and seeds, oils and scents into a paste.

'How much longer?' Alhena called. 'It must be getting late. I've been here most of the day.'

'Just getting the colour right, Mistress,' Nazira called over her shoulder. She reached for a tiny vial tucked away in the satin lining of her trunk. 'One more ingredient,' she said, more to herself than anyone else, tipping three drops of the deep red liquid into the bowl.

'What is that?'

Nazira nearly dropped the vial. She was startled by Alhena suddenly standing next to her, so close their skin was almost touching.

'This is the colour, Mistress. You asked for a deep pink.' She stirred the liquid in.

'But it's already the right colour.'

'This sets it. Although bathe tomorrow, or they may stain purple. But for now you will have deeply pink and desirable nipples for your special night, Mistress Alhena.'

The woman smiled lasciviously. 'Paint me. No slaves. I want only you to do it.'

Nazira nodded, stifling the desire to gag. 'Make yourself comfortable. And please, do warn your new husband that this will taste a bit strange. It may even make his lips feel momentarily numb, or turn a soft shade of purple. It's the tint reacting, that's all.'

Alhena shrugged. 'If it doesn't bother a zar, it shouldn't bother Qadiz.' She pulled off her robe to reveal her large, heavy breasts. She looked down proudly. 'I think he'll enjoy them, don't you?'

'Oh, yes, I do. Especially with this special treat you have for him, Mistress. Make sure you return his joy in your body. Kiss him deeply.'

Alhena glanced at Nazira with a new appreciation. 'For someone who knows so little about men, you give advice on them freely. I might even take it.'

Nazira smiled shyly.

The funeral for Qadiz of the Janisseries and Mistress Alhena was held five days later. No one ever knew what could have so tragically killed the newly married couple during their wedding night. Physics put it down to food that they alone ate at their marriage feast – for there were plenty of special treats formed for the celebrated pair.

It was a poisoning of some sort, the guild of physicians finally decided, for why else would their lips turn that particular shade of purple?

Three moons later, Mistress Farak insisted on paying for an intimate wedding celebration for one of her favourites.

Master Arif made an ebullient toast to the handsome young soldier who had married his sweetheart, the petite natir from the bathhouse, demanding that their first son be called Arif.

Dabbing a silken kerchief at her tears of joy, Mistress Farak turned to her companion and whispered. 'The perfume that Nazira's wearing is heavenly. Is it one of her own creations?'

'Oh, yes, Mistress Farak,' the young slave replied, 'Nazira told me it's the most beautiful fragrance she has ever created. She couldn't bear for anyone else to wear it but her.'

Farak shook her head quizzically. 'How strange, I could swear I have smelled that scent on someone before.'

Khaliya's lips lifted the scarred side of her face as she smiled.

In My Sister's Shoes

SINEAD MORIARTY

The following is an extract from my book In My Sister's Shoes. *It is the story of the complicated relationship between two sisters – Kate and Fiona. When Fiona is diagnosed with breast cancer, Kate comes back to Ireland to help.*

I woke up the next morning to my brother Derek banging on my bedroom door. I peeled my face from the pillow and shouted at him to go away.

'Yo, Mark's on the phone.'

'Tell him to fuck off.'

'He sounds kinda freaked.'

'Tough.'

'He said Fiona's locked herself in the bathroom and won't come out.'

While I had no intention of helping my cold-hearted

brother-in-law, my sister Fiona was a different matter. Ungluing my eyes, I shuffled over and unlocked the door. Derek handed me the phone. 'Yes?' I grunted.

'Kate, I need you to come over. Fiona won't come out of the bathroom and I can hear her crying in there,' Mark informed me.

'So deal with it. She's your wife.'

'She won't talk to me and the boys are getting upset. Maybe she'll talk to you. She sounds very distressed.'

'She has breast cancer. Of course she's upset. Welcome to reality, Mark.'

'Can you save the jibes for later and please come over?'

I was tempted to leave him alone to deal with his family issues himself for once, but I could hear Bobby howling in the background and I was worried about Fiona. 'I'll be over in ten minutes,' I said, and hung up.

I washed my mascara-streaked face and threw on my jeans and sweatshirt. On the five-minute drive to Fiona's I almost crashed the rental car twice as I remembered the holy show I'd made of myself the night before in the pub. How could I have misread the situation so badly? I couldn't believe I'd made such an obvious pass at my ex-boyfriend Sam and had been so publicly rejected. Oh, God, it was toe-curling humiliation. Could my life possibly get any sadder? Jobless, chubby, penniless – and now a social reject.

When I got to the house, the twins ran up to me. 'Mummy's crying and she won't come out,' they said, their sweet little faces flushed with concern.

'Don't worry. She's probably just a bit sick from the nasty medicine,' I said, hugging them. 'Now, you go and brush your teeth and wash your hands while I talk to your mum and dad. Okay?' I ushered them into the main bathroom and went to find Mark.

He was crouched on the bedroom floor talking to Fiona through the keyhole of the ensuite. Teddy was sitting beside him scratching the door with his paw and whimpering. For once, Mark seemed pleased to see me – well, relieved, at least.

'Thanks for coming. She won't talk to me,' he said.

'Fine. Go and take the boys to the park or something. I'll call you later.'

I knelt down in front of the door and tapped lightly.

'Fiona, it's me. Are you okay?'

I could hear her crying but she didn't say anything.

'Do you feel awful? Are you having a panic attack? Because freaking out right now would be extremely normal.'

Silence.

I lay down on the floor and put my eye to the bottom of the door. She was holding a clump of hair. 'Oh, Fiona, is your hair falling out? Is that it? You poor thing, is it bad? Can I come in and look? I'll get some scissors and we'll fix it up. Come on, there's nothing we can't sort out.'

She started sobbing.

'If it makes you feel any better, I made a pass at Sam last night, and after he'd ricocheted off his seat in revulsion, he told me he was seeing a young one from the office. My face is still bright red from the shame of it. Come on, open up and let me hide in there with you. I'm a danger to myself.'

The lock clicked and my sister's blotchy face peered out. 'Has Mark gone?'

'Yes.'

She sighed and pulled the door back, putting her hand protectively over her head. Clumps of hair lay on the floor.

'It started falling out in the shower and then I combed it – and *voila*!' she said, taking her hand down to reveal a large bald patch on the right side of her head. She looked so sad and vulnerable I reached out to comfort her, but she stepped back. Clearly I was a leper at the moment. No man or woman wanted me anywhere near them.

'What am I going to do? I look like a freak. I don't recognise myself. What have I become? Look at me!' she wailed, really letting her anguish out for the first time since the diagnosis.

'Come on, don't say that. Okay, losing your hair is a really rotten thing to happen, but you're still you, you're still gorgeous. We can fix this. You just need to shave it off. We'll go out and buy amazing hats and bandanas and wigs. It'll be fun.'

'Fun? I'm a bald 34-year-old mother of five-year-old twins, with lopsided breasts, whose husband hasn't gone near her in months. Mark's going to run a mile when he sees my bald head. I know he doesn't find me attractive any more and I don't blame him. I'm hideous!'

'Don't you dare say that! Now, listen to me,' I said, grabbing her by the shoulders and shaking her. 'You're the most amazing person I know. I've looked up to you my whole life. You're an incredible wife, mother, sister and daughter. Your hair – or lack of it – does not make you any less beautiful. Now, put some clothes on. We're going shopping.'

While Fiona got dressed I called Derek and asked him to get his best mate Gonzo to come over with his head-shaver.

'Dude,' said Derek, when he saw Fiona, 'you can't be going around like that. You look like someone's attacked you with blunt scissors.'

'I'm well aware of how appalling I look, thanks, Derek.'

'I think you need a number two,' said Gonzo. 'It'll be cool. You'll look like Sigourney Weaver in *Alien*. Hot!'

'Or Demi Moore in *GI Jane*,' I added, as Fiona did her best to smile.

Gonzo plugged in his razor. 'Don't sweat it, Fiona. I'm

good at this. Plenty of practice,' he said, pointing to his own tightly shaved head.

'Well, I can't look worse than I already do, so fire ahead,' she said, trying not to cry.

Gonzo shaved her head, gently and carefully, and then turned her around to admire his handiwork.

'Good job, bro,' said Derek, relieved to see that his sister now looked like a punk rather than an old woman with thinning hair.

Fiona took a deep breath and looked into the mirror. 'It's not as bad as I thought. I still look like hell, but I'm glad it's all off,' she said gulping back tears.

'Any time you need a top-up, just let me know,' said the newly appointed Vidal Sassoon.

I looked at Fiona's bald head. There was something incredibly lonely and sad about it. It was as if her cancer was now a badge. Without her hair, everyone would know she was sick. When she walked down the street, people would stare. She'd never be able to say, 'I'm great, thanks. How are you?' to anyone she met. It was as if she had an I HAVE CANCER sticker plastered across her forehead. She looked sick too. It was so much easier to pretend everything was going to be okay when she looked like her old self. But the image staring back at us was that of a sick person. A cancer victim.

'Well, I'll be off,' said Gonzo.

'Wait!' I shouted. 'Do me.'

'What?' he asked, confused.

'Shave my hair off too.'

'No way,' said Fiona.

'It's my hair, my decision, and I want it off,' I said.

'Awesome idea. Me too,' said Derek.

'I will not allow you to do this,' said Fiona.

'It's got nothing to do with you, so sit down and be quiet,' I said, already in *GI Jane* mode. I grabbed the kitchen scissors and chopped off my ponytail as Fiona stared at me. It felt fantastic. I was getting a huge adrenaline rush from doing this for her.

Gonzo set to work, and half an hour later, Derek and I were as bald as coots.

'You look hot,' whispered Gonzo into my ear and proceeded to nibble it.

For once I didn't swat him away or insult him. I knew what it was like to be rejected. Instead, I tried to pull my head away gently, but then he shoved his tongue into my ear so I thumped him.

'Newsflash, Gonzo. Women hate having a tongue rammed down their ear,' I snapped.

Gonzo and Derek looked at each other. 'Really?' Gonzo asked, put out. 'I thought chicks really dug it.'

'Well, this one doesn't,' I said. Even in my current male-famine, it did nothing for me.

Derek looked at Fiona. She shook her head. 'Sorry, guys. I'm not a fan of the tongue-in-ear either.'

Gonzo slouched out of the house to his car.

As Derek got up to follow him, Fiona stopped him. Looking down at the floor, she said, 'You both know I'm not very good at the whole emotions thing, but what you just did means . . . means . . .' She broke down.

Derek patted her shoulder. 'I get it that you're grateful. It's no biggie. Gotta fly. I need to get some lyrics down for my gig next week. Adios, muchachas.'

It was just me and Fiona, and suddenly I felt awkward. I didn't know what to say and I could see she was struggling too. She wanted to say so much, but it was too overwhelming.

'Kate, I . . .'

'Hey,' I said gently. 'I know, and you're welcome, and it's really no big deal. Now, come on, let's get this mess cleared up.'

Ten minutes later, Mark called to see how Fiona was. I told him about the hair shaving and said I'd pick the kids up from the park and take them off for lunch and let him go home to see his wife and spend some time with her for a change.

On the way to the park, I pulled the mirror down in the car to look at my hairless self for the first time. The person gazing back at me was a total stranger. I began to shake. Oh God, what had I done? I looked like a freak. I panicked. Would I ever look nice again? How long would my hair take to grow back? How long before I could go out in public without people staring at me and crossing the road to avoid me? I was a cross between a skinhead and a cancer patient. My hair had always been my best feature. Why, oh, why had I been so impulsive? I suppressed the urge to wail.

I forced myself to be calm. I had done the right thing. It had meant a lot to Fiona and she was so undemanding. After all, what was the big deal? It wasn't as if I had a job that required me to look good or a boyfriend I wanted to seduce. Gulping back the sobs that were threatening to escape, I tried not to think about the fact that my hair would take years to grow back and that no man would ever fancy me again.

When Mark saw me, he stared, open mouthed.

'You might want to work on your reaction,' I snapped. 'Fiona doesn't need to see you gaping at her in shock and horror. She needs you to pretend that it isn't that bad. She needs you to support her.'

For once Mark didn't have a snide retort. I must have looked even worse than I thought. He muttered something about seeing me later and hurried off, leaving me with the twins.

'Where's your hair?' asked Bobby, wide eyed.

'In the bin,' I said, as casually as I could. I wondered if I could take it out of the bin and bring it to a shop to have it stuck back on. They could do wonders with hair, these days. 'I decided to shave it off. What do you think?'

'You look scary,' said Jack, giggling nervously. 'Like an alien.'

'Well, boys, Mummy's hair is the same and so is Uncle Derek's. We all cut our hair off.'

'Why?' asked Bobby.

'Because we wanted to look like Kojak.'

'Who's Dojak?' asked Bobby.

'Bob the Builder's dad,' I said, pulling it out of thin air. I was getting good at this.

'Bob doesn't have a dad,' said Jack looking confused. 'He has Scoop the Digger, Dizzy the Cement Mixer and —'

'Pilchard the Cat and Wendy and JJ!' shouted Bobby.

'And Roley the Steamroller, but no dad,' added Jack.

'Maybe that's because Bob's dad, Kojak, lives in America.'

'Oh,' said the twins.

'Where does Bob live?' asked Bobby.

'In England,' I said.

'Is that where you used to live?' asked Jack.

'Yes, you clever boy, it is.'

'But you live with Grandad now,' said Bobby, not wanting to be shown up by his brother.

'Exactly,' I said.

'Can I touch it?' asked Jack, reaching up to feel the scalp formerly occupied by my lovely hair.

'Sure.' I knelt down so the boys could feel it. They squealed with delight as they rubbed my fuzzy head.

'Cool,' said Jack. 'I want to be bald.'

'When you're grown-up you can be.'

'I want to now,' whined Jack. 'I want to be like Bob the Builder and Mummy and Uncle Derek and Dojak.'

'Me too, me too,' said Bobby, slapping my head.

'First of all you have to let your hair grow and then when it's finished growing, when you're eighteen and you have a good job like Bob the Builder, you can have it cut off. But not now. Besides, I don't think Mrs Foley would like you turning up at school with no hair.'

'Is Daddy bald too?' asked Jack.

'No, sweetheart, but I think we should ask him to shave his hair off tonight when we go home,' I said, grinning at the image of Professor Mark Kennedy with his coiffed hair shaved off . . . knowing full well that it would never happen.

Breastfeeding the Girls

JOOLS OLIVER

I had always wanted to breastfeed our babies and I think that this was due to the fact that I didn't know any different. My sisters and I were all breastfed and so were Jamie and his sister, Anna. And now my eldest sister Nat was breastfeeding, too. So it seemed natural for me to do the same. I thought that it looked incredibly easy and a wonderful thing to do, so as I got nearer and nearer to my due date with Poppy it was definitely one of the things I was most looking forward to.

We were lucky at our antenatal group as we were offered an extra class exclusively about breastfeeding. At first I thought that it would be pointless to learn about breastfeeding when you didn't actually have your baby to try it with, but nonetheless I signed up for it. I thought it best to at least try; after all I still didn't have a clue how to do up a babygrow, let alone feed my baby! So off I went. The class was packed, with all the NCT (National Childbirth Trust) girls gathered round in the usual semi-circle. It was weird not having any of the men there – it was more relaxed and comfortable. (After all, if I was going to be getting my boobs out I would rather it be with just the girls, thank you very much!) It was all very helpful; even using little plastic dolls as our future babies I learnt a lot.

I was very shocked to learn that breastfeeding actually involves some quite skilled manoeuvring. I just thought it was a matter of putting your baby to your nipple and letting her do the rest! Of course it could never be that simple. There is a specific technique you have to learn in order to get your baby to 'latch on' successfully. It's all about angles really and letting your baby take charge! At the antenatal class we were given a diagram to show us how to hold the baby to the nipple, and so, armed with my plastic baby and the diagram, I set about practising my nearly acquired skill.

Okay, enough practising. It was now time for the real thing. As soon as Poppy was born she was handed straight to me. I laid her on my chest and within minutes she was foraging for my breast. I was shocked at her eagerness as I hadn't anticipated that. With a bit of fumbling she was on . . . no, wait a minute, she was off again. Hang on. She was a lot harder to manipulate than my plastic baby who had seemed to latch on perfectly first time and stay there for hours! With Poppy falling on and off my boob I decided to give in and relax. After all, I had just given birth and was too tired at this point to worry about breastfeeding. And obviously Pops wasn't too concerned because she fell asleep as well.

Undeterred by my first attempt and now back in the comfort of our little room on the ward, it was just me and Poppy, this time with no overzealous audience peeking in or (God forbid) tweaking my nipples to try and help the process along! For the first time since she had been born, I was now in charge and alone. I had been given a special typed-up sheet by the midwife, which had a chart to help me with my breastfeeding times. Apparently, I was to feed Poppy on one breast first and then write down which one I had chosen. Then on the next feed I was supposed to put her on the other breast. That sounded simple enough. It didn't say how long I was supposed to keep her on the boob but, hey, maybe I should be thinking for myself on this one. It was beginning to feel like school!

The second time I breastfed Poppy was much better. She seemed to latch on fairly quickly and, from what I could tell, she was content with her first proper meal! It only lasted about five minutes though. (Naturally I was timing the feeds to add to the work sheet – after all I wanted to receive top marks from the chief midwife on the ward. I wanted to be their best student!)

Okay. Feed number three. 'Shit! Where's my pen and work sheet?' as Poppy's screams reverberated through the ward during the middle of the night. I was faffing around trying to weigh my boobs with my hand, wondering which one was heaviest, and attempting to tally that up with my work sheet. 'Bugger,' I thought. So I decided to go with the left boob and on Poppy went again with no trouble. I had a pillow propped underneath my arm and Pops was laying on it clamped to my breast. I marvelled at the sudden quietness that ensued (as I am sure every other new mum does too)! And with only a flickering TV in the background for company I fell asleep in a state of bliss.

What was all this fuss about cracked nipples and sore boobs that we were warned about at NCT? Mine felt fabulous! And, may I say, Jamie thought they looked pretty good too! Now, remember, I am only talking day two here. By the time we had taken Poppy home for the first time and settled into a kind of breastfeeding routine, suddenly the pain everyone had talked about set in. Firstly, I noticed that every time Poppy fed from me I had the most searing pain like a crunching sensation in my stomach. It felt as if I had a very tight clamp strapped to my lower tummy, pulling tighter every time she sucked. At first I thought that maybe I had eaten something dodgy at the hospital, but once she had stopped feeding the pain ebbed away almost as fast as it had arrived. After a chat with my midwife she explained that breastfeeding helps the uterus to contract and that was what I was feeling. Perfect, I thought. At least that sorted out the first problem, and as time went on the nagging feeling subsided. After about two weeks it had gone completely and I didn't feel it again.

My next hurdle was incredibly painful, cracked nipples. They really were a sight. Every time Pops clamped her little gums and mouth on to the nipple I gave a yelp of pain if I was alone in the room and sometimes sat there crying with pain. I really had to grit my teeth as Poppy went hell for leather. I often found myself stamping my feet and grunting like a pig to deal with it. In fact, every time she fed from me I got myself into a grunting and stamping routine (much to the distress and disgruntlement of Jamie or whoever else was in the room at the time)! But the torture only lasted about a minute and as soon as she was settled there we both relaxed.

A good tip which my sister-in-law Anna-Marie gave me was not to slather my nipples in specialised nipple cream but to allow them to dry and crack as this way they would become hardened to it and within weeks they would heal. I did as she advised and it worked, although it's thoroughly tempting to coat yourself in cream, especially if it has been in the fridge for a while as it can be a really instant soother. I do remember, especially in those early days, sitting cross-legged on the floor in our sitting room with my tracksuit bottoms on and one of Jamie's shirts completely opened to the waist with no bra on. I sat eating my dinner with Poppy clamped to one boob and I held a bag of petit pois on the other exposed breast. What a sight, but at the time it was the norm and my mum and Jamie certainly weren't going to complain. (I don't think they would have dared!)

I actually found feeding Poppy the regular way (in the cradle position) quite hard to master at first, so my mid-wife showed me a different, more effective way for me by using one of those specialised 'boomerang'-shaped cushions which I could place around my waist and then put Poppy into position under my arm. (It's called the rugby ball position because it looks like you're carrying a rugby ball!) This seemed to work brilliantly and I soon became reliant on my super-sized boomerang cushion. I even phoned up my health visitor to ask if it would ever be possible for me to feed Poppy without using it as I imagined going for coffee with my NCT pals and whipping out my cushion!

For the first few days after giving birth the only milk supply that you have is called 'colostrum'. It's a yellowish colour and has the texture of skimmed milk as it's very watery. This milk is filled with all the essential nutrients that newborns need. I didn't actually get my proper milk coming in until about four days after Poppy was born. I had almost forgotten that it would be arriving and so was quite shocked to wake up one night to find massive wet patches circling my boobs and a completely wet sheet. I couldn't work out what had happened and thought that in my catatonic state I had poured water on myself from my glass on the side table. As I sat up I felt this strange sensation in my breasts. They were incredibly painful and heavy like you wouldn't believe. Looking down I no longer had to imagine what Jordan feels like every morning . . . they were massive! And as hard as rocks. They even felt bumpy to touch . . . so this is what they meant when they talked about your milk coming in!

My instinct told me that I had to empty these and fast. I couldn't bear to wake Poppy up to feed her so I decided that I would have to extract it myself. Luckily I had read up on this chapter when I was pregnant – hand expressing, I think it was called. It was simple enough. (I know that I could have just tried to use my breast pump, as this situation was exactly what they were designed for, but at three in the morning I was in NO mood to faff about with the instructions.) What I should have done is bought my breast pump well in advance and read the instructions so I knew what to do. Anyway, I went off to the bathroom and hand expressed some of my new milk. This was bloody fascinating! I was basically kneading my boobs from the outside in and the milk was coming out so fast. The relief it brought me was almost instant. At some points I didn't even have to push it out as it flowed out on its own. This only happened every so often; especially if Poppy had had a day where she fed little. My milk supply would be overflowing as she wasn't a great guzzler.

My breast pump often came in handy as I would just express the excess milk and either freeze it or throw it away. I would do this more frequently when weaning Poppy as she got older. As soon as Poppy had sampled real food, her intake of my milk lessened and it was inevitable that I was going to have this huge excess of wasted milk. At times it was just too painful to ignore. It got confusing, though, because I was told that if I expressed too much, my milk supply would increase. I felt like I was in a little bit of a no-win situation, but the odd sneaky breast pump here and there was okay as long as it was to get rid of excess milk. (It's beginning to sound like an addiction . . . you wait and see for yourself because quite franky it is!)

It always made us laugh when I put Poppy on the breast first thing in the morning when my supply was at its greatest. There is a process called the 'let-down reflex' where the milk rushes from your milk glands to your nipple and if Poppy happened to fall off my boob the milk would spray out like a fine shower all over her face. If I hadn't been taking any notice for a couple of minutes, I'd look down and see her little face covered in milk!

Now, the only way to stop all these wet mattresses,

sheets, pyjamas and clothes is to wear breast pads. I hated them so I rejoiced when it was no longer necessary to have them and gleefully chucked the whole supply in the bin. Basically they are like sanitary towels for boobs – what more can I say? But they were exceedingly helpful, especially in the early stages of breastfeeding when leakage was just par for the course. It is advised that you wear them at night, but for me they were just too fiddly and irritating. I would often find rogue pads in the strangest of places – under the bed, behind the sofa, and in Poppy's toy box of all places. They seemed to have minds of their own! It was never amusing to have a nice day out and find that, once you got home and looked in the mirror, your boob pads had been showing quite prominently all day through your T-shirt. Two wonky circular eyes peering out of your chest – now, that's attractive!

I was initially surprised at how little Poppy drank during the day. She always seemed to be asleep but, of course, it was a completely different story during the night time. For the very first few nights of Poppy's life, being woken up by her every few hours was a pleasure. We used to lie awake watching her little body – arms splayed out above her head – and will her to wake up so we could cuddle her, and then, as soon as she stirred, we would whip her out of her cradle. Jamie and I would both be vying for her attention and, of course, I would always win as I was the meals on wheels! Until week two . . . yes, it only took about fourteen days for us both (well, me especially) to realise that sleep deprivation was killing us!

Instead of lying awake willing Poppy to wake up, I would lie rigid in my bed praying for her to stay asleep. As soon as I heard the familiar little noises coming from the cradle I knew she was stirring. My heart would beat faster as I hoped it was just a mere murmur and not the full-on three-course meal beckoning! But, of course, within minutes she would be screaming her head off and I would have her out of her basket quicker than lightning in case she woke Jamie up. I found these feeds incredibly hard. In fact, if I'm being honest, the words I would use to describe them are 'pure punishment'. I couldn't believe that in two weeks I had gone from feeling pleasure to punishment. How could this be? I was doing three feeds a night (approximately midnight, three a.m. and six a.m.) and found the midnight one the hardest to deal with. Having gone to bed at nine, I would instantly fall into a deep, luxurious sleep only to be woken abruptly and put straight into action. My body was in shock!

Propped up against my pillows with Poppy attached to my boob, happily sucking away, I would feel my eyes getting heavier and heavier and I would end up dozing off. It felt like it was only for a couple of seconds but when I looked at the clock I would realise that in fact an hour had passed and Poppy had fallen asleep too. I would carefully place her back in her cradle, but no matter how careful I was, as soon as she was on her mattress her eyes would open and the look she gave me spoke volumes. I could have handled the look but it was the cry that followed that I couldn't fight! So, there we were again – me propped up staring into space like a zombie and Poppy back where she loved in the warmth of my breast. And as I looked over to my left there was Jamie sleeping like . . . a bloody baby! I really don't know which was more frustrating – the peaceful and relaxed sleeping Jamie or the incessant waking and feeding of Poppy. I had started to resent Jamie and thought, how dare he be enjoying his sleep when I couldn't. Of course this was not a rational thought. You have to trust me; when you haven't slept properly for weeks you start to go a little insane. God forbid if he started to snore midfeed; I think I might have killed him. When I look back now I want to laugh just thinking about the dagger eyes I would give him if he gently tried to stroke my back in sympathy whilst he made those unmistakable sleeping coos . . . it's not fair!

As cringeworthy as it is to reveal this, on really bad nights when I struggled to stay awake and keep my patience as little Poppy fed for hours on end, I used to make a very big fuss about getting her up and feeding her. I don't always think it was completely necessary to turn all the lights on in the bedroom or have the TV on for company in the background, but sometimes you just feel like the only person in the world who is awake in what seems like a very lonely place!

I remember on one of these particular nights, when I was up feeding my second daughter Daisy, I was watching *Dallas* on UK Gold (I say watching – I was actually rocking Daisy back and forth around the room trying to soothe her whilst catching glimpses of Sue Ellen and JR snogging after another drunken row!) when my mobile bleeped with a text message. It was from my mate Lindsey who had also just had her little baby, Joel. She was up breastfeeding him at that ungodly hour and it was brilliant to know that there was someone else out there in exactly the same situation – it certainly helped to keep me awake!

After a few weeks I managed to get myself into a regular daytime routine with Poppy and her feeding times, as I had decided not to feed on demand. I was quite surprised at first, when Poppy was newborn, that not every cry was for food, as I had assumed that that's the only thing she would want. I hadn't a clue what else she would need. However, you soon learn that it could be a dirty nappy or wind that needs burping. Once I had mastered all these other checks, if she was still crying I would then put her on the breast. On one particularly fraught morning my mum showed me that perhaps a little cuddle and a wander round the room would be just as satisfactory as putting her on the breast and at once she instantly relaxed and stopping crying. Seeing this allowed me to learn to establish a good routine of my own that worked for me. It involved feeding her roughly every four hours, with the first feed at around seven a.m., then eleven a.m., three p.m. and finally seven p.m. Of course, at first none of these times were guaranteed, especially if we had had a bad night. I just tried to stick to some sort of routine that felt natural to both Poppy and me. I know all babies are different, but this is what worked for me. After only a few months she had it sussed and I started to feel a bit more ordered in my head.

Not feeding her on demand also allowed me to realise that in between the feeds, the cries and agitation would be down to something else. It was so illuminating when I worked out that Poppy had different cries for communicating different things to me. I know that it sounds a bit like mumbo jumbo but you really can tell, especially the cries for tiredness and hunger. It's all a matter of getting to know your baby and believing in yourself!

I felt that we were quite lucky with Poppy as after only three months she had started to sleep through the night with her last full feed at seven p.m. and her next at about seven a.m. I am not sure why she was so easy in that way. By this time I found breastfeeding to be a wonderful, exciting and bonding experience. It lasted for about six (mostly) blissful months. So it was with great joy and anticipation that I looked forward to breastfeeding our second baby. Little did I know that this experience was going to be totally different and one that I hope won't put me off breastfeeding any other babies we might be lucky enough to have in the future.

I don't want to put *you* off (if you are planning to breastfeed for the first time) but I feel I should tell you about my bad time as it is all part of the experience (and I had no idea this could happen).

I was eight months pregnant with Daisy when we went to celebrate Poppy's first birthday with our NCT class. Being the first mum out of our group to get preggers for a second time, I was a source of fascination to all the girls. My friend Sarah asked what I was most looking forward to about becoming a mum for the second time and I said . . . breastfeeding four months down the line!

When Daisy was born a month later she was given straight to me, as Poppy had been, but instead of having difficulty latching on she fed straightaway and with vigour for at least an hour. I was chuffed that I'd got past the first hurdle – done and dusted, or so I thought.

Daisy seemed to latch on well but she would break off after only a couple of minutes. I assumed it was because she wasn't hungry, as it seemed to be happening all the time. I would continually try to get her on the breast, arranging her time and time again so that she would sit on there happily, but no matter what I did, her latch was weak and I often found myself hunched over trying to fit my nipple into her mouth (which I knew was incorrect and would only cause me pain).

After about two weeks I had managed to get used to it, but I knew that something wasn't right. It was on one of my midwife's visits that I decided to discuss this matter with her. I felt a little foolish, as I assumed she would think that by now I had it all sorted as Daisy had gained a really good daily weight, so what was wrong? The midwife I had was quite vague, and after letting her see how I was feeding she said that there was nothing wrong with Daisy or the technique with which I was feeding her. I was still totally unconvinced. When I looked at Daisy a little closer it looked like there might be a problem with her tongue. We never did get to the bottom of it but one day she suddenly latched on properly and then she was off!

Within days of my midwife's visit I awoke one morning to find that my left breast was burning hot and covered with red blotchy marks starting from my armpit and spreading down towards my nipple. I had never felt anything like it before and could only assume that I had developed the dreaded mastitis. I could not believe that I had managed to avoid it with Poppy and now it had caught up with me!

It was so painful that if I touched it I felt sick. I should have known that it was coming, as the day before I had started getting flu-like symptoms and had assumed that I was just run down and tired. But apparently this was a sign that mastitis was setting in. When I woke up the flu-like symptoms had worsened and I was dripping with sweat and shivering under the duvet. I couldn't bear anyone touching me. This was going to be impossible as I was on my own looking after Poppy and Daisy. And of course the first thing that Poppy wanted in the morning was a huge cuddle and the first thing Daisy wanted was my inflamed boob . . . you must be joking, girls.

I couldn't believe that my body could react so badly to a simple blocked milk duct. The first thing that I knew would ease the pain was a warm bath. Submerged in the water I could feel the pain ease, but I knew that this was only a temporary solution – sooner or later I would have to get out! With the knowledge that the best thing to do with mastitis is to allow your baby to feed off the breast till it is empty (I know, it seemed crazy to me too) I thought I was going to be letting myself in for torture. But the reason that you have to continue feeding is to drain the milk away, otherwise it will lead to a build up and eventually an abscess – this I did not want. I also tried to do a bit of hand expressing, especially around the tender areas. It seemed to ease the pain for about half an hour, then my breast would harden and inflame again – it was so tiring, especially as I was trying to look after Poppy too. Four hours after getting up that day, I was weeping into the sofa cushions, unable to do anything. The flu symptoms, coupled with my extreme tiredness, had made me a wreck. On my own and alone (Jamie was at work) I felt the lowest I had felt since I had given birth to Poppy.

I then tried a classic remedy that my health visitor had suggested – cabbage leaves! With both babies set down for a nap I took out two fat green leaves from the fridge and placed them in my bra – hmm, that was one way to boost a cleavage! Then I lay out in the sun to try and get warm, even though I was burning up already. I really don't think the cabbage leaves did anything, but the fact that they were ice cold was a relief in itself. Plus, I don't think that I was beginning to smell that good. Later that afternoon my bra was emulating a scent that resembled smelly socks and rotting veg! Yuk, no thanks! I then decided to use special gel-filled breast pads, bought when I was pregnant with Poppy, which you could either stick in the fridge or boil up in a saucepan to make cold or warm compresses. I decided on the latter and found that to be quite a relief. Daisy was still feeding off both breasts but nothing seemed to help. By late afternoon I couldn't take it any more. I felt as if I had tropical fever and I didn't look much better either. I will never forget how I was feeling. I was slumped over Poppy's high chair trying to feed her, whilst holding Daisy at the same time. My cheeks were burning red and my face puffy from crying and, for some reason, I had decided that it would be a good idea to have a new fringe cut in (à la Catherine Zeta-Jones). My hair looked dreadful – a cross between

Humpty Dumpty and a Purdey bowl cut! Very wrong –
I would advise you never to do drastic things with your
hair whilst high on hormones!

So with me in this state, Jamie decided enough of the
herbal remedies – it was time to call the doctor. It was
such a relief to see someone medical. I had begun to think
that maybe it wasn't mastitis after all but something more
sinister! After a quick examination from the doctor he
confirmed it was mastitis and a course of antibiotics was
prescribed. I couldn't get down to the late-night chem-
ist quick enough. It was amazing – within one day I was
back to my normal self. My breast no longer had the red
splayed blotches all over it and my flu-like symptoms had
completely disappeared.

I was so relieved I could now carry on breastfeeding
without any pain and discomfort. Four happy days passed
until the fifth when I woke in the morning to find that I
had those all too familiar feelings of pain and soreness in
my body but this time it was the other boob that had the
red blotches and the nagging ache. I couldn't believe it.
I was still on the antibiotics – how could this be? After a
quick visit to my doctor he decided that I should be put
on to slightly stronger medication. Again, within hours I
was back to my normal self. I hoped that I had beaten it
but it was not to be. Five months down the line and I had
battled through seven hideous bouts of mastitis – it was
an ongoing nightmare.

Each time I was struck down I would read up about it, determined to get to the bottom of why this was happening. After all, it was threatening my decision to carry on, although I was determined to try and see it through as I wanted to feed Daisy for as long as I had fed Poppy. It was really getting me down. I ended up visiting three different doctors, who each gave me different opinions. Two of them suggested that I give up and start bottle-feeding, and the other suggested that I feed Daisy through the pain as it would help. I was so confused. I was dying to pack it in, to feed her from a bottle, but that would have left me feeling guilty and I was also driven with a desire to beat it. On the other hand I was fed up with plying my body with endless antibiotics – what the hell were they doing to my insides?

During one of my reading-up sessions I discovered that sometimes your baby can pass bacteria to you through your nipple and each time she feeds she is simply putting it back into your body, which results in mastitis. Armed with this knowledge, I confronted my doctor and, under my instruction, he analysed a sample of my breast milk to see if it contained any bacteria. I felt like Miss Marple! Alas, no bacteria were found. I was so disappointed as I really wanted to discover what was causing it. Finally, I decided that enough was enough. I was going to stop breastfeeding – I had managed for five and a half months. If only it was that simple . . . Daisy didn't want the bottle; she wanted the boob. Let the next battle commence!

Pops' transition from breast to bottle was not an easy one but if I had known how hard it was going to be with Daisy I never would have complained with the Popster! I persevered with Daisy for many weeks but in the end I decided the best thing would be to introduce someone completely new into Daisy's life to try and get her off the breast. And that someone came in the shape of a maternity nurse called Barbara – my lifesaver. By this point I was feeling extremely emotional, tired, guilty and worn down, and she was just fantastic. I booked her to come over every day for a week but if I'm honest I didn't have all that much faith. Being a mum twice over made me feel that I should have known what to expect by now and how to cope, but one thing that I've learnt is that all babies are not the same and each experience is completely different. I never would have thought that with my second child I would have to call in extra help for what would be deemed as a very simple mummy task! Like a miracle, Barbara had Daisy sucking contentedly on her first bottle of formula on Day Two!

This whole episode made me realise that I shouldn't feel guilty about calling on other people for help. I really wanted to achieve everything with my two girls and cope with the rough stuff without having to rely on outside help, but it was such a relief to step aside and let go for a minute. After seven rounds of mastitis I would have let Mr Blobby in to help me.

Farewell to the Sisters

DEBRA OSWALD

I need to admit something that's a little embarrassing.

When I was in Grade Six at Burnside Public School, there was a lot of competition to get the juiciest roles in the end-of-year play. Eleven-year-old me was going for the part of The Barmaid. I worked damned hard on the cockney accent I felt the role required. And blimey, whaddya know guv'nor – I was cast as The Barmaid, and for years afterwards I nursed a secret pride in my cockney accent.

Ten years later when I was working as a real barmaid in an RSL club, the truth hit me like two thumps in the chest. My cockney accent was lousy. I was only cast as the barmaid because I was the one kid in Grade Six at Burnside Public who had anything to hang over the bar.

The sisters grew early and they grew large. Not dainty

B cups, sizeable Cs or even bounteous double Ds. We're going deeper into the alphabet where the Es, Fs and Gs live. E for enormous. F for freakishly huge . . . until I was finally G for gigantic.

Did you know there's a medical term for huge knockers? Gigantomastia. Sounds made up but it's deadset true. Along with gigantomastia comes chronic back pain, headaches, permanent dents in each shoulder. Imagine lugging two 3-kilogram bags of sand around on your chest wall, day after aching day. The weight on the rest of my body can fluctuate up and down, but the sisters just keep on growing bigger, like triffids.

So that's why, in thirty minutes' time, I'm going to be on the operating table for a breast reduction. When I tell people about the surgery, everyone gasps, 'Oh! But without your breasts you won't be *you* any more!' Bloody hell – is that true? It's got me worried. I mean, is my personality located in these? When the surgeon goes the knife on the knockers, will he be removing a chunk of my selfhood? I've lived with the sisters so long that maybe I don't know what's me and what's us any more.

You get used to the reality of being huge-breasted. For example, when shopping for rockmelons you need to be careful that you're not charged for four when you're only carrying two. When it rains, you have to be ready for the rain-shelf problem – the windward versus the leeward side of the twin mountains (the trick is to hold the bottom half of your shirt out to get an even soaking of rain.) Then there's the small milk-hungry babies grabbing for you in supermarkets: 'There must be some boosy-juice in those big mamas!' And the leers from tradesmen can be hard to take sometimes. When I was younger, walking past building sites made my body feel like it was merely a transport and blood-supply system for my humungous knockers.

Clothing enormous bosoms is a matter of problem solving rather than girly consumerist delight. Follow me into the intimate apparel department of my local department store. No, don't linger over the gaily spinning displays of sexy lingerie. We're heading into the dark recesses of the back corner, set aside for the gigantomastic woman. This isn't lingerie any more. This is the no-nonsense surgical supplies section.

Don't even look at those red and purple bras – frothy little morsels designed by stick-insect models and spun out of lace by fairies. No, it's time to make your selection from the vast expanse of beige cotton and heavy-duty elastic designed by structural engineers and rivetted together by fitters and turners. Complete with steel girders.

I realise mammograms aren't fun for anyone but when I walk in, the radiographers get an eyeful of the norks and groan, 'I'll get extra X-ray plates.' A mammogram of these babies requires a series of connecting maps like a street directory. Map 32 adjoins map 34. And when they squash each chest puppy between the two plastic torture shelves – ooh. I know it hurts for everyone, but for some of us, the sheer acreage of pain is especially memorable.

Along with other huge-breasted women, I've noticed how many men in the world suffer from the same debilitating eye-muscle control disorder. No matter how witty or fascinating a woman might be, these poor men cannot seem to keep their eyeballs from dropping down to chest level again and again. For years, when chatting with such eye-to-tit conversationalists, I tried staring at their codpieces in a 'tit for tat' manoeuvre. Sadly, that doesn't seem to be a disincentive. It only encourages your average breast-ogler.

You get used to the stares – from men, women, clothes-shop bitches and fellow beach-goers. I know they're not thinking, 'Ooh, what attractive breasts.' They're thinking, 'How freakish is that! How does she get around? Does she need counterweights to stay upright? A backpack? Can she ever sleep on her stomach?'

One friend of mine has admitted that, because of his extreme short-sightedness and the extraordinary protrusion of my chest, he has very little idea of what I look like. My face is merely an out-of-focus blur in the background, beyond the first few centimetres of cleavage.

Don't get me wrong. I've loved the bazookas over the years. I'd rather have these than two fried eggs on my chest. They form a handy battering ram to move through crowds – proud and strong like the prow of an ocean liner. Some men do seem to like them. And a few of the big boobs jokes are funny.

Sometimes it's preferable to be freakish instead of just another dumpy forty-something woman. Moving through the world with something this extreme leading the way, I've had to make a choice – I can either hunch over and wear baggy sweaters to hide them, or I can be as bold as my mammaries. If the knockers are out there – huge and proud – then I have to act accordingly. There is nothing a drunk bloke in a pub can say to me that would make me blush. I thank the sisters for that.

I'm not having the reduction because I'm embarrassed or self-conscious. I would've done it ten years ago if that was the reason. I simply want to be rid of the back pain. Not the boosies.

Under this gown, my boobs have texta lines drawn all over them. They're going to remove a kilo from each one. I suppose there's a limit to how much they can fit in the hospital incinerator in one day. Afterwards I'll still be huge, just not freakishly huge. You should see the texta lines. I wonder what it's going to feel like to be stitched together like that. Frankentits.

And afterwards, will I still be me? Well, yes. Just me

with less back pain. Huge knockers have helped make me who I am, but that won't be taken away surgically. I won't be losing anything except two kilograms of tissue. If the sisters helped to make me, that's not going to be lopped off with them. I am not this body part.

It's time for me to say goodbye to my current bosoms. Look, girls, it's over. You two dames have been wonderful company most of the time. Together we fed two happy babies. You've brought pleasure to me and countless others – well, not countless. A few. Anyway, it's been good. And this is nothing personal, nothing hostile. Just practical. You've become a pain in my neck. It's time to go.

Farewell, sisters.

Ellie's Jellies

ELLIE PARKER

The jelly paused for a moment, brilliant in its splendour, its turrets gleaming, its towers towering – then it began to walk towards the edge of the plate. It spread on all sides until the rim of the plate curved upwards, then it stopped . . . What should have been two exquisite jelly castles had become two huge pink breasts with cherry nipples.

At any time my grandmother was a resourceful woman and in an emergency she was doubly so. She took up the pastry tube that Maggie had filled with whipped cream and swiftly she put those mighty breasts into a whipped-cream bra.

Judy Cuppaidge, *The Balloon Flyers: Tales of an Australian Childhood*, 1988

I was nine when I first read a story about two huge jelly breasts and their cherry nipples. I was smitten by the naughtiness of food becoming boob. The connection was so feasible, yet so ridiculous. Even at nine years of age, I was captivated by the possibility that food not only told a story, but that it embodied the story itself. The jelly *was* the boob and the boob *was* the jelly.

I suspect that this is why I became a freelance food writer. Food is a language that I adore. It speaks directly to the senses. It is disarming and amusing in its honesty. Most importantly, it is a language loved and understood by all.

About a year ago, I scammed a job writing a weekly column for a newspaper. I'd heard that the paper was looking for a new food critic. The city's incumbent food critic had choked on a *pomme noisette* and died. The fat old bastard had finally got his just deserts. Before there was any time to think it through, I was on the phone to the editor-in-chief.

'Can I please have the job?' I blurted.

'Sure, along with the 300 others who've already called this morning,' he snapped. 'What makes you so different from all the other wannabe food writers out there?'

I paused. If I didn't answer, I wouldn't have the job. Then suddenly, from the strange blank depths of my brain, rose the image of those two mighty red breasts with their silly cherry nipples.

'Boob food,' I replied. 'Boob food is my point of difference.'

There was another pause. Then the editor agreed to give me a restaurant-reviewing job on the condition that I wrote a regular column on boob food. The topic appealed to him no end. He thought it would attract a younger, sexier readership. I couldn't believe it.

Neither of us knew what 'boob food' actually meant. The first day on the job, I informed my boss that I was going 'out into the field' for research purposes. I was desperate for inspiration. All I knew about was what happens if you make two jellies on a hot summer's day. Beyond that, boob food was anyone's guess.

I contemplated my own set. They'd always been the butt of jokes. My mother-in-law once suggested I eat more hormone-infested chicken in the hope that it would plump my breasts up a little. Past boyfriends had told me that they were nice 'even though they were small'. Girlfriends had remarked that my padded bras were misleading and deceptive to the male population and that I had a responsibility to dress 'honestly'.

Yet my breasts, and breasts generally, had always been relatively insignificant to me. They were hardly ever on my list of hot topics for conversation. I rarely washed them. I popped them in and out of bras without thinking. Other people always seemed far more preoccupied with them.

I realised that even though I knew a fair bit about food, I couldn't profess to be much of an expert on boobs. And so began my foray into the world of bosoms and their relationship with food.

In the weeks that followed I entered into a strange, slightly deranged phase of boob-watching. If I were a man, you would simply call it perving. I told myself that my honourable, educative investigations put me above any accusations of lechery or loitering. My DVD collection suddenly blossomed with documentaries on Greek statues, Hindu goddesses and ancient fertility idols. I attended every life-drawing class on offer until I felt I had satisfactorily canvassed all the female nude models in the metropolitan area.

Then, at home one day, I reached for a cookbook. It was a well-loved cookbook with a broken spine and the remnants of many meals. It was one of those cookbooks you read like a novel, over and over again.

I pulled the book off the shelf with Tarte Tatin in mind, only to find myself staring at a photo of breasts on the front cover. The coquettish image featured a naked woman's body wearing only a skirt of fresh garfish. Her breasts were at the top of the page, peeping out from above the book's title. My parents had given this book to me on the cusp of puberty, and in the years following I had somehow overlooked the naked woman on the cover. I had begged my parents to buy me this book for my fifteenth birthday. Despite its luscious, delicious, sexual imagery it was easily digestible to my tender, self-conscious fifteen-year-old self. There was no embarrassment in these suggestive images. In fact, they made a lot of sense to me. Osso Buco and a woman's buttocks worked very well together, I thought.

That evening I sat down and read the book properly. Interspersed between recipes for Malaysian fish-head curry and risotto Milanese were images of breasts posing alongside certain foods. One photo featured breasts snuggling up to a variety of small, smooth, curvaceous eggplants. Another page showed papaya halves, with their glistening, winking little seeds nestling in the centre of the fruit.

I loved the natural harmony created by these images. Both the food and the boobs were represented in strong, bold forms but held a uniquely sexy subtleness. There was a natural affinity between the two.

My mind wandered back to the childhood story of the jelly breasts. They, like the eggplants and papayas in the book, were symbols of the boob. Just how many foods emulate the shape, texture and consistency of a breast? I had found the material for my column.

I quickly descended into booby-food madness.

My fridge filled with oval, round, smooth, shiny fruit

and vegetables. At restaurants I refused to order anything leafy, crunchy or pointy. At home I replaced my set of Global knives with a melon baller and an ice-cream scooper. My pantry was stuffed full of gelatine leaves, aspic, agar-agar, glacé cherries and those ridiculous pavlova pre-mix 'eggs'. *Fior di latte* (flowers of milk) balls became a regular feature at mealtimes, replacing parmesan and cheddar. Melons crowded into the crisper. For my birthday, my mother gave me a kaleidoscope of moulds – big squishy silicon ones and small antique metal ones. I even threw out my old ice-cube trays, replacing them with trays that created perfect little ice spheres. The Heinz ketchup bottle was immediately siphoned off into a round, red, tomato-shaped squeezy bottle.

Boob food became my new culinary repertoire. I was committed. My cookbooks fluttered with little yellow Post-it notes, each marking a sympathetic boob-food recipe. I read up on experimental approaches to create foams, hot jellies and 'spherification'.

Before serving rice, couscous, pilaf, burghul or mashed potato, I would place it in a Chinese teacup, pat it down and then up-end the domed form onto the plate. A little nipple – a sultana, pistachio or olive – always adorned the top.

I found dumplings and ravioli to be incredibly successful boob foods, as they hid all manner of non-conforming ingredients within their velvety bulge. Floating atop a rich broth, my dumplings provided the perfect textural slipperiness. A big, fat raviolo, drizzled with olive oil and filled with a mixture of silky goats' curd and beetroot mash, delivered an unctuous ooze that only a breast aficionado could appreciate.

Rotund little patties, made from mince, chilli and garlic, provided a great base for a boob. Topped with puddles of aioli or dollops of ketchup, they looked the part. For dessert, soufflés and mousses were always supremely satisfying on both a textural and visual level. The soft curvature of their domes, the wobbly movements and the pillowy bounce made for a perfect mouthful of boob.

Breakfasts were generally confined to three options. Melon balls came with a perfect scoop of yoghurt plopped on top. Eggs Benedict, though clichéd, was the ultimate booby hangover cure. And then there was the brioche. I spent weekends waking up at the crack of dawn to bake these perfectly formed little beauties. Their little nipples popped up out of a smooth, sugary, yeasty, nut-brown, mushroomy bloom. It was impossible not to bite the teat off immediately. Italian bombolone were another delightful discovery. These chubby cinnamon-coated doughnuts had a slight dimple in their middle from which a little dollop of strawberry jam pouted out. Then came the real joy – the ooze of molten jam once you bit through.

Dinner parties became breast festivals. My husband

and friends were conscripted to the cause of boob food. Upon arrival, I always served slippery nipple cocktails. Loaves of bread and slices of butter were replaced with rosetta bread rolls and little butter balls (the melon baller was coming into its own here). Insalata Caprese made from bocconcini and baby egg tomatoes were a regular feature during such evenings, followed by moulded salmon mousses wrapped in cabbage leaves. I was happy to point out to my guests that the cabbage belongs to the *brassica* family of plants. While I was dubious as to the exact connection between cabbages and bras, I was confident in telling my guests that cabbage leaves were brilliant in soothing the engorged breasts of pregnant women. Baby cream meringues and frightfully pink cupcakes with raspberry nipples served as appropriate dessert options. Alternatively, in the summer months, bright red Champagne berry jelly wobbled its way out of the kitchen along with vanilla-bean ice-cream.

Expeditions to the cinema invariably involved purchasing a choc-top complete with coloured Smartie teats. Instead of watching the trailers, I was always curious to observe how people ate their choc-tops. Most men tended to crunch enthusiastically into the chocolate coating and sink their teeth into the ice-cream below. Most women preferred to place their lips around the chocolate mound and suck for a little bit, ensuring that the chocolate was soft enough to chew without it splintering into their laps. Did this mean that women are subconsciously more sensual? Or were they simply more fastidious than their male counterparts?

In just under a year, my boob-food column reached cult status. People bought the paper on a Thursday simply to read my article. It was heralded as *Sex and the City* for foodies.

I was amazed with the wealth of material available to write about. Readers sent me photos of 'boob food sightings', and confessed to also having no desire to eat anything other than something round and soft.

But, column inches aside, I had also apparently increased the inches in my waistline. Since the column's inception and the beginning of my fattening boob-food obsession, I had grown into something rather unsightly.

I caught a glimpse of myself in the mirror. Mortified, I realised I was all boob. The bulging, curvy, prominent bits had taken over. Worse still, I no longer recognised the very boobs that stood in front of me. Somehow, in the year I'd spent searching for bosom buddies in the world of food, I had lost my own. It was as if all the boob food had gradually morphed into two large amorphous balloons on the front of my chest. My god, had I fed my boobs too many boobs?

Like two blancmanges on the run, my boobs were an embarrassment. My boobs had let themselves go in the most undignified of ways.

All boob food was immediately abandoned. I jettisoned the copious balls of mozzarella from my life. The morning bombolone habit had to go. The weekend brioche were bumped. The French onion soufflé evenings were retired indefinitely. My round, smooth, creamy world was turned upside down like bavarois up-ended from its mould.

Horrified, I began eating leafy, crunchy, pointy things again. Things that were long and thin and hard. Texturally, I was challenged. Identity-wise, I was in crisis. My boobs were adrift, and on their own. Until such time as they arrived back to the point at which they began, I was having nothing to do with them.

Fortunately, boob-friendly food is the antithesis of boob food. The healthier I ate, the further boobs were cast from my mind. All the foods that promised low-GI, low-fat, and low sugar content, and therefore promised to reunite me with my old boobs, shared similar characteristics. In direct contrast with the supple rotund shapes that I was so familiar with, I was now confronted by long, turgid, tuberous, spindly foods. It was not until I returned from the markets with my first basket of shopping that I realised how complete the transformation had been. Was this a joke? Was some goddess in the heavens having her own private little laugh at the fact that I was now having to chow down on phallic foodstuffs in order to reclaim my original lady bits?

Bananas became my new breakfast. Celery, cucumber and carrot sticks were a staple snack. Turnips, sweet potato and snake beans featured heavily at dinnertime. Sourdough baguettes served with olive oil replaced the rosetta rolls and balls of butter. Lamb backstraps and loins of pork were barbecued side by side with zucchini and asparagus spears. I marinated and cooked an entire slippery eel in miso. I even endured one sea-cucumber dish of which we shall never speak again.

In the throes of my old-boob revival, I bought a mincer and started making my own sausages (using über-lean mince of course). I madly pumped out streams of exotic meaty worms: traditional pork, lamb and rose-mary, chicken and sage, and hot spicy little chipolatas. Pigs in Blankets were religiously served when watching the football. I only occasionally indulged in cock-tails. For my birthday my mother gave me an oversized pepper grinder.

And somewhere in the middle of my mad phallic frenzy, my boobs returned. My beautiful, little alabaster domes. On reflection, I think it quite fitting really. I had become top heavy. I needed balance from down below.

My weekly column followed this journey throughout. The change in direction, from boob food to health food, caused outrage in some camps and delight in others. Readers were desperate to know what happened next. I received threats in the mail telling me that I'd let the sisterhood down. In the end, I begged the editor to let me stop writing it – I felt like I was held captive by my boobs and the craze they'd created.

It made me realise that breasts are like recipes in a cookbook. You're attracted to the glossy picture on the front cover, but somehow the meal never turns out as it's meant to. Boobs are mischievous. They have a mind of their own. They sometimes stray from where they belong.

I thought I owned my breasts. I thought I was in control of them. But, like desire, like memory, like the first taste of childhood, mine somehow got the better of me.

Quote from *The Balloon Flyers: Tales of an Australian childhood* by Judy Cuppaidge (McMahons Point, NSW: Chapter & Verse, 1988). Reproduced with permission.

The Hen's Night

ADELE PARKS

'So, what are we doing, exactly?' asked Bev's mum, as she plopped onto the squashy settee and reached for a sausage on a stick.

Jess had been unsure about how to cater. Champagne and salmon canapés seemed too frivolous for the occasion, but egg sandwiches and sherry seemed too funeralesque. In the end she'd plumped for sparkling white wine and nibbles on sticks.

'It's an intervention,' said Jess, Bev's best friend since infant school. 'It's an American concept. We all agree that Bev should not be marrying Todd, don't we?' Bev's friends and relatives exchanged glances (ranging from guilty to assured) and nods (ranging from apologetic to emphatic). 'Well, the purpose of tonight is to persuade her to ditch him. For her own good.'

'But she thinks you've arranged her hen's night?' asked Kate, Bev's cousin.

'Yes.'

For a moment Jess's confidence and conviction wavered. She should have stopped Bev buying a new outfit for tonight, the night on the tiles that was unlikely to materialise. At least not if Jess had her way. It's such a shame, thought Jess. Bev really does look knockout in those new skin-tight jeans and the frilly black top, and she's looked more and more fabulous over the last few weeks – probably because of the upcoming wedding. Jess was stabbed with feelings of guilt. How could she inflict so much pain on her best friend?

Jess breathed in and reminded herself that the creepy Todd had as good as assaulted her. His drunken pass was so obvious and insistent. It wouldn't have been so bad if he'd been shamefaced or repentant the morning after, but instead he had winked at her over the cornflakes in Bev's kitchen! Even so, Jess would have probably left well alone if the incident had been isolated. But when she'd mentioned it to Fran, the other bridesmaid, Fran said that he'd had a crack at her too. Then Jess whispered her misgivings to Kate and Kate confided that none of the family liked Todd much either.

'He owes me money,' said Bev's aunt. 'I paid for the wedding cake and the cars. I wouldn't mind, but he's always talking about how much he earns yet never spends a penny of his own. He could peel an orange in his pocket.'

'He didn't notice that Bev has lost nearly a stone for the wedding and she's been working so hard at her diet and exercise,' said one of the cousins.

'He called her lardy the other day. Lardy and lazy. I heard him with my own ears or else I would have doubted it,' pointed out Fran, shaking her head in disbelief.

'He's the one that's idle,' added Bev's mother. 'Bev does everything for him. She even cuts the lawn at his flat.'

'And he knocks the booze back,' added Kate.

'Nothing wrong with liking a drop in,' said Bev's dad. 'But he doesn't know when enough is enough.' It would be his sole contribution for the evening; no one expected him to offer much more. It was good of him to turn up. Interventions were newfangled and American; it was agreed that they were women's work. Bev's dad was only here in case things turned ugly. He had a calming presence. His wife of forty-two years claimed he couldn't get into a lather in a bath full of Imperial Leather body wash.

'And he has shifty eyes,' concluded Mrs Davis. Bev and her son had courted for two years when they were teenagers. She'd always hoped . . .

'Okay, so we have our reasons,' said Jess, more to convince herself than anyone else. The crowd was baying for blood, but Jess knew it wasn't going to be easy. She understood how much Todd meant to Bev and how much time and effort Bev had put into planning the wedding. *The wedding*, which was due to take place *next week*, with a string quartet, fireworks, and six small flowergirls. Oh, lord. If the wedding was cancelled Bev's nieces would never forgive Jess.

Jess had long suspected that Todd was not the right man for Bev. Bev never seemed relaxed and happy in his company. More often than not they were fighting or Bev was walking on tiptoes to avoid a quarrel. But they'd rubbed along for months, and months had turned into years, and then years had turned into an engagement. Todd didn't go down on one knee and produce a ring. Nothing as formal as that. Apparently, one of Bev's great-aunts had died and left Bev a sapphire ring. Todd had joked that it would save him a bob or two if they ever did get hitched. After that Bev had started to wear the ring on her third finger, left hand.

Where had confident, carefree Bev vanished to, thought Jess. Who was this downtrodden woman left in her place?

Jess understood the need for companionship. She understood the embarrassment of attending friends' *second* weddings, let alone first weddings and children's christenings, without the chance of reciprocating the invites. She wanted to meet the one, fall in love and get hitched too. She was old-fashioned enough to think it would be a nice thing to do – but not with just *anyone*, or worse, someone like Todd. It had to be *The One*. Bev used to say the same thing. How could she be thinking of compromising?

The final straw had been when Todd started to go on about Bev getting a boob job. Apparently he didn't like 'tiny, itty bitty titties'. That was probably why he'd felt entitled to grope Jess and Fran, who were both well-endowed. Jess had the sort of boobs that shuddered just a little when they escaped from her bra at night. Fran had proudly breastfed for the best part of a year. It seemed that when Fran heard a hungry baby cry, her breasts, unbidden, would jump into action – even if it wasn't her own child.

Bev had been waiting for her breasts to grow since she was ten. Now, twenty years later, she accepted that Jordan – the glamour model – must have received the share God had intended for Beverly Clarke. Still, Bev saw it as a good thing that people never glanced at her chest when she was talking to them, at least never more than once. Todd had said that he didn't know how fat birds could be so flat-chested. He'd said Bev was a freak of nature. He'd started to cut out articles and adverts about plastic surgery from the back of Sunday supplements. He'd said that instead of a honeymoon, perhaps he could go away with the lads for a few days and Bev could get her boobs 'done'.

Jess shuddered. It wasn't right. Why couldn't Bev see that it wasn't right? She checked her watch. Bev was due any minute. Never mind butterflies – Jess had kangaroos in her stomach. She needed the loo. She needed a drink. She needed the night to be over. Maybe she should keep her trap shut. They could drink the fizzy wine and then go to a club. This could be Bev's hen's night after all. No one wants to hear that their man is a loser. What if Bev didn't believe Jess? Or, she believed her but still hated her for making it impossible to ignore his lecherous ways? Many messengers had been shot for less.

The front door banged. This was it. Bev strode into the small sitting room crammed with her friends and family. She was wearing her new jeans and looked as wonderful as Jess had expected.

'Oh hello, Mum, Dad, Mrs Davis. I wasn't expecting you here.' Bev wore an expression that Jess, her oldest friend, didn't recognise. She appeared triumphant, terrified, excited and depressed all at once.

'I invited them,' explained Jess.

Bev looked surprised, then relieved. 'You are so *the* best friend,' she whispered. 'You knew, didn't you?' Jess tried to smile to hide her confusion. Knew what?

'Jess has done absolutely the right thing in gathering you all here,' Bev declared. 'I don't know how she does it, but she's read my mind. I have something very important to announce. I'm sorry, but the wedding is off.'

Stunned silence. 'Did you find out he made a pass at Jess?' asked Kate.

'No,' said Bev, shooting a quizzical look at Jess.

'You know he owes me money?' asked Aunt Lil.

'No.' Bev looked sorry.

'You're sick of his moody, greedy, rude behaviour?' asked Fran.

'No,' said Bev firmly. 'Well, maybe.'

Jess wanted to ask if it was because he'd been obsessed about the outer package and never considered Bev's inner beauty. But she couldn't quite bring herself to talk boobs in front of Bev's dad.

Bev turned pink and shrugged. 'I've met someone else. Rick, you can come in now. It's as good a time as any. Come and meet my mum and dad.'

The Fisherman and his wife

MEG ROSOFF

There once was a lowly fisherman who lived with his wife by the sea. They were a sun-creased, windswept couple with work-roughened hands, and they lived modestly in a wood and tarpaper hovel on the beach.

One day, as the fisherman bobbed gently on the water in his boat, he noticed a beautiful blue and green fish, the likes of which he had never seen before. It flapped frantically beside him, its tail tangled in fishing line, and he leant over the edge to look at it more closely. As he stared, the fish startled him greatly by speaking.

'Untangle me, please, fisherman, and let me swim away,' begged the fish in a high silvery voice. 'For I am not good to eat, and I value my freedom above all else.'

The fisherman merely goggled at the beautiful blue and green fish.

'Help me, please, kind fisherman!' urged the fish once more.

And so the fisherman took hold of the tangled line, working gently and carefully to untangle it and free the unhappy fish. It took some minutes, during which the fish lay still, observing the fisherman with wise, unafraid eyes.

At last, the tail came free, and the fisherman steadied the fish under water until it recovered its strength. And then, with a great joyous swoop, the fish dove deep into the sea, leaving a hollow of water behind him that did not fill up for some time.

Well, well, well, thought the fisherman. What an odd day I have had at sea. And he set off for home, pleased with himself for having such an interesting adventure to report to his wife.

But when he returned home and told his wife the story of the beautiful fish, she became furious and began to beat him about the head with a slipper.

'You fool!' she cried. 'You miserable cretin! You half-witted bumbling imbecile!'

'But, my darling,' protested the fisherman. 'What have I done?'

The woman slapped him again. 'Any ordinary fool would have recognised a *magic fish* when he saw it. That fish might have granted us any wish in all the world. If only you hadn't been such a boneheaded bumpkin!'

The fisherman looked abashed. 'I am sorry, dear wife. But what would we have wished for? We are happy with our simple life.'

The woman snorted. 'Happy? Look at me! My hair smells of rotting fish, my breasts sag to my waist, and my face could be mistaken for a crocodile's.' Here she began to sob. 'No one would ever imagine I was once young and beautiful.'

'True,' admitted the fisherman. 'But I barely noticed you growing old. I, too, stink of fish and am not as young as I once was. Yet I still love and admire you as you are.'

'How can you?' wept his wife. 'Any man would prefer a smooth-skinned, pert-breasted young girl to a horrible, wrinkled old harridan.' She sobbed bitterly, and although the fisherman tried to reassure her that she was wrong on this point, and many others as well, it was no good. At last he knelt down before her.

'Please, dear wife. If only you will cease your wailing, I will set out first thing tomorrow and find the beautiful fish. I will ask him whatever you wish me to ask, and if he is, as you say, a magic fish, your wish shall be granted.'

At this, the wife stopped weeping. She sat up at once and dried her eyes. 'All right,' she sniffed. 'Tell the fish that your wife wishes for the restoration of her youth and beauty.'

'But surely there is a better —'

'Go and tell the fish what I have asked for.'

So the next morning, the fisherman guided his little boat out to sea, and soon found the place where he had caught the beautiful fish. Feeling somewhat foolish, he called out to the blank green sea.

'Magic fish? Magic fish? Are you out there, oh, fish?' And before many minutes had passed, a splashing and a flash of colour announced the presence of the beautiful fish. It poked its head out of the water beside his boat.

'Hello, my saviour,' said the fish in his silvery voice. 'How can I help you?'

'Oh, fish!' cried the fisherman. 'My wife has sent me to ask if you would grant her a wish. '

'Tell me her wish,' said the fish.

'My wife would like to be young and beautiful,' said the fisherman, and he blushed with shame.

But the fish merely shrugged. 'It is done, fisherman,' he said. 'Go home to your beautiful young wife.' And with that he dove deep into the sea, leaving a great gaping hole in the water that did not fill up for some time.

A little while later, as the fisherman winched his boat up onto the shore, a graceful young woman greeted him. For a moment he did not recognise her.

'It is I! Your wife,' said the young woman, fluttering her lashes and shaking her youthful booty. 'How do you like me?'

'Well enough,' said the fisherman, though he could not hide the uncertainty in his voice.

Later that night in bed, the fisherman ran his hands along her youthful curves with disbelief, and it was many exhausting hours before he managed to satisfy her youthful desires.

For a few days, the fisherman and his wife lived in peace. But one morning, he awoke to find her whispering in his ear.

'Husband, I am not happy with the youth and beauty I once had. I want to be younger and more beautiful than ever before. I want great big breasts and legs up to my armpits. I want cascades of blonde hair and huge blue eyes. I want bee-stung lips and the complexion of a ten-year-old girl.'

'Oh, wife,' begged the fisherman, 'Please think again! It is not right to ask for these things.'

'Never mind,' said his wife. 'That is my desire. Go and tell your fish.'

The man's heart was heavy. He did not wish to summon the fish again, and for such a wish as this! But his wife beseeched and implored him, and in the end, he gave in.

Bobbing far out on the blank green sea once more, he called out: 'Magic fish? Magic fish? Are you there, dear fish?' And before many minutes had passed, there came a splashing and a flash of colour, and suddenly the beautiful fish poked its head out of the water.

'Hello, my saviour,' said the fish in his silvery voice. 'How may I help you now?'

'Oh, fish!' cried the fisherman. 'My wife has sent me back to ask if you would grant her another wish.'

'Certainly,' said the fish. 'What does she require now? World peace? An end to hunger and disease? That all men and women shall be happy?'

'No, fish,' said the fisherman mournfully. 'It is none of those things. She wishes to be younger still, with huge breasts and blonde hair, legs up to her armpits, bee-stung lips, the face of a ten-year-old girl and big blue eyes.' He took a deep breath.

'How peculiar,' said the fish. 'Why would she desire such things?'

The fisherman shook his head. 'I do not know, fish.' And a tear trickled down his cheek.

The fish shrugged. 'Never mind. It is done,' he said. 'Go home to your big-breasted wife.' And with that he dove deep into the sea, leaving a hole in the water so deep, it did not fill up for nearly an hour.

As the fisherman winched his boat up onto the shore, a woman arrived to greet him. She had huge breasts, a vast mane of blonde hair, legs up to her armpits, puffy swollen lips and skin so fine and white he feared it had already begun to scorch in the sun. He stared for a moment in disbelief.

'How do you like me now?' asked his wife, joggling her huge breasts and tossing her vast mane of hair.

'I like you well enough, wife,' choked the fisherman,

aghast, and he had to turn away to hide his disgust.

That night, when they went to bed, the fisherman lay as far away as possible from his deformed wife, and pretended to be asleep.

For a few days, the fisherman and his wife lived in peace. He found that if he avoided looking at her, he could pretend she was still the woman he loved. But she was not.

'Husband,' she cried, one morning as he set out in his boat. 'I am still not happy with my appearance.'

'Oh, wife,' murmured the fisherman wearily. 'No more changes, please, I beg you.'

She frowned. 'Go back and tell your fish I require bigger breasts, and thinner thighs. Tell him my thighs should be no wider than fishing rods and each of my boobs must be big enough to fill a bucket.'

'I can not tell the fish these things,' replied the fisherman, shaking his head with sorrow.

'You can,' said his wife. 'For I desire it. Go and tell your fish my wish.'

The fisherman's heart was heavy. But his wife shouted and cajoled and wheedled, and in the end the fisherman set off once more. The weather had begun to change, and he guided his little boat out across a wild rolling sea filled with dangerous peaks and troughs. The boat groaned with protest, and the poor fisherman wondered whether either of them would survive the journey.

'Fish?' He called out from the crest of a wave, straining to be heard over the storm. 'Magic fish, magic fish? Are you out there, sweet fish?' There came a howling wind, the sea leapt up even higher than before, and the fisherman had to grip the gunnels of his little craft to avoid being thrown overboard. But before many minutes had passed, he spied a flash of colour near the side of his little boat, and the beautiful fish poked its head out of the water.

'Hello, my saviour,' said the fish in his silvery voice, which managed to carry over the sound of the raging storm. 'How can I help you this time?'

'Oh, fish!' wept the fisherman. 'My wife has sent me back insisting that you grant her one final wish.'

'Well,' said the fish. 'I may grant her one last wish, and I may not, but tell her she must come and ask for it herself.'

So the sorrowful fisherman returned to shore, and despite the fact that the storm showed no sign of abating, the fisherman's wife (pleased that the fish wanted to meet her in person) set off immediately. Once out in the middle of the crashing green sea, she wasted no time calling out.

'FISH!' she screamed. 'FISH! WHERE ARE YOU, YOU OLD TROUT? I WANT MY WISH!!'

The beautiful fish rose from the sea, more beautiful than ever. The fisherman's wife had to cover her eyes, or the intensity of his colours would have blinded her.

'Yes?' said the fish in his silvery voice. 'May I help you?'

'YOU JOLLY WELL CAN,' shouted the fisherman's wife. 'GIVE ME BOOBS AS BIG AS BUCKETS AND LEGS LIKE A GIRAFFE! GIVE ME LIPS LIKE INNER TUBES, AND THE SKIN OF A ONE-DAY-OLD BABY! GIVE ME HAIR AS PALE AS MOONLIGHT, AND —' Her eyes were wide and glazed with ecstasy. '— MAKE ME A SIZE ZERO!'

The fish thought for a moment. 'Why do you wish for these things?' he asked.

The wife stared back, shocked. '*EVERYONE* WISHES TO BE YOUNG AND BEAUTIFUL. IT'S OBVIOUS.'

'No,' said the fish, 'everyone does not wish for these things. Some wish to be healthy or happy or wise. Some wish to be loved. Some wish to put a stop to suffering and pain. Perhaps you'd like help imagining another wish, one that might last longer than a week. Perhaps, for instance, you might like . . . a child.'

'STRETCH MARKS!! VOMIT!! SLEEPLESS NIGHTS!!' shrieked the wife.

The fish thought for a moment, while the fisherman's wife drummed her fingers. 'World peace?'

'NOT INTERESTED,' shouted the wife. 'IT'S TOO BLOODY PEACEFUL AROUND HERE ANYWAY.'

'A cure for cancer? Hatred? AIDS?' Despite the crashing storm, the fish's low, silvery voice rang out clearly.

'FOR A FISH, YOU SURE GAB A LOT. WHAT DO I CARE ABOUT THOSE THINGS? ANYWAY, IT'S NOT MY FAULT PEOPLE LIVE IN AFRICA AND START WARS.'

'All right,' said the fish. 'I shall grant your wish. But only if you'll tell me how you grew to be so stupid and selfish.'

The wife sighed. 'IF I'D KNOWN I WAS GOING TO GET THE THIRD DEGREE, I'D HAVE SENT A TELEGRAM.'

The fish waited.

'MY LIFE IS EMPTY,' shouted the wife. 'I AM ALONE ALL DAY WITH NOT ANOTHER SOUL TO TALK TO. MY HUSBAND LOVES FISH MORE THAN HE LOVES ME. I'M BORED AND USE-LESS AND UGLY. FOR ALL MY LIFE IS WORTH, I MAY AS WELL BE DEAD.'

The fish said nothing for a moment. 'Very well,' he said at last. 'It is done.' And with a huge crash of thunder, he disappeared into the sea leaving a hole as deep as the abyss, and was never seen again.

The fisherman's wife was never seen again either. Her bucket-sized breasts overbalanced her body and she top-pled over the side of the boat, hurtling down, down, down to the very bottom of the abyss, where she was eaten by coelacanths.

And as for the fisherman?

He soon remarried a plain, flat-chested woman with a cheerful disposition and 172 recipes for mackerel.

And they lived happily ever after.

The Rain Queen

KATHERINE SCHOLES

Only a few chosen women were allowed to witness Annah's initiation. It took place in the Old Queen's hut, with the rest of the Waganga, including Mtemi, waiting outside.

Patamisha sat behind Annah supporting her body, while the Old Queen unveiled Annah's right breast and gently washed the skin with ivy water. Annah closed her eyes, absorbed in the sensation. It was like being licked by a cat's tongue, she thought. Smooth, yet rough. She was aware that she was not thinking, not feeling, clearly. An hour before she had drunk a pain-killing potion prepared by Zania. As it had taken effect, she had felt her anxiety diminishing, her surroundings growing strangely distant. She seemed numbed, and yet at the same time, acutely aware of the details of things. Like the cat-licking movements. And Patamisha's kind murmurings fluttering like a moth close to her ear. Then, at last, the gleam of Annah's own scalpel, reaching towards her skin.

Stinging pain. Moving in a slow line.

Bated breath around her; eyes staring at the sight of the blood. A white woman's blood, shed in their midst. So shockingly red on the pale delicate skin.

From within the haze of the drug, Annah watched the parting of her flesh. It appeared to her like a vision, a presage to the opening of her body that would take place on the night of her wedding. She welcomed the blood now, as she would then. The love blood, blood of love.

Blood of a lover . . .

The cloth returned. Not cat-licking now, but dab-dabbing, blotting the wound.

Annah closed her eyes. Her whole body seemed focused on her breast, tracing the path of three bent lines as they were slowly and firmly etched deep. The mark of the royal house of the Waganga.

A handful of ash was rubbed into the seeping lines, the mound of flesh becoming a battlefield of grey smeared with red.

'It is finished.' The Old Queen lifted her head as she spoke. Then she began to ululate, the other women picking up the high fluting sound, joining in.

Annah rested against Patamisha's slender body, letting the bright, shattering noise flow over her. Her breast throbbed and burned, but the pain was held down by Zania's medicine.

'Now,' Patamisha spoke into Annah's ear. 'You must go out and show yourself.'

Annah shook her head. She couldn't imagine that she would be able to stand, let alone walk.

'You can,' Patamisha assured her. 'It is like the moment after childbirth. Your body has been torn open. Yet, you are still strong.'

The women crowded close around Annah as she got to her feet, so that it was impossible to tell if they held her up or if she stood alone. Slowly they moved towards the door, then out into the sunshine.

The men watched in silence as Annah was borne slowly along.

'See the Regent,' said the Old Queen. 'He cannot believe his own eyes. He hoped that your courage would fail.'

Suddenly the women melted away, leaving Annah alone.

But not alone. Mtemi was beside her, standing tall and proud.

The warriors raised their spears to the sky in a mark of respect. Then a familiar word rose over the crowd like a cheer.

'*Maji! Maji!*' Rain! Rain!

Kitamu's voice broke through.

'Welcome our Queen! Welcome the bride of our Chief!'

Annah looked around her. Even in her dazed state, she was aware of a sense of deep joy at the thought that her place among these people was now sealed. She felt safe and loved. Even the thorn trees bending over her looked like sheltering canopies. And the sky above was a soft, kind blue.

Annah stood with Mtemi and the other members of the royal family in front of a crowd gathered around the meeting tree. Zania was to conduct a rainmaking cere-mony. It was Annah's first formal occasion since her initiation into the tribe. Three weeks had passed since then, and her wound, treated daily with an ointment pre-pared by Zania, was nearly healed, the pain gone.

Patamisha had helped Annah dress for her debut appearance, carefully draping the tall fair body in fine old cloths that smelled of camphorwood, frankincense and dust. When the white woman had walked out in front of the tribespeople, there had been murmurs of approval. But it had been Mtemi's response that had touched Annah most. He had smiled, openly admiring, as she was led to join him. He too was in ceremonial dress – he looked just as he had on the night of the ngoma.

The two stood side by side, waiting for the ceremony

to begin. They were close, without touching. But when Mtemi moved, his leopard-skin cloak brushed against Annah's bare forearm. A sleek, velvety caress.

A flutter of laughter passed over the crowd as the safety doctor strode to the front and kicked one of the village mongrels away from the trunk of the tree. The dog's back leg had been cocked and it half fell as it yelped angrily away. The disturbance raised a cackle of alarm from some caged chickens that had been dozing peacefully in the sun.

The safety doctor stood behind his ritual altar, resting his hands on the wooden benchtop which was worn smooth and deeply stained with old blood. He prepared for the ritual by laying out five perforated stones – rain-making amulets inherited from his ancestors – in a straight line down the middle of the altar.

Annah's gaze travelled over the man's proud, ageless face; his bony body draped with skins; his neck, wrists and ankles hung with relics. She was suddenly reminded of Stanley's grandmother, the solitary woman who had refused to accept the teachings of the Mission. With a sinking feeling of dismay, Annah realised that, faced with a similar dilemma, Zania would make the same costly choice. Yet, he loved his people so deeply. Caretaker of both body and spirit, he looked over their births, chased demons from their houses, and prepared them for death. He tended to their every need and ill. The thought of him having to become a lonely exile was unbearable.

Annah frowned, caught up in her thoughts and only dimly aware of Zania's careful rearrangement of the pattern of sacred stones. It occurred to her that Kiki might have been right to encourage the Old Chief to stand against the influence of the German Mission. But what did this mean for the whole idea of being a missionary, of spreading the Christian faith? Were they all – Sister Barbara, the Bishop, Sarah and Michael – labouring under a delusion?

The questions turned over in Annah's mind. She could see no simple answer. The certainty and clarity of Zania's beliefs, and the sense of balance and harmony that she had witnessed in the village, were only parts of the whole. She was aware of something else, an abiding fearfulness that touched almost every strand of life for the Waganga. The ancestors could be inspirational one moment, and malevolent the next. The dark could be a benign presence, and then an alien realm, dense with menace. The seasons, the sky, the rain – all evoked joy and awe, but also apprehension and suspicion. This binding fear was something that Stanley, as a Christian, seemed to have escaped. There was, by contrast, an almost tangible aura of peace and confidence about him. And yet his position was complicated as well . . .

Annah tensed at the sudden sound of loud squawking. Zania had grasped the first chicken by the neck and hauled it out of the cage. The bird's beady eyes darted left and right as the safety doctor held its head down on the altar and raised his sharp knife. Annah steeled herself. She had to watch, she knew – had to observe, unflinching, the severed neck spurting a fountain of blood, and the mindless wings flapping.

Zania sacrificed seven chickens in all, spilling their blood over the stones in a calm, almost business-like manner, before sending their carcasses off to be plucked and cooked. Remaining behind his crimsoned table, he called out to the sky, using an ancient form of the tribal language that only he could understand. When he was finished, he paused, immobile, for several long minutes. Then he gathered up his stones and turned and walked away. The rainmaking ritual was complete.

The tribespeople stayed where they were, craning their necks to study the clear blue sky as if expecting clouds to appear before their eyes.

Annah glanced around her at the aftermath of the ritual. Stray feathers were scattered on the ground. Fresh blood spattered the dust. The air was tainted with the smell of it baking in the sun. It was hard to see how any of this could be connected with the summoning of rain.

She leaned towards Mtemi, speaking in an undertone. 'Can he really make it rain?'

Mtemi smiled. 'A safety doctor learns to interpret the behaviour of insects and to notice other signs in nature. When rain is expected, he performs the ceremony to encourage the ancestors to help bring a good rain.'

'But it doesn't always work,' suggested Annah.

Mtemi shook his head. 'Sometimes there are droughts.'

'So . . . although Zania is a rainmaker, he doesn't actually have the power to make it rain.'

Mtemi turned to face Annah. 'Does God have the power to make it rain?'

Annah flinched at the directness of his question. 'Of course.'

'But if Christians pray for rain,' Mtemi continued, 'do they not find themselves in the same position as Zania? It may rain. It may not. And God is more likely to answer your prayer in the wet season than in the dry . . .'

Annah looked away. Remnants of Bible verses came to her mind.

Ask and it shall be given you . . .

. . . for he sendeth rain on the just and on the unjust.

She frowned, confused.

'Meanwhile,' Mtemi said, 'we are all here together. The whole tribe. We are thinking about rain. Nothing but rain. How the rains will feed the gardens. How the gardens will feed us. We are remembering all the good harvests that we have had. That, too, is a part of the ceremony.'

Annah nodded slowly. She felt she was on the brink of glimpsing a completely different way of thinking; one in which yes and no – or fact and story – were not opposites, but rather, different ways of viewing the same thing. The thoughts were vague and half formed, but in them she saw the glimmer of something strange and new, alarming and enticing.

Mtemi's voice broke into her thoughts. 'I heard, once, that some rainmakers were employed by the Tanganyikan Agricultural Corporation Ranch.' Annah turned to him to listen. 'They had eight thousand cattle to feed and the rains were late. The rainmakers came all the way from England with their scientific instruments packed in cases. Lots of maps and papers.'

'Did they make it rain?' Annah asked.

Mtemi didn't answer straightaway. He teased her with silence. Then his face broke into a grin.

'They took a long while getting ready,' he said. 'In that time the rains came.'

Annah laughed. She wanted to keep laughing. The warm sound bubbled freely up, fed from the deep spring of joy that seemed ever present inside her. She was aware of Mtemi watching her face.

Suddenly he leaned close to her. His lips were almost touching her ear.

'Tonight the moon will be full,' he whispered in English. 'I want you to see how it shines on the water.'

He paused, looking around and nodding casually to anyone who met his eye. Then he spoke again, slowly and clearly. 'When you have said goodnight and gone to your hut, wait until the village is quiet. Then meet me at the lakeside. The place where the old tree has fallen into the water.' He glanced away again.

'Have you heard?' he asked, slipping back into Swahili.

Annah nodded. Her heart drummed in her chest. 'Indeed, I have heard.'

On the shores of the silver lake, smooth mud gleamed like satin. Annah felt its coolness licking the soles of her feet as she walked, a fine surface slurry oozing between her toes.

The old tree was not far from the place where the track emerged from the forest. Annah fixed her eyes on its ragged shape as she approached. Drawing nearer, she searched the shadowed space around it.

She saw the leopard-skin cloak first, black spots standing out against a field of yellow ochre. Then the dark outline of Mtemi's body became clear. Annah walked steadily towards him. The sense of anticipation that had been gathering inside her was softened by an aura of unreality. It seemed impossible that they were to be together, alone, after so long.

She was still wearing her formal robes – the cloths swirled around her limbs as she moved, releasing wafts of frankincense. The perfume rose briefly to her nostrils, then lost itself in the earthy breath of the lake.

The two figures met without words. They stood side

by side watching the full moon hanging in the clear still sky. A silence pervaded the scene, surviving somehow in spite of the night birds' keening, the croaking of frogs and the steady hum of thronging insects.

Annah was the first to speak, nervousness throwing her back onto childhood training – Eleanor's insistence that conversation should never be neglected.

'When I was a little girl . . .' Annah's voice was low and tentative. 'I believed there was a man in the moon.'

Mtemi shook his head.

'Not a man. It is a rabbit. There are his ears.'

He pointed towards the moon. Annah let her eyes travel slowly along the contours of his arm.

'But I did not call you here to study the sky.'

Mtemi's voice drew Annah's gaze back to his face. To his dark, warm eyes. Slowly his words settled into a shape that held meaning. A wild, impossible meaning . . .

'Are you willing?' Mtemi asked. His voice was soft and deep. 'You must say.'

Annah stared at him in confusion. So much had been said about following the rules of the tribe. Could it be that they were now free to choose for themselves? Set free, somehow, by the silver touch of the moon, or the quiet grace of the lake.

Annah reached towards Mtemi, two pale hands suspended in the half-light. Petal fingers curved, like lilies floating.

'I am willing.'

He led her away from the water, towards a swathe of long dry grass that bordered the trees. There, he took off his cloak and laid it down, flattening the soft blades into a bed of hay. Then he moved to stand close to Annah. She waited, scarcely breathing, for him to touch her. But instead he spoke.

'I want you to kiss me.'

Annah felt a moment of surprise, before she remembered that the gesture would be foreign to him. The knowledge made her feel bolder, stronger. She took Mtemi's face between her hands, palms cradling his cheeks and chin. She let one finger travel up and follow the curve of his lips. Soft-skinned, yet firm. Then she covered his lips with her own parted mouth. A chain of memories flickered past – other mouths pressing kisses on her lips. But now, here, it was she who led, following the calling of her own senses.

Mtemi wound his arms around her back, pulling her closer to him, pressing her breasts to his chest. His fingers buried themselves in her long red hair, grasping and tangling in its thickness. Annah closed her eyes. She let her own hands move over Mtemi's body, feeling the muscles of his back, finely moulded beneath lean flesh. And his smooth skin, thinly veiled by a single draped cloth. Her lips, touching his shoulder, tasted salt.

It took only a few movements to loosen the robes that

had been so carefully folded and tucked by Patamisha. The royal fabric became a tangle about Annah's feet and she was a long, pale shape bathed in moonlight. Mtemi, naked also, was a matching shape of opposite colour, the secret shadows of the treetops mirrored in his midnight skin.

One dark hand came up to touch Annah's right breast – to trace the blackened scar of three bent lines. Mtemi bent his head, his mouth covering the mark. Annah felt the warmth of his tongue smoothing the etched lines. She tipped back her head, long hair fanning out behind her. Moonlight glowing red through the lids of her closed eyes.

Mtemi lowered her onto the leopard skin. His own body followed her down, knees easing between her legs, pushing them apart.

The hidden spear.

Ordena's phrase came to Annah's mind as she felt him pressing against her. Hard but gentle. A touch that reached every nerve in her body. All else seemed gratuitous, her ears still needlessly hearing, feet and legs stirring, futile, against the dappled hide.

Her spine arching, she rose to meet him. Her fingers pressed into his back, pulling him closer.

The hidden spear, plunging deep. Filling her up, and making her whole.

A Great Set of Ta-Tas

CAROL SNOW

In Southern California, where I live, there seem to be three basic breast sizes: big, huge and 'Oh my God, call a chiropractor'. At my local shopping mall, even the white plastic mannequins are stacked – which gives a whole new meaning to the term 'fake boobs'.

And then there's me, size 34A. Well, on my right side, anyway. My left is more like 34AA. But if I tighten the straps on my 'Thank Goodness It Fits' bra, things more or less even out. With the exception of a year or so in early puberty, when there was still a chance that the Tittie Fairy would cast her magic spell, my poor endowment has never bothered me. I'm short with a small frame, and anything too big in the chest department would look out of pro-portion. When I was pregnant and nursing, and my cup size ballooned to an almost-B, the bouncing and jiggling just annoyed me. Besides, my husband of fifteen years has always insisted that he likes me just the way I am – and since he's a terrible liar, I choose to believe him. Really, it's okay. The way I figure it, someone has to be on the small side of the bell curve. Only around here, the bell curve doesn't look much like a bell. It looks more like a mountain: a big mountain that disappears into the clouds so you can't see where it ends.

I grew up in a suburb of New York City, where the weather is colder and the women wear more clothes. I've lived in California for almost seven years now, surrounded by large-breasted women all along, presumably, but I never really noticed them until recently.

It all started during a beach outing. My friend Stacey and I were sitting in our canvas beach chairs, chatting and drinking Diet Cokes, just a couple of soccer moms watching their sunblock-slathered children play in the waves. Stacey wore board shorts, a tank top, and big sunglasses, while I had on a skirted bathing suit and a baseball cap. (Now that I'm over forty, I've decided I can wear skirted bathing suits without apology. My breasts may be small, but my thighs are most definitely not.)

Stacey is a few years younger than I and several degrees cuter, with streaky blonde hair, an easy laugh and a fondness for tomboy clothes. She's thin with girlish curves and a pair of skinny thighs I'd kill for. Until that day, I'd never really noticed her breasts. But then, until that day, I'd never really noticed *anyone's* breasts.

We were chit-chatting about the usual stuff: home improvement, kid improvement, plans for the summer. Then the conversation shifted to 'when we were young' – and that was when she dropped the bomb.

'When I graduated from college, my parents offered to buy me a car,' Stacey said casually, flicking the sand with her painted toes. 'And I said thanks, but I'd rather have a boob job instead.'

I tried not to look shocked.

I looked shocked.

I've never really approved of Californian indulgence. It's bad enough that parents buy their children cars. But *breasts?*

'My mother had hers done years before,' Stacey explained with a shrug. 'So I wanted them too.' Put that way, silicone implants seemed like a genetic inheritance, like blue eyes or detached earlobes.

At that point in the conversation, I did what anyone would do: I checked out her rack. And I must say, she has a great set of ta-tas. Nevertheless, Stacey regretted her decision immediately and spent the next several years hiding her body in oversized T-shirts, embarrassed by her big, gravity-defying melons. Time and two children settled them down, though, so now she just looks great in a tank top.

But still.

How prevalent is breast enlargement in this part of the world, I wondered? After that day on the beach, I went through a brief phase of paranoia, eyeing all of my well-endowed friends' chests and thinking: *Has she or hasn't she?* Most hadn't, I finally decided, though it seems everyone has a breast-enhancement story.

Like this: My friend Michelle's sister-in-law needed surgery for a deviated septum. Because she was going under anaesthesia, she figured she might as well get her boobs enlarged at the same time – kind of like when you take your car in for new brake pads and ask them to change the oil, too. (I asked Michelle whether the same surgeon did both procedures, but she didn't know.)

Or this: In college, another friend, Heidi, worked at a bridal store. One day, a bride came in for a second fitting and threw a tantrum because the dress was too tight. She swore she hadn't changed sizes, a claim somewhat undermined by the bandages across her chest and the small drainage tube peeking out from behind the satin. (*Ew.*)

Despite these stories, not everyone around here sees monster boobs as a must-have accessory – the perfect complement to a Coach bag or a pair of Jimmy Choo shoes. My friend Jean moved to the States from South Korea when she was three years old. Now in her late thirties, she and her Korean–American contemporaries were brought up to see breasts as – get this – a way to feed babies. (So, if you're thinking about opening a Hooters franchise in Seoul, you might want to reconsider.) Assimilation is a powerful force, though. While Jean can't think of a single middle-aged Korean–American with fake boobs, she knows of three women in their twenties who have had the procedure done. Astonishingly, one set of the girls' parents hasn't even noticed that their daughter jumped from an A-cup to a D-cup in the space of a weekend – that's how non-breast-focused the culture is.

I make no claims to being an all-natural woman. I dye my greying hair, wax my unruly eyebrows, whiten my tea-stained teeth. But breast surgery is something entirely different. The American Society of Plastic Surgeons' website (which suggests that breast implants can 'enhance your self-image and self-confidence', which is the whole idea, I suppose) lists a few risks associated with the procedure: unfavourable scarring; bleeding; infection; poor healing of incisions; temporary or permanent changes in nipple or breast sensation; formation of scar tissue around the implant; implant leakage or rupture; wrinkling of the skin over the implant; anaesthesia risks; fluid accumulation; blood clots; pain, which may persist; deep vein thrombosis, cardiac and pulmonary complications; and the possibility of revisional surgery.

Understandably, many women who have undergone mastectomies feel that the benefits of breast reconstruction and implants outweigh the risks. But for healthy women with normal (read: imperfect) breasts? I just don't get it – especially when you consider that breast implants can get in the way, quite literally, of accurate mammogram results.

According to fifty-year-old Nina, it all comes down to a (Pilates-toned) arms race of sorts – especially for single women. 'Everyone around here looks good,' she said, explaining her motivation for artificial breasts, eyelashes and hair (bleached with extensions). 'Everyone's got the hair and the boobs and the make-up. You have to do all this just to compete.' Nevertheless, there are times when Nina longs for a simpler world: 'I bet I'd stand out if I moved to South Dakota or someplace.'

Not that there's anything wrong with a generous endowment. My former college roommate, Kim, is blessed with big, round melons (I think the Tittie Fairy gave her my share) and, perhaps more crucially, an 'if you've got it, flaunt it' philosophy. For as long as I've known her, she's been using push-up bras and tight, low-cut shirts to her advantage. Nothing makes her face light up like an admonition of, 'You can't wear that shirt – everyone will stare at your breasts!' Partly, she likes to defy expectations. An economist with three degrees, Kim wants to expand her identity beyond 'tax-reform nerd'. And partly, she just likes it when people stare at her breasts.

While breast augmentation was never a consideration, Kim once faced a plastic surgery decision of a different sort. Her parents never tried to buy her a car (being from New York, she didn't even get a driver's licence until she was almost thirty), but they once offered to pick up the tab for a nose job. Although she hates what she calls her 'witchy-poo nose' (I think it gives her character), she immediately turned down the offer, scared off by the thought of unnecessary surgery and pain. But it was more than that. 'I thought it would be so obvious that people would notice. And a Jewish girl with a nose job – it's just such a cliché.'

Growing up, I had several friends who got nose jobs, and I've got to say, most of them looked better after the procedure. But Kim's comment made me think. When Jewish girls begin sporting button noses and Korean girls sprout enormous breasts, doesn't the world get a little less interesting? Is there really just one standard of beauty? Do we all want to look alike?

I haven't just been looking at women's breasts lately; I've been checking out little girls, too. My daughter is twelve years old: coltish, quiet, beautiful, immodest. She didn't inherit my thighs. Just starting to scale the fence that separates girlhood from womanhood, she has abandoned her Barbie dolls and Beanie Babies in favour of instant messaging and iPods, but she still cuddles up to me and runs through the house naked (which makes her little brother cackle and her father duck for cover). The sight of her changing body makes my chest ache with pride in her beauty – and with sadness for the child I am losing. In her bedroom she has a shelf covered with plastic bottles of scented body lotions and a drawer stuffed with thin, almost-unnecessary bras. She lags behind most of her friends in physical development. If that bothers her, she hasn't let on.

But still. I know what lies ahead. I've been there myself, after all. She will work her way up to the top of that fence and tumble over to the adult side, never to return. She will tame her eyebrows, which are unruly like mine but so much prettier. She will trade her glasses for contacts (as I did), pierce her ears, add blonde highlights to her brown hair. And after that – what? Will she like the way she looks? Will she like herself?

Driving through Los Angeles recently, my daughter and a friend were chatting in the back of the car when we passed an enormous billboard. At first glance, it looked like a promotion for a strip club (which are frequently advertised, oh-so-classily, along LA highways). There were the oversized, over-round breasts and the revealing garment. There was the sprayed hair, the plump lips, the bright white teeth. But when I looked more carefully, I realised that the sign wasn't aimed at men; it was targeting women. And it wasn't paid for by shady club operators; it was funded by plastic surgeons. 'Breast Augmentation', the billboard said in big, big letters. The model smiled with an implicit promise of happiness. *This could be you,* she seemed to say (and maybe did; I wasn't exactly taking notes). She didn't have to say the rest: *Because right now you're not good enough. If you want to be happy, become someone else.*

In the back seat, my daughter and her friend continued talking and laughing. We whizzed past the sign. They never even noticed it.

The Peonies

BRENDA WALKER

Peonies are like small fat breasts, floating on thin stems. I buy them whenever I can. It's a few days away from Christmas and I'm standing on a footpath with a bundle of peonies in my arms, sweet as a new baby and almost as heavy. It's that time of light excitement when strangers carrying ribboned parcels smile and speak on the street. The man in the shoe-repair booth has just told me a story about finding a fruiting apple tree in the wilderness when he was trekking in Canada. Another man, a stranger, stops me mid-stride and says *You must have been very, very good.* It comes as a surprise: that sudden half-forgotten crackle of flirtation, like tinsel in shop windows. I look down at the peonies, skin-pink in my arms, and say *No. They're not mine. They're for a surgeon. And he was very good.*

I'm on my way to my reserved and purposeful surgeon with a bunch of flowers. I think he'll like them. He's a breast surgeon. There. I've almost said it. There are times when I can think of nothing but the moment of my diagnosis, the vertigo as I listened to my doctor's explanations, the hard grip of concern for my son, the way that these two things can coexist: a sense of falling, unsupported, and a sense of being crushed. I speak about being sick. *I was sick, for a year or so*. More correctly, like a great many women, I once had breast cancer. My surgeon has a sign on his door: Diseases of the Breast. Three years have passed since that diagnosis, I'm tired of the subject, tired, and I haven't really begun to talk about it yet.

Ten years ago, in Palo Alto, I first learned about the diseases of the breast. I was writing a book on Edgar Allan Poe. Stanford University has a great collection of Poe material and I was working my way through it. I read and slept in a hotel room that fitted me like a nutshell. There was space for a bed and a suitcase and at night I sat cross-legged on the bed with my books in front of me. At the foot of an old lift, a lift made of brass and wood and glass reinforced with chicken wire, there was a big lobby with excellent coffee and back issues of the *New Yorker*. Someone was always playing the piano and the desk clerk would dart across the great expanse of empty shabby flooring from time to time to explain that this was not allowed. It made no difference; insomniac pianists just disobeyed him. Chopin drifted up the lift-well to my room. By day I walked into the university, down a long corridor of phoenix palms, to my other room on the first floor of a research institute. It had been a house once, the elegant clapboard retirement home of the first president of the university, who lived on his own campus, into old age. I have always loved wooden houses; the way they take in wind and sound. Footfalls are different in a wooden house. My room had plenty of shelving and a desk that a child, a grandchild of the president, might once have used. Here, in the daytime, I did my work on Poe.

Poe writes about men who cannot steady their minds; about ailing women, frail in life yet killingly capable after they die. Sometimes they don't have to lift a finger, these dead women. Their lost men mourn so terribly. The men are fearfully alone, deranged, busy with self-destruction. There is no recovery. Poe's characters don't, in the cruel and shallow phrasing of our own time, *move on and form new relationships*. Grief is not like that.

These days we've turned our faces to the wall in this matter of death and loss. We're just not looking. In the nineteenth century, people couldn't look away. One of Poe's rivals, Rufus Griswold, remained with his wife's corpse for thirty hours. He's quoted as saying *I kiss her cold lips, but their fervor is gone*. I'm not sure what he expected. Something more, certainly. Something more than simple extinction. We all expect more than that.

So there I was in America, reading everything I could about women and death in the nineteenth century. But it wasn't all fun. The food was shameless. At my childish desk I ate exhaustingly huge burritos and plate-sized cookies studded with chocolate. I normally lived on fruit and lean meat and salad. In America I drank coffee with cream. I also read everything on the shelves in my room, which were full of books that I couldn't buy at home, books written by other women in the Institute, and one of them was Marilyn Yalom's *A History of the Breast*.

What stayed in my mind, over the following years, was one of her epigraphs: *When poets speak of death, they call it the place 'without breasts'*. I was, of course, working on death at the time; I was susceptible to quotes about death. In Marilyn's book I read about nursing mothers, about pornographers and political displays of the breast by revolutionaries and liberationists. I saw the breasts of the Virgin as the painter Jean Fouquet imagined them: high and spherical with a blank small nipple. I read about breast cancer with detached concern. It was terrible but remote. Nobody I knew had ever had it. It didn't happen to women like me, or so I thought, fit women with no family history of cancer. I was disciplined about food and exercise. Like the woman in Don DeLillo's novel

The Body Artist, I *worked my body hard*. DeLillo's character is *the dictator* of her body *and also the oppressed people*. I understood this, when I read it. I too worked hard in the swimming pool and on the walking track and I had confidence in the health and submission of my body. It did what it was told. When I read about women with breast cancer in Marilyn's book I thought *poor souls*. It's a phrase my grandmother used. She never spoke of happy souls. The soul was always pitiful, it seemed, and when a person was in difficulty you looked to the suffering of their spirit. Back in Australia I tucked a copy of *A History of the Breast* on my shelf and it slept there until I suddenly, badly needed it.

Just before I was told that I had cancer I saw a strange exhibition. A German artist, Wolfgang Laib, sieves hazelnut pollen into great squares of softly luminous yellow. There must be difficulties in gathering this quantity of pollen and transporting it, but the result is deeply soothing, without perspective, without the need to decide which part of the work is more or less important. Laib also uses stone and beeswax, so his exhibitions have the slight perfume of late-night conversations when the candles burn low. Laib was once a doctor and although he now spends his time laying down floors of pollen and shaping wax and stone he feels that he has never stopped being a doctor. I don't know exactly what illness his art might remedy. The human illnesses of disproportion and loneliness, perhaps. The big ones, bigger than cancers and worn-out hearts. There is this to be said for cancer, too: it gives a great sense of proportion. Everything goes flat. The fizz goes out of ordinary anxieties as well as happiness. It can be calming, in a way. It would be a pleasure, this freedom from ordinary emotion, if only the ordinary was not replaced by a single, constant fear. And there's plenty of company. Cancer is almost as common as the flu.

Here's how it began. I saw a dimple in my right breast, as if someone had pressed it with a fingertip and the skin hadn't popped out again. There were no lumps in my breasts, just masses of soft dense tissue. They'd always been like that. Weeks passed, the dimple lengthened. It was like a shadow when I held myself sideways to the mirror. Nothing, really. I went to the GP as efficiently as I might pay a routine bill. It was likely to be nothing, he kindly agreed. But I'd better have a mammogram. It wasn't nothing. As I undressed for the biopsy I caught a reflection of my breasts in a small mirror that someone, for some reason, had hooked low on the wall. I was bent over, looking down and across at my shoulders and the unmarked tops of my breasts. I was thinking *but I have a son*. He was fourteen. I couldn't leave him. He was my field of pollen, the sense of him stayed in my mind like a colour after my eyes were closed. I just couldn't leave him. And he still needed me.

My doctor told me about the cancer. *A big tumour*, he said, and *you'll need all the support you can get*. That's when it came, the sense of falling and the sense of being crushed. I asked him if I would live. *Yes*, he said. *I believe so*. He was entirely confident, although really he couldn't know. He wrote me a script for Valium, for the fearful times when I wasn't sitting in his surgery in the full light of his confidence. He had swum the English Channel in a relay. There were photos of it in the waiting room. He knew what he was doing.

It was still morning. I drove home but I couldn't sit and I couldn't stand still.

All the small things I once enjoyed suddenly lost meaning and power. What was the point of my photographs, my books and things? If I didn't survive my son would look at them, alone. Was there any point in a porcelain Chinese pillow shaped like a cat, bought in an antique shop in Charlottesville, Virginia? Someone long dead had dreamed on it. Every trace of their thought, their breath and memory had disappeared. Only the human mattered and the human was so quickly gone.

I was demolished, stupid with grief and fear. I paced swiftly, arms folded, from one window to another. Somewhere I heard, or read, that a particular French executioner had a trick to help the condemned take up their position on the scaffold. As he led them forward he told them to mind the step. They looked at their feet, not up at the blade of the guillotine. The small fear of tripping preoccupied them briefly and they were able to move sensibly to their deaths. For a time I was like a prisoner who has looked up instead of down, a prisoner who has glimpsed the blade. I was terrified.

I calmed down enough to phone my father, in the east. He too was calm, questioning me, thinking ahead to the next step: telling my mother. Of course the news destroyed them, briefly. My eldest brother told me they looked as if they had been shot. I felt deeply guilty for causing them such pain. I was ashamed. Then I too thought about the steps that I must take, those light sure-footed steps away from death, those people who would come with me, the people who would stay behind.

I'll spare us both the story of the medical procedures. From the point of view of the person with cancer, this is really an unfashionable story of fear, of patience and obedience to the instructions of the surgeon and those moments when patience and obedience fail. For everybody else, there are words and pictures. Surgery, chemotherapy, radiation, further medication and the results of all the clinical trials. You can read survivor stories on the internet. You can see photographs of women's scars. So many of us have had breast cancer and our stories are everywhere in print and conversation and online. The particulars are heartbreaking. Pregnant women birthing their babies at the earliest possible time, taken directly from their newborns into cancer surgery. My own story is unremarkable. You can walk to raise funds for breast cancer on Mother's Day, as I do now, with my son, and every participant wears a number with a name, or list of names of women they love who are alive, or not, and there is a great hum of stories rising from these names. I am just one of the names, a woman like so many others who lived, as most do, through the standard cancer treatment. Besides, illness has demanded so much of my attention, for so long. I need cancer to sink into the background of my life.

On Boxing Day, a week after I've delivered the Christmas peonies to my surgeon, I'm having lunch with a group of women I barely know. I'm close to the woman at the head of the table. We were neighbours once, and walking companions, exchanging the pleasures and irritations of our days. All around me are the friends she made in her twenties, long before I met her. The woman next to me mentions breast cancer. I'm silent; my friend is silent too. Nobody else at the table knows. This is a great relief. It's almost as if the last three years happened to someone else. As if I got away clean.

Once I read a story about an old woman who, at the

end of an eventful life, decides to go back to the convent she had run away from as a girl. She expects to have to explain herself to the women who had lived their peaceful routine lives within the convent walls. In fact nobody noticed that she was gone. The Virgin Mary had disguised herself as the little wayward nun and performed all her duties in the time she was away. The Virgin knew her way around the convent; she was good at being a nun. I'd like to pretend that something like this has happened to me. Someone else, someone who knew what she was doing, went through the cancer medicine in my place. I appreciate what she did, I offer thanks for what she did, but I don't want to be her; I don't ever want to live the life that she lived in that time.

The problem is that cancer is physically unforgettable. My false breast was the saddest thing I'd ever seen, a shark-fin of plastic, the colour of a doll. The opposite of, say, a peony. Instead of laying it in its shapely container overnight I tossed it on the floor. Yet without it I was conspicuously unbalanced, I crept about in loose clothes with rounded shoulders. It hurt at the end of the day. I felt as if plastic was strapped painfully to my irradiated ribs, which indeed it was. The afternoons were often a matter of slight endurance. I also faced the risk of having to go through cancer treatment again with the remaining breast, perhaps much later, when I was old and frail. There was a solution. I knew the details of reconstruction surgery, apparently bizarre reassignments of flesh and muscle from one part of the body to another. Recovery might be difficult, a lot of women were unhappy with the results, and if you were unhappy there wasn't a lot you could do about it. On the other hand, it's hard to be wholly happy or even to think straight when you have predictable low-grade pain, and occasional moments of sharp fear. There was a chance, too, of getting something like my own breasts back. This meant a lot to me. And what do breasts mean in our culture? Everything, apparently. *We are born reading*, writes William S. Wilson, *The infant reads the breast.* And the adult? *You cannot read but of the breast. And probably can't go to the movies, or look at a painting either. Or dream.* Of course you can. But if you're missing a breast you might find yourself, from time to time, standing to one side of the general audience. You might feel deeply alone. I talked it through with the brother who is closest to me in age. He said *If you could do it in a blink, would you do it?* I said *yes*, notwithstanding the strangeness of the surgery, the implanted silicone. There was a risk that it would be like having the shark-fin prosthesis on the inside rather than the outside of my skin. But I still said *yes*. He said *Then it's just a matter of time and pain.* And there it was. A gift from a brother. My decision in favour of a little extra time and pain.

In 1930 the American model, photographer and, later, war correspondent Lee Miller produced two photographs of a table setting: a placemat, cutlery and a plain white plate. On the plate, as a kind of meal, is a medically severed breast with leathery dead skin and a glossy, jellied interior. Pictures of breasts are not supposed to look like this. She's reminding us quite harshly of the diseases of the breast and the fact that breasts are there, in the first place, to provide us with nourishment. There are plenty of shots of Lee Miller's own breasts, some by the surrealist, Man Ray. She's standing behind a window, her boned gown pulled down over her hips. Her breasts are small and lovely. She's self-possessed. She knew what she was doing with breasts.

I scheduled my surgery well in advance. I used the time to build strength and fitness and I propped Man Ray's picture of Lee Miller up on my bookshelves to give me heart. After all, she knew breasts inside and out. In the first part of her life she was fearless. Then she changed. She was one of the war correspondents in Dachau after the liberation and the experience broke her. She's testimony to Edgar Allan Poe's understanding of grief. We cannot entirely recover from some of our experiences. We live through terrible things, common terrors like cancer and, for some, the vast horror of large-scale human destruction. Nobody can take our place in our lives, nor should we wish them to.

In spite of this, we look forward to what we might salvage of our lives. *I am the poet of breasts*, said my cosmetic surgeon grandly and we laughed at one another. On the night before my surgery he drew, freehand, what seemed to be leaves across my back and lily pads on my chest. When I woke from the anaesthetic I was wrapped in white gauze. It looked like the bodice of an adventurous dress, covering an area of tight muscle and sliced skin, the source of many surgical drains. Under these wrappings and incisions I was secretly hoping for the shape of peonies.

References

Don DeLillo, *The Body Artist* (London: Picador, 2001), p 57.

Kenneth Silverman, *Edgar A. Poe: mournful and never-ending remembrance* (New York: HarperPerennial, 1992), p 217.

William S. Wilson, 'loving/reading,' in Daniel Halperin (ed.), *Antaeus: Literature as Pleasure* (London: Collins Harvill, 1990), pp 200–01.

Marilyn Yalom, *A History of the Breast* (London: HarperCollins, 1997).

NOTES ON THE CONTRIBUTORS

Maggie Alderson was born in London, brought up in Staffordshire and educated at the University of St Andrews. She has worked on two newspapers and nine magazines – editing four of them – and contributed to many more, including her well-loved weekly column in *Good Weekend* magazine. Her fifth novel, *How To Break Your Own Heart*, was published in 2008. She has also released three books of columns and co-edited three anthologies of short stories, most recently *In Bed With*. She is married, with one daughter, and lives by the sea.

Kaz Cooke is an author, cartoonist and part-time bosom arranger. Her books include *Up the Duff: The Real Guide to Pregnancy*; *Kidwrangling: The Real Guide to Caring for Babies, Toddlers and Preschoolers*; *Girl Stuff: Your Full-on Guide to the Teen Years*; and two picture books for children, *The Terrible Underpants* and *Wanda-Linda Goes Berserk*.

'Hermione's Up the Duff Diary: Bosom Bits' by Kaz Cooke,

from Up the Duff: The Real Guide to Pregnancy, *Penguin Books, Camberwell, 2009.*

Sarah Darmody is the author of the prize-winning novel *Ticket to Ride – Lost and Found in America* (Random House, 2005). She worked as a journalist and film critic in the USA, and in the American film industry in New York. She returned home to a book called *Film: It's a Contact Sport* (New Holland, 2002), and later contributed to the short story collection *Take Me With You* (Random House, 2005). Sarah has worked in publishing for Penguin Australia, and for the Australian Broadcasting Corporation. She is an ambassador for the National Breast Cancer Foundation, and underwent a prophylactic double mastectomy in 2007 at the age of twenty-nine.

Jessica Dettmann is a Sydney-based editor and writer. She is a graduate of the University of Sydney and a postgraduate student at the Bread Loaf School of English, Middlebury College, Vermont. She likes cats, puns and food. She was expelled from the School of Hard Knockers.

Merridy Eastman is a NIDA graduate who has worked for over twenty years as an actor, especially for the Melbourne and Sydney Theatre Companies. Although she's had major roles in most Australian soap operas and television dramas, Merridy is best known for being a *Playschool* presenter.

In 2002, Merridy's first book, *There's A Bear In There, And He Wants Swedish*, a memoir of her experience as a brothel receptionist, became a national bestseller. In 2006, Merridy's second book *Ridiculous Expectations* followed her search for true love in London, and the third, *How Now Brown Frau* is the hilarious sequel as she begins life as a writer, wife and mother living in Germany. *A Full Fitting With Irene* was originally commissioned for *Breast Wishes*, the new Australian musical supporting the National Breast Cancer Foundation.

Excerpt courtesy of Breast Wishes, *a small musical about big issues.*

Mia Freedman is an author, columnist, social commentator and blogger. She began her career doing work experience at *Cleo* and worked her way up through the ranks until she was appointed editor of *Cosmopolitan* at 24. She has been a passionate campaigner for a more positive portrayal of women in the media and pioneered the regular use of women of all shapes, sizes and nationalities in the pages of magazines. Mia was appointed Editor-in-Chief of *Cosmo*, *Cleo* and *Dolly* before she left magazines for a brief flirtation with TV. She quickly decided she just wasn't that into TV and left corporate life for more balance. She writes a popular weekly column for the *Sun-Herald* and *Sunday Age*, does corporate speaking and freelance feature writing as well as a daily blog at mamamia.com.au. Her first book, *The New Black*, was published in 2005 and her second book, *Cereal For Dinner*, is a memoir of magazines and motherhood and will be published in late 2009. She has three beautiful children and one excellent husband.

The granddaughter of Frank Hardy, **Marieke Hardy** was born on or around the set of *The Sullivans* and has remained in television ever since. From inauspicious beginnings as a lisping child actor in *The Henderson Kids II*, she has both appeared in and written for many Australian dramas from *Blue Heelers* to *Always Greener* to *Something in the Air*. Her first storyline was accepted by *Altogether Now* when she was 14 and since then she has forged a career in scriptwriting, winning an AWGIE award for her children's series *Short Cuts* which she wrote single-handedly. She also wrote and co-produced the series *Last Man Standing*, which *Herald Sun* television critic Robert Fidgeon adored to the point of erotic obsession. In addition to writing, Marieke has a radio show, a political fashion label, a go-go dancing career, a regular DJ gig and an award-winning blog. People often find her irritating and say she swears too much, but no-one ever accuses her of being tall. Her dog's name is Bob Ellis and she has four tattoos. She's currently writing a feature film and attempting her first novel.

Kate Holden is the author of *In My Skin: A Memoir* (Text Publishing), about her years as a heroin addict and prostitute in Melbourne. First published in 2005 and re-issued in 2007, her memoir was shortlisted for awards in Australia, and has been sold to ten countries overseas. Kate and her family featured in an episode of *Australian Story* (ABC) in 2005. She is a graduate of the University of Melbourne and RMIT, where she is completing a Master of Arts, and has recently returned from an Australia Council for the Arts residency in Rome. Kate has had a short play performed, several short stories and memoir pieces published in anthologies, and is now a full-time writer of reviews, essays, and a fortnightly column for *The Age*. She has two breasts of which she is very fond, although she feels the right-hand one is slightly more wonderful.

Jin Xing is one of China's foremost ballerinas. She is a mother of three and lives in Shanghai. Her memoir *Shanghai Tango* was first published in English in 2007.
'Becoming a Woman' by *Jin Xing, from* Shanghai Tango, *Atlantic Books, London, 2007.*

Marian Keyes is the international bestselling author of *Watermelon, Lucy Sullivan is Getting Married, Rachel's Holiday, Last Chance Saloon, Sushi for Beginners, Angels, The Other Side of the Story* and *Anybody Out There*. Her latest novel is *This Charming Man*. She is published in twenty-nine different languages. Two collections of her journalism, *Under the Duvet* and *Further Under the Duvet*, are also published by Penguin. Marian lives in Dublin with her husband.

'Chicken Fillets and Plus Sizes' by Marian Keyes, from This Charming Man, *Penguin Books, London, 2008. Reproduced by permission of Penguin Books Ltd.*

Kathy Lette first achieved *succès de scandale* as a teenager with the novel *Puberty Blues*, which was made into a major motion picture. She has written ten internationally bestselling novels, two of which have been made into motion pictures. Her novels have been translated into seventeen foreign languages and are now published in more than 100 countries. *How To Kill Your Husband and Other Handy Household Hints* was a number-one bestseller in 2006. Her latest bestselling novel is *To Love, Honour and Betray – till divorce us do part*.

'An Ode to the Barbie Doll on Her 40th Birthday' by Kathy Lette, from Girls' Night In, *Penguin Books, Camberwell, 2000. Reproduced with permission by Penguin Group (Australia). This story first appeared in the* Daily Mail *(UK) and* ELLE *(Australia).*

Kate McCartney is an animator, writer and illustrator. She has written and performed for television, most notably *Big Bite*, *Hamish and Andy* and *Kath and Kim*. Her animated film *The Astronomer* was nominated for a 2006 Australian Film Industry award for Best Animated Short. Kate lives in Melbourne.

Sarah Macdonald is a writer, broadcaster and journalist. She has presented radio shows on Triple J, Radio National and 702 ABC Sydney, and appeared on ABC TV's *Race Around the World* and *Two Shot*. Her bestselling book *Holy Cow – An Indian Adventure* has sold around the world and been translated into several languages. She has also edited the collections *Take Me with You* and *Come Away With Me*. She currently lives in Sydney.

'Mother's Love' by Sarah Macdonald, from Holy Cow!: An Indian Adventure, *Bantam, Sydney, 2002.*

Monica McInerney grew up in a family of seven children in the Clare Valley region of South Australia, where her father was the railway stationmaster. She is the author of the bestselling novels *A Taste for It*, *Upside Down Inside Out*, *Spin the Bottle*, *The Alphabet Sisters* and *Family Baggage*, published internationally and in translation. In 2006 she was the ambassador for the Australian Government initiative Books Alive, with her novella *Odd One Out*. Her most recent novel, *Those Faraday Girls*, won the General Fiction Book of the Year at the 2008 Australian Book Industry Awards. She has also published a collection of short fiction, *All Together Now*. She currently lives in Dublin with her Irish husband.

'The Role Model' by Monica McInerney, from All Together Now, *Penguin Books, Camberwell, 2008. Reproduced with permission by Penguin Group (Australia).*

Fiona McIntosh left London to travel, and has since roamed the world for her work in the travel industry. Over the last two years she's settled down to full-time writing. McIntosh lives with her husband and twin teenage sons. She admits to a helpless obsession for chocolate and runs an elite competition, over which she alone presides, for the supreme chocolate products around the world . . . from best hot chocolate to best gelati . . . and everything chocolatey in between. According to Fiona, Paris presently leads the charge and she is still recovering from last year's chocolate macaroon experience.

Sinéad Moriarty was born and raised in Dublin where she grew up surrounded by books. Her mother is an author of children's books. Growing up, Sinéad says she was inspired by watching her mother writing at the kitchen table and then being published. From that moment on, her childhood dream was to write a novel. After university, she went to live in Paris and then London. It was at the age of thirty, while working as a journalist in London that she began to write creatively in her spare time. After a couple of years toying with ideas, she joined a creative writing group and began to write *The Baby Trail*. Shortly after the novel was published, Sinéad had a baby boy – a very happy ending to her own Baby Trail. Since writing the book, Sinéad has moved back to Dublin where she lives with her husband, her two sons and baby daughter. The second and last titles in the *The Baby Trail* series – *A Perfect Match* and *From Here to Maternity*, are also published by Penguin. Sinéad's latest novel is *In My Sister's Shoes*.

'In My Sister's Shoes' by Sinead Moriarty, from In My Sister's Shoes, *Penguin Books, London, 2007. Reproduced by permission of Penguin Books Ltd.*

Jools Oliver lives with her husband and two little girls in London and Essex. She is the author of *Minus Nine to One*, a down-to-earth account of pregnancy and motherhood, and *The Adverntures of Dotty and Bluebell*, a collection of stories for children.

'Breastfeeding the Girls' by Jools Oliver, from Minus Nine to One, *pp 114–34, Penguin Books, London, 2006. Reproduced by permission of Penguin Books Ltd.*

Debra Oswald is a huge-breasted Sydney writer. Her stageplays include *Gary's House*, *The Peach Season* and *Sweet Road* (all shortlisted for the NSW Premier's Award). In 2008, her award-winning play *Mr Bailey's Minder* was produced in the USA and *Gary's House* was performed in Japan. She has written three plays for young audiences – *Dags*, *Skate* and *Stories in the Dark*, which won the 2008 NSW Premier's Award. She has written three Aussie Bite books for younger readers and five novels for teenagers. Debra's television scripts range from *Police Rescue* to *The Secret Life of Us* to *Bananas in Pyjamas*.

Ellie Parker is a freelance journalist who has written for publications such as *The Age*'s *Epicure* and *Poster* magazine. Ellie has always had a love affair with food and the wee little words that describe this passion. Ellie is currently the editor of breakfastout.com.au, a new web magazine that focuses on the best places to eat breakfast in Melbourne. Ellie is tireless in her search for the best Eggs Benedict in town and is fearless when it comes to black pudding at 8 a.m. She particularly loves dipping a cheese kransky into a runny yolk.

Adele Parks lives with her husband and son in Guildford, England. They are, in her opinion, the most enchanting beings on the planet. She is an Aquarian, northern and she wanted to be a writer since she was a little girl. Since 2000 when the *Evening Standard* identified Adele as one of London's 'Twenty Faces to Watch', Adele has written eight *Times* Top Ten bestsellers, including *Playing Away* (debut bestseller of the millennium), *Husbands* and *Tell Me Something*. She sells throughout the world. Two of her novels have been optioned as movies. She has written articles and short stories for a number of magazines and newspapers. Since 2006 Adele has been an official spokeswoman for World Book Day. Adele thinks being healthy and happy is the new rich and famous. Adele would choose champagne over chocolate but an ideal day would include both. She thinks people can be astoundingly brilliant and stupid; often the same person can be both and that's what she writes about – the beautiful complexity of being human. Her greatest dream is that more people make their own happy endings every day.

Meg Rosoff was born in Boston, educated at Harvard and St Martin's College of Art, and worked in New York City for ten years before moving to London permanently in 1989. She worked in publishing, politics, PR and advertising until 2004, when she wrote her first novel, *How I Live Now*, which won the Guardian Children's fiction prize (UK), Michael L Printz prize (US), the Die Zeit children's book of the year (Germany) and was shortlisted for the Orange first novel award, has been translated into 28 languages, and is being made into a film. Her second novel, *Just in Case*, won the 2007 Carnegie Medal, and her most recent book, *What I Was*, has been published for both the adult and teen market. Meg lives in London with her husband and daughter.

Katherine Scholes was born in Tanzania, East Africa, the daughter of a missionary doctor and an artist. She has fond memories of travelling with her parents and three siblings on long safaris to remote areas where her father operated a clinic from his Land Rover. When she was ten, the family left Tanzania, moving first to England and then settling permanently in Tasmania. As an adult, Katherine moved to Melbourne with her film-maker husband. The two worked there together for many years, writing books and making films. They have now returned to Tasmania where they live on the edge of the sea with their two sons. Katherine is the author of three international bestsellers: *The Rain Queen*, *Make Me An Idol* and *The Stone Angel*. Her fourth novel, *The Hunter's Wife*, was published by Penguin in 2009.

'*The Rain Queen*' by Katherine Scholes, *from* The Rain Queen, *Pan Macmillan Australia, Sydney, 2000.*

Carol Snow is an American author who writes fiction for adults and teens. Her titles include *Been There, Done That*; *Getting Warmer*; *Here Today, Gone To Maui*; and *Switch*. Originally from New Jersey, she now lives in California with her husband and two children. For more information about the author and her books, visit carolsnow.com or myspace.com/carolsnow.

Brenda Walker has written four novels. The most recent is *The Wing of Night*, which was shortlisted for the Miles Franklin Award in 2006 and won the Nita B Kibble Award in 2006 and the Asher Award in 2007. She is an Associate Professor in English and Cultural Studies at the University of Western Australia.

Cathy Wilcox was born in Sydney and has spent most of her life there, apart from some extended stints in France. She has been drawing cartoons for the *Sydney Morning Herald* since 1989 and for *The Age* since 1993, and has also illustrated numerous children's books. She has breastfed two sons in spite of the mess, and wears a size 34C.

ACKNOWLEDGEMENTS

With a book like this, built entirely upon acts of kindness and goodwill, it's almost impossible to thank everybody. The village of people it has taken to get this book to you is extraordinary. Two massive organisations, Penguin and the National Breast Cancer Foundation (NBCF), spent a year answering questions ranging from 'Can we make the holy, sacred orange Penguin *pink*? He would like that, really. He's a sensitive bird,' to matters left for lawyers and experts in foil finishes. No one chucked a tanty. Everyone said yes. They said yes, and yes, and how can we help, and it has made my heart swell to bursting.

Every author deserves a special, golden thank you for giving so freely of their time and talent – their two most precious attributes. One author had just a single day in her publishing schedule in which to write something. Did she get a manicure? A drink with an umbrella? No, she strapped herself in and wrote through the night.

The crew at Penguin who worked on this book were

large and generous, in particular its publisher, Ali Watts, editors Jessica Crouch and Anne Rogan, special people like Ben Ball, Dan Ruffino and Louise Ryan, who believed in it from the very start, and all the sales and marketing team. I would love to mention all of them by name, but it's been a company-wide effort, and every single person played a very generous part, from the CEO down. That's a very long list to share.

And for me, for my thank yous, how can I leave out every single person I've met on my journey here? The research team at kConfab? My surgeon Dr Narine Efe? My GP Dr David Burgin? My family, my friends, my mum, who gave in to my desperate pleading and broke me out of hospital by stuffing my drainage tubes in a green enviro shopping bag slung over my arm. (Bye bye! Back soon. Just off to the park!)

The CEO of the NBCF Sue Murray, who should be running the country, deserves a very special thank you, as do all the incredible staff of that organisation. Special Agent Fran Moore, who supported this project even though I haven't made her enough money for a latte since 2006. And how can I leave out the elderly woman who inspired me to do this in the first place, by raising $120 000 for NBCF research simply sitting at her local shopping centre, day in, day out, just sitting there smiling with a tray of $2 pink ribbons? Her son-in-law had breast cancer. She told me, 'Well, we've all got to do our bit for the people we love, don't we?' And yes, I thought, yes we do. And shopping centres wouldn't work for me (spend the proceeds, go to jail), but books I understood. So thank you to her and her son-in-law, too.

Thank you for buying this book. Each of you. You are saving lives and building futures. When we fund advances in breast cancer, it helps the fight against all cancers, and when people like me see you carrying this book on the train, or wearing a pink ribbon walking down the street, you may never notice our smiles, but inside we say thank you, thank you, *thank you*.

Special thanks to The Boy, who, as if they were a rock band, claims to like the boobs' new hits better than their classics, and who came up with the title for this book. A very special thank you to my parents and my family, for feeding and housing me intermittently so I could work on a non-paying gig, and to my brother, whose life-long control of type 1 diabetes (he has a James Bond-like nemesis arrangement with his condition, and he always outsmarts it handsomely and gets away) is a giant kick up the pants of perspective when I get sookie over one faulty gene and plastic boobs.

Thanks aren't big enough for artist Abbey McCulloch, who gave me strength when I didn't have any, and opened her heart and home to a stranger.

Thank you to James Geer, a very talented photographer with a big heart, and to luscious MOR Cosmetics, for treating our authors to a fragrant pink 'thank you' for donating their time.

Thank you, Danni, for giving your blood to save my life, and for giving us all Sally D to love now that you can't be with us any more.

And lastly, thank you to the cancer researchers who should be given fifteen minutes at the end of the nightly news to talk about what a good game they played that day, and how far they've come as a team, just the same as our sporting greats. We're behind you, guys. Keep going.